"Traditionally companies have just sought shareholder value; this is what is taught at leading business schools worldwide. Millennial customers, however, are taking a more holistic approach to consumption, and demanding that companies produce products and services that serve a greater purpose, rather than simply shareholder value. In this fascinating book, Tsolkas shows how crises can foment innovation that create shareholder values in purposeful ways that are more than just lip service."

JONATHAN LEVAV, Professor of Marketing at Stanford Graduate
School of Business, Palo Alto, California, USA

"This is an eye opener, how companies today can differentiate and grow while helping the world to become a better place. A recommended read from cover to cover."

DR. NICOLAS DURAND, CEO Abionic, Lausanne, Switzerland

"'Christos is a genuine believer in his theory 'purpose rising from crisis' which is carved from firsthand experience. He presents his mantra in an honest manner and each reader is certain to extract their own personal gem from this treasure trove."

NAAVA MASHIAH, Author, Private Equity/Wealth Management expert,
Geneva, Switzerland

"Sometimes, crises come into our lives. They are troubling, unwanted, take us out of our comfort zone. We typically find ourselves wanting desperately to get back to comfort, out of the unknown. Though there is no going back but, usually, that is where the opportunity lies. Ultimately, the question is whether we choose to freeze in panic or embrace this opportunity. *The Gift of Crisis* is a brilliant real story with insights and practical instruments to use in order to ride the waves of change and turn it into opportunity. Highly recommend to leaders who are looking for their 'blue oceans'."

ANNA DEREVYANKO, Executive Director European Business Association,
Kyiv, Ukraine

"Christos donates a transcendental view on crises and their relationship to us. His book provides a much-needed philosophical system for contextualizing the significance of the perpetuity of adverse events and the confluence of crises. He has taken the time to diligently study the 'new norm' of persistent volatility and draft an aspirational manual for us all."

THOMAS ANTONIADIS, Managing Director Critical Publics, London UK

"Having seen Christos deal with multiple crises as an international executive, I was very pleased to see that he decided to share his learnings and insights with the world and write this book. I know his book will be of great help to all those seeking to take their leadership skills to a new level of conceptualization."

GREG KRASNOV, Serial Entrepreneur, Founder and CEO Forum Capital, Singapore

"Christos Tsolkas has written a must-read primer for those that MIGHT go through a crisis. After reading this book you will have a roadmap and the confidence to sail through it with Purpose."

TRINI AMADOR, Author, Managing Director, Global Brand Marketer, BHC Consulting, San Francisco, CA

"A practical framework backed by rich stories on *how* to prepare yourself to seize the next inevitable crises to galvanize your teams to high performance through meaning and purpose."

FRED MOUAWAD, Founder, Chairman & CEO Synergia One Group of Companies, Singapore

"Humble and witty at the same time, Christos shows how purpose is not just a buzzword, but it can trigger fundamental changes in everyone, and thus change the world."

GIANPAOLO TURRI , President Adamant Namiki, Tokyo Japan

"This is an excellent read in which the author, Christos Tsolkas has developed a very systematic approach to defining "purpose" for an individual or an organization. Christos bases his findings on his own experience in which he succeeded to manage, with good will, a real crisis scenario. I was able to immediately relate to his experience to another similar experience that I personally had. The book is very non-academic and I highly recommend any daring entrepreneur to read it."

AYMAN HIJJAWI, Chairman The Hijjawi Foundation, Nablus Palestine

Christos Tsolkas and his experiences around the world, at the highest levels of management and within the throws of crisis, give a clear and poignant view of not only surviving turbulent times, but utilizing the energy and uncertainty of crisis to refine and hone one's purpose. When purpose of the individual compliments purpose of the organization, the results create a strength and momentum which is greater than the sum of its parts. A very timely read for all organizational levels and job types, *The Gift of Crisis*, explores a methodology for self-exploration and the tools needed to make real, positive change. A change that benefits the individual, the company and the society in which they live."

ANDY PAPATHANASSIOU, Professional Motorsports – Director of Human Performance, North Carolina

"In todays fast changing world the ability to manage teams through a crisis is an absolute "must-have" skill for any manager. The best ones turn such events into fires which forge the biggest competitive advantage any company can have: a purpose. Having an insight into Christos's experiences and views on how to not only survive, but strive in rapidly changing environments is absolutely priceless. An absolute goldmine of knowledge for any manager, especially those working on emerging markets, where crisis situations of various types come pretty much every year ..."

ANDREW OLEJNIK, Entrepreneur, Founder Homsters, Istanbul

"Christos Tsolkas uses brilliant storytelling coupled with a pragmatic guide and methodology to show how organizations can rediscover themselves, modernize their purpose in 'tech-novative' ways, and aim for success while helping the planet. You can have it all and Tsolkas shows you how."

CHARLENE LI, bestselling author of *The Disruption Mindset* and Founder & Senior Fellow at Altimeter, a Prophet company

"At many points during our lifetime, answers to our most exigent queries pass by without us paying the slightest of attention as they are not necessitated - even if so subconsciously. There are times however, when in some otherworldly way, what we need the most falls right in-front of us and paves the way. The latter is what Christos' book reflects for some of us, a gift from up above, at the right time."

GEORGE KORRES, Chairman of the board at Korres Natural Products, Nicosia, Cyprus

THE GIFT OF CRISIS

THE GIFT OF CRISIS

How Leaders Use Purpose to Renew their Lives,
Change their Organizations, and Save the World

CHRISTOS TSOLKAS

For information about this title or to order other books and/or electronic media, contact the publisher:

Christos Tsolkas, Business Advisory, Switzerland

www.christostsolkas.com

contact@christostsolkas.com

ISBN: 978-1-7341696-0-7 (Hardcover)
ISBN: 978-1-7341696-1-4 (Softcover)
ISBN: 978-1-7341696-2-1 (eBook)
ISBN: 978-1-7341696-3-8 (Audio book)

Printed in the U.S.A. and U.K.

Cover and Interior design: 1106 Design
Illustrations: Andreas Aggelopoulos, Comixing

BEFORE READING THIS BOOK

In advance of diving into this book, take a moment to answer the following questions and check off all that apply:

- ☐ Have you ever faced a personal, family or business crisis?
- ☐ Do you ever wonder how to deal with a potential new crisis before it knocks on your door?
- ☐ Do you believe in the power of teams to solve problems individuals can't manage alone?
- ☐ Do you worry about the enormity and number of global problems that threaten our collective future?
- ☐ Do you think that governments and nonprofit institutions alone are unable to make the world a better place?
- ☐ Do you see a new kind of leadership on the rise?
- ☐ Are you impressed by the technological revolution of our times, and do you hope that technology can help serve a broader cause rather than create more problems?
- ☐ Are you seeking new ways to re-invigorate your life, your team or your company?

If these questions intrigue you, turn the page …

CONTENTS

FOREWORD

In over four decades of work as a coach and advisor to senior executives and leaders around the world, I have encountered many fascinating business leaders who are quietly making their teams, organizations and the people around them better. I learn from each and every one of them.

My friend, Christos Tsolkas, taught me something unique: How a sense of purpose, born in response to crisis, can accelerate team and leadership growth.

I first met Christos in Palm Desert in 2010, where he was attending the Global Institute for Leadership Development, an annual gathering I founded and co-chaired for twenty years. He struck me as another young, curious executive whose ambition and energy for the job was matched by his interest in self-development.

We didn't talk much at first. Then, I noticed him again during some exclusive small-group sessions with the great leadership teachers Warren Bennis and Jim Collins. Christos was one of the more engaged and curious participants. In his questions, he revealed a hungry mind, willing to challenge existing paradigms and the status quo. I took note of him as someone who might turn out to be a "mover and shaker" in his global organization.

A couple months later, I received a call from Christos. He seemed hesitant or even timid about reaching out, but he soon got to the point. Christos told me he needed help in his own leadership development journey, and he wondered whether I would be available to provide him with some one-on-one coaching. He worried, however, that he might not be significant enough in position to warrant my attention. It was a very false assumption. We got started the next week.

Our work started on a very personal level. We focused not just on Christos the executive but also on Christos the person. I won't go into much detail except to say that he had, like a lot of people in their forties, come to question his purpose and path in life. He wanted to be a more effective business leader, but this was tied to a craving for more meaning and fulfillment, too.

In a sense, he had encountered a personal crisis. We enjoyed monthly phone calls and a number of long walks over the next two and a half years. I saw Christos turn his uncertainty and personal chaos around, in a very authentic way, by developing a more profound and energizing sense of purpose. His personal development was very fast. It was a sign of things to come.

Around this period, Christos was leading a sizable and important organization in Greece. As the old blessing and curse goes, "May you live in interesting times." I watched from a distance as Greece descended into social and political turmoil with a devastating economic collapse. And I watched how Christos weathered his own doubts and confusion to lead his organization into stability and eventually a return to growth.

It was a bravura performance, and I knew how Christos pulled it off. He'd applied what he knew about personal purpose to his own team, and he coached and encouraged them through a very difficult time to achieve great results and great satisfaction.

Christos was rewarded with a well-deserved posting, a bigger territory based in Kiev, Ukraine. This time, he didn't want to wait for a crisis to develop his team, so enlisted me to use proven team performance improvement tools to get that process started. We began by assessing the team's current level of performance. Christos made some personnel moves accordingly. Then we got going on the work.

The team started as a Level 3—about in the middle of the bell curve based on SYMLOG research. The goal, as always, is to strive for Level 5 status, which describes a high-performance team that is basically self-sufficient, and in which the senior leadership team is leading with the objective of being the team of teams, i.e., that is committed to developing high performing teams throughout the organization.

Under ideal circumstances, with the right resources, focus and continuity, this can take up to three years on average. Christos' team accomplished this in just one year.

How did he manage the transformation so quickly? The difference was leading from a common purpose and then the crisis.

A few months into our work together, Ukraine spiraled into disruptive turmoil that made Greece look like a day in the park. I had nightmares imagining what Christos and his people were going through. During these dark days, we frequently Skyped to discuss the situation and how to guide and hold his people together. Christos did not see the crisis as a reason to abandon our work on team building, rather as a reason to work even harder. He believed, very simply, that his organization and people would only survive if his team came together at a higher level around a new purpose that all could share.

He was right. Crisis did not throw his team's leadership development process off track, it accelerated it. When we measured the team's performance level a year later, it had achieved Category One status, i.e., they were inextricably woven around mutual accountability for staying on course.

Offered Christos one additional and unusual piece of advice during this period of crisis. Suggested that he take good notes. I wanted him to write everything down in the moment—not only the technical challenges, and the events, but also the experiences and the feelings. In this way, he could record what it was like to lead during a crisis and how that could help others later.

That was the genesis of this book The Gift of Crisis. It is a fascinating personal story and an adventure that combines insights, research, experiences and personal advice from someone who lived and breathed what he writes about.

It reflects an evolution in Christos's thinking and my own. Any crisis—personal, organizational or geopolitical—can be turned into an opportunity, a new beginning of rediscovery and reinvention, one that connects purpose and meaning with development and growth.

Am also proud that in producing this work, Christos took the ideas even further. He believes deeply in what he writes about and has built the business case for purpose as an organizing principle for driving the kind of innovation that tackles the world's biggest problems.

At a time when crisis is everywhere, and it is so easy to get off track or to fall into cynicism and helplessness, Christos's book is a gift to us all.

Dr. Phil Harkins

Author of *Powerful Conversations, Everybody Wins, In Search of Leadership, Skin in the Game, The Art and Practice of Leadership Coaching, Best Practices for Succession Planning, Best Practices in Leading the Global Workforce*, and *Best Practices in Knowledge Management and Organizational Learning Handbook.*

January 15, 2020

INTRODUCTION

My Pitch to You

This is a book about purpose and the role it can play in improving our lives, our work, our organizations and our world.

I call purpose "The Gift of Crisis" because for me it was an unexpected (and, frankly, unwelcome) surprise that led to major, positive changes in my personal life, my career and the way I practice leadership and support others.

At the time I was working as an executive for a global company, heading up territories headquartered in Athens, Greece and then Kiev, Ukraine. As you'll read in Chapter One, I had the strange experience of going from one geopolitical hotspot to another in very quick succession. In both scenarios, our business plans got flipped over like a card table. In Kiev, even our lives were in danger. But our teams came together in ways that showed me the power of fighting for something bigger than business and even bigger than ourselves.

Later, inspired by the insights I'd gained in the field, I explored the power of purpose in other scenarios, experiencing it firsthand in startup environments and studying it through the work of others. My early thinking on the relationship between purpose, crisis and innovation was published in the *Harvard Business Review*. Out of that great honor, I gained opportunities to speak before audiences all over the world, and I started to help companies and leaders engage with their most urgent challenges in new ways that spurred cultural transformation, innovation and explosive growth.

This book is about that story, those insights and the practical ideas and tools that others can use to catalyze their own growth and the growth of their teams and organizations. It starts with crisis—something we all try to avoid—but crisis can be a gift. And if there's one thing I've learned over the past decade, it's that there's always another crisis around the next corner.

The Practice of Purpose

I started working on this book in 2015, which is four years ago now as I write this introduction. My ideas have evolved and grown over that period. Many things have happened in politics, the economy, the environment, internationally and through technology to affirm and prove my theories. I've honed and updated my views in the face of things I've seen and learned firsthand and through the experiences of others.

I'm still just as excited about those ideas and their power to produce real business results as I was when I first encountered them. When I started, the word "purpose" was not used as extensively as it is today. However, even though it is a more common term now, and there has been an increasing amount of research and publications about it, I still believe that practical understanding and use of purpose is off the mark. When I talk to audiences of leaders or to executive teams, I need to explain at the outset that "purpose" and "business" are not operating in different universes, but mutually supportive; that purpose is not about philanthropy, corporate social responsibility (CSR), public relations activities or spirituality, but about business, competition and growth; that it's not just for individuals in their personal growth, but hugely significant for leaders, teams and organizations; that it's not about being a good corporate citizen, but a competitive, innovative organization; that it's not only about doing what's right for customers, but also about finding urgent problems, developing transformative solutions and driving exponential business growth.

In that sense, purpose, crisis, leadership, innovation and growth come together in a single formula which I will explain and illustrate in the pages to come. I believe it's a formula that can potentially change the way your organization succeeds. In the chapters that follow, I will talk about how crisis can give birth to purpose, how that changes our understanding of leadership, and how it leads to innovation, market success and global impact. We will look at:

- How talented people and teams can flourish in the face of crisis by adopting a galvanizing sense of meaning; (Chapter Two)

- How leadership can and must evolve to meet the new ways people demand to be led; (Chapter Three)

- How business models can incorporate purpose to meet urgent challenges and even global problems; (Chapter Four)

- How that mode of doing business can help an organization flourish in a very new societal and economic environment that is revealing its rules to us so quickly many corporations will soon become lost and outdated; (Chapter Five)

- How the combination of purpose and crisis leads to transformative innovation that can steer a company into profitable "Blue Ocean" territory; (Chapter Six)

- How significant global problems (I call them Level One problems) can be embraced to catalyze exponential corporate growth; (Chapter Seven)

- How technology has never been more available to facilitate and achieve our biggest, most ambitious business plans; (Chapter Eight)

- How you can craft a blueprint for driving innovation and growth through purpose. (Chapter Nine)

It is not my intention or hope to sell millions of books, I know I won't. Although I have been a "salesman" my whole career, I have a different ambition in mind now. My goal is to help people (a few or many) think differently about meaning and work. In the process, I want to give them the capacity to shift their team and even their organization toward a new direction by putting these ideas into practice. The ideas are not all mine. I've been very influenced by the stories and insights of others. But I believe I have brought them together in a new way.

I'm a very ordinary leader with an ordinary career. But I have found purpose to be of great use to me personally and professionally. I'm a happier, more engaged and more successful person as a result. More importantly, I've seen how purpose can engage and energize the people around me and direct their talents and capabilities to accomplish something bigger together. We live in a time when groups—and businesses in particular—have the power to do great and amazing things.

This book is a road map for any organization of any size or stage of development to follow. It will help such organizations stand out from their competition, differentiate themselves to customers, disruptively innovate, expand into new markets and grow exponentially.

It's time we get serious about why we're in business and learn how to make our work matter. In the process, I believe we will uplift our lives, energize our careers and save this precious planet we call home.

CHAPTER ONE

A Test Every Leader Will Face

Every crisis is its own story.

For my team, our crisis started quietly on November 21, 2013, when the Ukrainian President, Viktor Yanukovych, decided to suspend plans for developing closer ties with the European Union. I had moved to Ukraine a few months before to serve as a managing director for my company. Like any international executive working in Eastern Europe, I knew the political situation in Ukraine was volatile. But I had no idea how suddenly and dramatically the country was about to descend into chaos.

Yanukovych had close ties with Russia. Everyone knew that. Russian President Vladimir Putin wanted more control over Ukraine because it had been a major territory within the Soviet Union until its independence in 1991. That was common knowledge too, although few imagined how far he would go. Many Ukrainian people, especially students, were angry and upset by Yanukovych's decision to move Ukraine "back" toward Russia rather than "forward" toward Europe. They felt their future was on the line. So, they gathered in Kiev's Independence Square to protest. Those demonstrations became known by their Twitter hashtag as the "Euromaidan" movement.

For the first few weeks, the protests felt relatively calm and peaceful, even hopeful. The students chanted and sang and demanded an end to Yanukovych's government and called for investigations into corruption. Optimists wondered whether this was Eastern Europe's version of the Arab

Spring of 2010, a movement that had combined protests, demonstrations and social media activism to bring more democracy and transparency to the Middle East. My work colleagues and I were less naïve, but I wasn't too worried yet, even though I definitely had concerns about where the political showdown was headed.

By the end of the month, we began to see how bad things could get. The Yanukovych government became more defensive. Clashes between the police and the demonstrators grew violent. In December, we canceled our annual Christmas party. This was a disappointment, but we were worried that if employees came to Kiev for the party, many would want to join the protestors in Maidan Square. We wouldn't be able to guarantee their safety if they did so, but we didn't want to deny them the right to express their political beliefs, either. As a compromise, we decided to ask everyone to stay home instead.

By January, hundreds of buses were arriving in central Kiev every day as the regime brought in thousands of counter-protesters. The clashes between pro-government and anti-government groups became more tense. On January 22, 2014, the violence finally exploded. Three protestors were shot that day by snipers hiding on the rooftops around Maidan Square. A fourth was kidnapped and found tortured and dead in the woods. That was the first day we met as a team to figure out how to handle a situation that seemed like it could quickly spiral out of our control.

Knowing the crisis had reached a grave new level, we began to exercise more caution in our daily lives and took concrete steps to reduce risks to our employees. We started instituting nightly head counts. Every manager sent in a report every night that all their employees had made it home safely that day. We canceled an annual commercial conference that eight hundred employees were expected to attend from all over the country. Any movement was risky, so we deferred non-essential travel and increased the level of daily communication from my management team to the field force. We prepared a countrywide relocation plan just in case. Even so, we got frequent reminders that the situation could turn quickly in unexpected directions. One night, for instance, one of our company cars was destroyed in an arson attack. We suspected the perpetrators were pro-Russian groups targeting vehicles with out-of-town license plates.

On the morning of February 20, 2014, my driver, Fedir, drove me to the office, as he did every day. We took the riverside route because the roads leading into the center of Kiev were still barricaded. I was tired that morning, having stayed up late the night before watching live streaming and international news about what was happening in my "adopted" country. The past two days had been particularly bad. The police, by all accounts, had begun shooting live ammunition instead of rubber bullets, and there were more reports of sniper fire from rooftops. A dozen or so people were dead. Despite that chaos, the traffic was much lighter than usual that day, a calm that only gave me a strange feeling in my stomach. I asked Fedir what was going on, but he didn't know any more than me. The closer we got to downtown, the emptier the streets became. By the time we reached the office, we could both smell fire.

I rushed inside. Many of our employees were already at the office, but they were all sitting wide-eyed in front of their laptops or standing in front of the big television screens at the coffee corner watching live streams from Independence Square. A few blocks away, the police had opened fire on

the protestors again. Bullets whizzed through the air as the snipers shot everyone in sight. They aimed for the neck because that was the unprotected area between helmets and flak jackets. Before the day was over, sixty-seven protestors had been shot dead, bringing the three-day count to one hundred. Kiev—that beautiful, hopeful, vibrant city—was bleeding.

For my organization, this was the end of any sense that the crisis outside our walls could be managed or contained. We had no idea how we would get by or what was in store for us. Fortunately, we figured out how to work together in a very new way.

Crisis and Its Outcomes

We live in a time of crisis. At any moment, order and normalcy can be overturned by unexpected developments.

From my perspective, this sense of constant crisis has been growing since 9/11. Before then, of course, the world was no stranger to crisis. The '90s saw the dot-com crash. The '80s witnessed the spread of AIDS, the breakup of the Soviet Union and the first Iraq War. The '70s had the oil crisis, stagflation, terrorism, conflict in the Middle East, and the Vietnam War. The '60s had the hippy movements, the rise of rock and roll and anti-war protests in the U.S., Europe and Japan. The '50s seemed peaceful but only because the world had just finished a half century of global war and economic depression.

Still, since 9/11, crises have come fast and furious. The U.S. invaded Afghanistan and then Iraq. Terrorism spread as Al Qaeda and then ISIS inspired attacks around the world. Faith in business was shaken by the Enron scandal, then faith in our entire economic system was rocked by the financial crisis of 2008 which generated the worst global recession since the Great Depression. Many companies went bankrupt, the economies of some European countries nearly collapsed, millions of people in America lost their jobs, savings and homes. A sense of deep uncertainty set in, and feelings of resentment and distrust of the establishment began to grow as the wars and slow economic growth continued year after year.

The populist revolutions in the Middle East and later in Central European countries like Hungary and Ukraine appeared to be positive signs at first, signaling the possibility that waves of change could make the world a better place. Social media seemed a force for good, creating more political transparency and helping to support people who'd been powerless before. Authoritarian dictators got overthrown. Democracy spread.

But then the tide turned. Protests turned into revolutions and then civil war. Millions of refugees flooded into Europe. Authoritarian governments cracked down on democratic freedoms. Social media got used increasingly to spread hate, fear and fake news. In America, the rising stock market seemed to make the rich richer while leaving the middle class poorer and giving millions the belief that the system is rigged. Meanwhile, the opioid epidemic spread across rural America and small towns, killing more people every day than AIDS did at the height of that epidemic. During this same period, austerity measures in Europe led to more unrest and prolonged the economic stagnation and joblessness.

In the wake of all this turmoil, it shouldn't be surprising that we are now witnessing the the rise of nationalist movements and populist authoritarian leaders everywhere. Britain stumbled through Brexit. In France, Austria, Germany, Italy, Hungary and Poland right-wing extremist political parties are on the rise. In America, the election of Donald Trump turned the political establishment on its head. Every tweet creates a new firestorm. Every day is a new surprise. No one, and certainly no company, is immune to crisis anymore.

If you are a business leader managing an organization or a team when crisis comes, you may easily feel overwhelmed by circumstances that are too complex, confusing or fast-moving to control. Maybe the crisis is the result of new competition, a financial scandal, a data breach, political instability, an environmental disaster, a sharp economic downturn or a terrorist attack. Suddenly, your carefully developed plans, strategies or processes can seem pointless. The support you've always relied on—clear communication channels, sufficient organizational resources, a team of people trained to do specific jobs, stable regulations—may not be available to you. The organization itself might feel threatened and vulnerable. As the ground shifts and the rules change, you will have to figure out, in real time, how to survive and navigate a new reality.

Is crisis a curse or a gift? We're hardwired to avoid crisis, if at all possible. Nobody wants to see the world get tipped over or lives and livelihoods get disrupted or become endangered. But leadership is also about facing tough moments and doing what can be done to make things better in the short and long run. A crisis can tear apart a team or an organization, but it can also bring people closer together. A crisis can destroy plans, but it can also lead to better ideas or innovations. A crisis can cause great distress and anxiety, but it can also make people feel more alive and empowered than they ever have before. A crisis can cloud thinking and create confusion, but it can also sharpen your sense of right and wrong and generate great clarity around what to do next and what a better future could look like.

Despite all of the turmoil, distress and damage that can come from a crisis, the leader who faces one is also lucky. Because crisis is where purpose is born. And it is through purpose, more than any other force, that people gain a sense of meaning, and organizations come together and grow.

Standing at the Front

Here's a story that will help illustrate what I mean.

In 1999, before Enron and the dot-com crash, one of the oldest companies in America, a little-known pharmaceutical distributor called McKesson, experienced a financial crisis that nearly destroyed it.

McKesson had been a sleepy company for many decades, selling pharmaceuticals mostly to independent pharmacies around the country. In the 1990s, it began to grow through acquisitions and new market strategies. McKesson was headquartered in San Francisco, the heart of the dot-com sector. As the tech boom took off, McKesson was not immune to the excitement of rising stock prices. Every McKesson office had a video monitor tracking that day's market movements. Then, like other "brick and mortar" companies looking to get into the tech scene, McKesson decided to buy a dynamic healthcare information technology business called HBOC for $14.5 billion. Almost overnight, McKesson became a Wall Street darling with one of the best-performing share prices in healthcare.

John Hammergren was an executive vice president reporting to the COO, who'd been with the company for a few years at that point. Still a young man in his early forties, he'd worked his whole career in healthcare. He'd grown up in central Minnesota in a close family and spent summers traveling with his father who was a hospital supply salesman. Hammergren was only sixteen when his father died suddenly. That tragedy changed his life. He no longer had any financial safety net, and realized it would be up to him to provide for himself and his mother and pay his own way through college. He needed to make a decision about the type of person he would become, and he turned to his family values (trust, honesty, accountability) for guidance. He grew up very fast.

At a number of different healthcare companies he proved himself to be a diligent worker and a good decision-maker who was not afraid to take risks because he believed that's where the best opportunities could be found. He rose quickly through the ranks. At McKesson, he was positioned near the top of the leadership team but outside the inner circle where the key strategic decisions got made. His career looked promising.

McKesson formally acquired HBOC in January 1999. At the end of April, the company held a board retreat which coincided with a special dinner with the senior HBOC team. Hammergren wasn't part of the board retreat, but he went ahead to the dinner. The McKesson and HBOC executives waited at the restaurant for hours for the senior executives and board directors to show up. When the top group finally did arrive, much later than planned, their mood seemed dark and anxious, but they offered no explanation for their delay. Nobody outside the senior group could tell what was wrong.

The next morning, leaving the hotel and about to get into a taxi, Hammergren was handed a press release by a colleague. In the car, he read an announcement. McKesson would need to restate its earnings for the previous year in light of certain accounting irregularities at HBOC. He knew this was bad news, but he didn't know how bad. Eventually, it would be discovered that the leadership at HBOC had inflated its own earnings prior to its acquisition by McKesson by concocting nonexistent deals and backdating sales contracts. This fraud would earn several executives prison time.

That morning, however, Hammergren didn't grasp the gravity of the situation until he saw what happened to the company's share price when the market opened. The $150 million dollar restatement immediately destroyed $9 billion in McKesson's value. The stock price was in free fall, and Hammergren's own personal net worth had been wiped out overnight. He felt shell-shocked.

In the midst of this turmoil, Hammergren got a call from the CEO. He expected some insight into the company's troubles, but instead the CEO asked him to fly to Hawaii in his place. The HBOC sales team was already there on their annual award trip. Someone from McKesson needed to help them absorb the news. Hammergren had nothing to do with HBOC, but he understood why the CEO needed to stay behind in San Francisco, so he agreed to go as the McKesson representative.

Arriving in Hawaii, Hammergren found the HBOC sales group devastated. One minute they'd been celebrating a record year with their spouses and colleagues, the next minute their world had come to an end. Even worse, they felt responsible for the catastrophe since it was HBOC's accounting troubles that had caused McKesson's crisis. People were frightened and looking for answers. Hammergren called a general meeting. Once everyone had gathered in the room, he stood at the front with the senior HBOC team and expected them to say a few words. To his surprise, they were unable or unwilling to address the group. It was as though they wanted or needed someone else to do the talking.

Seeing the dejection in the room, Hammergren tried to raise the spirits of the sales team. He told them, as confidently as he could manage, that they and the organization would get through this. He believed in the quality of the HBOC people and in the quality of their customer base. Together, they'd find a way. His speech was all he could offer them in the moment, but it seemed to help.

Unfortunately, the news didn't get any better over the next few months. The accounting irregularities were just as serious as they'd appeared. The CEO and CFO of McKesson soon resigned. Other top executives were fired. In a turn of events unimaginable a year before, Hammergren found himself one of the last executives left standing. The board asked him to serve as the new co-CEO.

It was not an easy assignment. The company was adrift. McKesson's share price continued to plunge, even as the dot-com boom roared on. Employee morale was terrible and customers were angry. On top of everything else, Hammergren wasn't sure what to do about HBOC. Did its problems go deeper than just accounting errors? He decided to visit the HBOC headquarters in Atlanta and examine the business closely. While there, he went to a major customer meeting to say a few words. The room was packed with about 250 customers, all angry and looking for someone to blame. Hammergren and a colleague figured they would take the stage for fifteen or twenty minutes and answer questions. The Q&A went on for a brutal three hours. It was like a scene from the *Blues Brothers* where Belushi and Akroyd perform behind chicken wire while dodging beer bottles and vegetables thrown at them by the hostile crowd. The anger was much more intense and the problems deeper and more severe than Hammergren could have guessed. Still, the experience helped clarify what needed to be done. He told the room that McKesson would make good on its promises and invest in the future, rather than off-load its problems or cast anyone—customer or employee—aside.

Privately, he wondered how to turn things around. Even though normal business operations continued, the company was in disarray and the people were walking zombies. But he believed that beneath the rubble a great company still had a chance to rise again if he could only inspire hearts and minds. To that end, he developed a set of shared principles for the enterprise, called ICARE, which encouraged people going forward to act with complete integrity and do the right thing on behalf of the customer, no matter what. These values gave everyone something to rally around. Hammergren earned credibility by acting with accountability and talking straight. He backed up all the rhetoric with a formal scorecard for the business in which the measures of success were no longer tied to Wall Street. Instead, the company would evaluate its progress based on customer and employee satisfaction, operational success and financial success that went well beyond stock price.

Finally, he helped employees understand that McKesson was a company that could make a real difference in healthcare and in people's lives. Though McKesson's businesses didn't touch patients directly, the McKesson people made sure that patients and caregivers received critical support in terms of medicine, supplies and information. The way Hammergren described it, employees could see a parallel between the experiences of McKesson and the healthcare system as a whole. The U.S. healthcare industry was on the brink of its own disaster. Companies like McKesson needed to step in to meet those enormous challenges. This perspective helped employees develop a shared sense of purpose, and gave them the hope and resiliency they needed to re-engage with their work and turn the company around.

Eighteen years later, Hammergren was still CEO of McKesson until he finally retired. The once-sleepy pharmaceutical distributor grew dramatically over that time, on all fronts, from number of employees, to global footprint and huge revenues. Today, McKesson is one of the most valuable companies in the world and sits in the top ten on the Fortune 500. That dramatic growth would not have been possible without the crisis that nearly destroyed the company.

The Power of Purpose

In the early 2000s, financial crises like the one McKesson faced were relatively common. Enron, Arthur Anderson, WorldCom, Tyco, Swissair, Parmalat, HIH, Barclays, Barings, and Lehman Brothers were among a host of acclaimed organizations around the world that also got caught up in financial scandals and were either destroyed or only exist today in a diminished state.

Other companies, like McKesson, have met crises, faced potential catastrophe and discovered or rediscovered the sense of purpose needed to turn things around. Johnson & Johnson, IBM, Ford, etc., have made it through different challenges and emerged stronger and more focused than ever.

Then there are the countless stories we never hear about. A crisis does not have to be so large that it threatens an entire organization or industry sector. A small family-owned business or a sales or product development team can face a crisis that is just as serious in terms of its threat. The best way to turn a bad situation into an opportunity for renewal and growth is to sharpen focus on a clear sense of purpose. A crisis helps us think about and understand what really matters to people.

There's an old saying in the military, "There are no atheists in foxholes." It means that people who are in great stress or danger will always turn to God, even if they aren't normally true believers. When problems are too big to handle, only God can help.

I've developed a slightly different view. I think that when human beings find themselves in difficult situations, the support they really need comes from a sense of purpose. For some people this is God. For others, it's a national flag, a family to protect, a major goal, something that matters personally.

All of these things—God, flag, family, goal—come down to meaning. That's what purpose is: a sense of meaning. Viktor Frankl, the Austrian psychiatrist, determined that a sense of meaning or purpose can help a human being survive the most horrible experiences. As a Jew during World War II, Frankl was forced into a Nazi ghetto where he worked as a physician because of his training as a psychiatrist. Later, he was given the task of monitoring the mental health of inmates and helping new people overcome their shock and grief. Then, he and his wife were transferred to Auschwitz where Frankl worked as a slave laborer. In those horrifying, dehumanizing and brutal conditions, Frankl observed that many people simply gave up and died. The ones who had a sense of higher purpose seemed better equipped to survive. As Frankl put it, "Those who have a 'why' to live, can bear with almost any 'how.'"

Crisis/Krisis

I can't fully know how a concentration camp survivor or even the CEO of a company uses a sense of purpose to get through a crisis. Instead, I can tell you about my experience and break that down.

In reality, my crisis story started in Greece, not Ukraine. In 2009, I had just been appointed managing director and was stationed in Athens. It was my first position as the head of a large corporate territory, and I was incredibly proud and excited. I'd grown up in Athens and worked there earlier in my career. Returning as a managing director made me feel like a conquering hero.

Things were a little rocky economically when I started my new position. The global financial crisis had hit the year before, and Greece, like most countries, had just entered a serious recession. Still, I felt pretty confident and saw the downturn as a chance to make up some ground on the competition. I knew the Greek market like the back of my hand and had personal connections with many of the people who would now be my suppliers and partners. I focused immediately on developing the quality of my team and building a culture in which we all felt inspired and energized. We launched our first new factory in over eighty years—a proud moment for me—and I felt like I was setting our company up for strong future growth.

You can imagine how sick I felt in late 2009 when Greece's debt crisis suddenly exploded and the economy collapsed almost overnight.

The downturn was so much bigger than anything I'd ever experienced before. All the confidence we'd felt, and even the general prosperity of the country, suddenly seemed like an illusion. It wasn't just businesses that got clobbered, Greek society fell apart. Jobs evaporated. Political leaders seemed completely lost. Greeks woke up from their dream of good economic times, realized that it had all been built on government debt they couldn't pay off, and reacted with panic and anger. Massive protests ensued. People flooded the streets in scenes reminiscent of the Great Depression. The government responded with severe austerity measures, and businesses started to lay people off. Not surprisingly, workers got angry and launched national strikes, making a terrible situation even worse. Violent riots erupted next. People broke shop windows, burned cars and fought like gangs in the streets. I couldn't believe the chaos and anger. It was incredibly distressing to watch my homeland fall apart before my eyes.

For our business, the collapse was just as brutal. To counter the economic strain, the government implemented a series of heavy austerity measures. Suddenly, no one had any disposable income. The loss of market demand decimated our profitability overnight by more than three quarters. I could think of no way to stop the slide.

I remember actually looking out my window, desperate for answers. That's when I realized that I was facing the Salamina sea pretty much from the same spot where, 2,500 years earlier, King Xerxes had watched his fleet destroyed by the Greek navy in one of the most famous battles of Ancient Greece. I laughed at the comparison, but I was also distraught. The stress was affecting me physically, emotionally and mentally. For months, I had ice-cold hands, a sick stomach and no appetite. I developed a slipped disc in my back, had difficulty sleeping and my thoughts were often muddled. I had a short temper and I felt frustrated all the time.

It helped to talk with some very understanding bosses back in Switzerland. They told me that they didn't hold me responsible for the steep decline in profitability because the financial, political and social turmoil was obviously not my fault. Instead, they would measure my performance and growth as a leader by how I dealt with the crisis. In other words, the crisis wasn't personal, and it was not necessary or even helpful for me to feel responsible for events that were clearly beyond my control. But it was my responsibility to manage it as best as possible for the sake of my team and the company. While that might seem self-evident to someone outside the chaos, I think it's a lesson that every young leader must learn and absorb.

That advice really helped me to focus on what I could do, not what I couldn't, and what my team needed from me to weather the storm. Soon, the crisis became a catalyst for a sharpened sense of purpose. I knew people didn't care as much about brand or market share when the world was falling apart. So we put aside all the many different things that we'd been worried about before—and focused on what was truly critical and mattered to everyone. We all needed jobs. We wanted Greek society and the Greek economy to get better. We knew our company could help. We had eight hundred employees, and we didn't want to cut our workforce in half to keep our margins up. We also didn't want to cheapen our brands to secure easier revenue. We wanted long-term success. So we decided that our new purpose would be to do whatever we could to put our business in a position to survive the turmoil and emerge stronger when it was over.

We called that approach "We never stop," and it became a rallying cry that helped us all work harder, stay resilient and come up with creative solutions for many different complicated problems.

In the end, we did survive and we kept our eight hundred employees and our brand position. Many businesses in Greece didn't make it, and the economy is still struggling more than ten years later. I don't think that Greek society has recovered its sense of purpose and vision for a better future even today.

When I reflected later on the difference that leadership can make during a crisis, I thought of something interesting that perhaps only a native Greek or a classically trained scholar would know. The word crisis is Greek in

origin, but the Greek word "krisis" has a second meaning that goes beyond the English usage. As in English, a *krisis* is a time of chaos and confusion. But the Greek word also means to apply judgment and discernment, or to separate the components of a problem. In other words, to extricate ourselves from a crisis, we must also exercise *krisis*.

That was the mindset I learned to incorporate to weather our problems in Greece. Leaders feel responsible by nature, but that sense of accountability must be balanced by some emotional detachment and sound judgment. They must be able to separate themselves from the turmoil and see the many confusing facts in a clear-eyed and objective way in order to make good, prompt decisions and take appropriate actions.

While I don't think previous crisis experience is essential for a leader, my experience in Greece helped me immeasurably in reacting more quickly and confidently to the confusion I encountered in Ukraine.

Preparing for Black Swans

When I came on board as the new managing director in Ukraine, I was excited to experience life in a new country and to take over an even bigger territory. I had a new apartment, a new gym and a new team of talented international managers. I was looking forward to the challenges of leading a business division with a large market and lots of opportunity. These are the normal things that business people get excited about at the midpoint of their careers.

I hit the ground running and ran into some roadblocks right away.

I think it's a common experience for a leader to take on a new position in a department or organization that seems to be functioning well, turn over a few rocks, and find unexpected problems. Early on, I discovered that our organization was in some trouble. We were losing market share. Our people had no motivation. Most importantly, my management team didn't have a winning attitude or a sense of urgency and was missing some critical leadership traits. I realized I'd need to shake things up to help us reach a higher level of performance.

So I got to work doing the normal kinds of things that any leader in that situation would do. Within six months, we established a shared vision and set of values organized around a campaign called "We Better." We wanted to grow and get better as an organization and as individuals. Things started to click. We stopped losing ground and turned our apathetic attitude around. Our business began to pick up substantially and the numbers jumped. The organization felt revitalized, and it was suddenly exciting to be part of our group. We were on the move.

The crisis, it turned out, would accelerate that progress dramatically.

I can't see the future, and I had no idea what was about to happen to Ukraine, but I'd learned a lesson from Greece that a serious emergency can overturn everything. So I asked an experienced American coach I knew to help us develop a crisis management plan just in case. Nassim Taleb calls unpredictable high-impact crises "Black Swan" events. Our coach helped us think through what we'd need to do in a number of different scenarios that might affect our communication channels, our ability to work from headquarters and how we would delegate decision-making if anything went wrong.

We scheduled a training day for the end of the year to test out that plan and practice implementing it. Ironically, by then, the Black Swan had already arrived.

The Fog Fear

The protests and riots, the unpredictable police violence, the mysterious kidnappings and horrible assassinations, the alarming military activity by Russia … as the crisis worsened, almost everyone became frightened, me included. I remember one ordinary night, waking every half hour to check my phone for updates, when the sudden sound of explosions made me break out into a cold sweat. Was the Russian military attacking Kiev? For the next long minute, I debated whether I should initiate our evacuation plan. Then I looked out of the window and started laughing. The sound of exploding bombs was just fireworks from a nearby wedding ceremony.

In my best moments, I tried to be detached and objective—to exercise *krisis*. But the panic and confusion that we all felt was very real, and I knew that I needed to acknowledge those feelings and allow people to express them so they could learn to manage themselves productively. This was a balancing act at times, but it was particularly tough during the early stages of the crisis before we got used to the "new normal." Later, we came to expect that confusion and fear could escalate rapidly with any sudden trigger.

We had over 1,400 employees. Those of us in Kiev were at the epicenter of the demonstrations and clashes. But eight hundred of our employees worked in a factory very close to the area where Ukrainian troops and Russian-backed rebels were fighting, and many of our field offices were near this hot zone. What would happen if the conflict expanded and Russian troops occupied the area? Our employees were afraid for their physical safety and the safety of their immediate families and relatives. They worried about the future of Ukraine politically, about the ability of the economy to continue to function, and about doing their jobs and managing their responsibilities under extraordinary stress.

Experiencing that level of unrest is truly a helpless feeling. There are so many things we take for granted under normal circumstances in a developed country. The rule of law. Justice. The availability of groceries. A stable currency. Reasonable political leadership. Personal safety.

You feel very small when that goes away, and increasingly vulnerable, as if you have little control over your life; and the violence and insanity of larger events can sweep over you in a minute and wipe everything away. You also become closer with your friends and family and can even feel close to strangers very quickly. People support each other—and help each other out. That part really makes you feel good about humanity.

How can a business leader help the people in an organization manage that much unpredictability and abnormality? Even though we had made plans before the conflict began to hold a simulation exercise on crisis management, the reality of what we actually did experience and how it overturned our world reinforced the notion that it's extremely difficult to plan for chaos. Geopolitical conflicts, pandemics, or natural disasters are events that go well beyond the operational and strategic scope of a business and the normal responsibilities of a management team. I soon realized that the way we responded as a senior team to the daily barrage of unpredictable events would be the real difference maker.

I was very aware that how I appeared to others mattered a great deal. People take their cues from the leader even in normal times, and often model their own attitudes and behavior accordingly. The leader is watched especially closely during a crisis when panic and confusion can rule. I wanted to be the calm and decisive captain who was also visible, hands-on and active. I also needed to be "present" for others. Some leaders hide their emotions and try to appear heroic, all-knowing and supremely confident. Others reveal everything about what they are thinking or feeling and share their vulnerability. I felt that a middle path was appropriate, admitting that I had concerns and worries while being strong for others. Sometimes I had people come into my office and close the door to discuss their fears and even cry on my shoulder. I comforted them with understanding and an ability to help them see options and positive possibilities.

I tried to lessen their burdens as much as possible. I wanted every employee to know that we were looking out for them, and that their most important responsibility was to be safe. This was a challenge, of course. Foreign employees knew that they and their families would be evacuated from the country at the first sign of collapse. We had a plan for that. But the safety of domestic employees became even more difficult to ensure as the conflict went on and some of our people got conscripted into the military.

I also wanted our place of work to feel like a refuge or escape from the harsh reality outside. Mimicking offices I had visited in Silicon Valley, I put in some games like billiards and minifootball to give people a laugh and a way to expend some physical energy, especially when the hours became long. I believed it was important for us to have a good time together.

In Greece, we had turned to the well-known story of Shackleton, the polar explorer, to reflect on the fortitude, resilience, and adaptability needed by a team to overcome daunting odds. In Ukraine, we had recently heard a motivational speech by a modern Antarctic adventurer, Sean Chapple, who introduced us to the concept of "Tent Time." According to Chapple, his exploration team bonded because they spent time together in a tent at the end of every day, sharing stories, memories, and worries in casual conversation. Similarly, the more time we spent together in Ukraine, and the more we were able to share with each other, the calmer and closer we became as a team.

Email sent to our Crimea employees one day before the Referendum which led to the Russian Annexation on March 14, 2014:

Dear colleagues,

I want to let you know that you are not alone in the tough situation you are facing in your homeland at this moment. I also want to assure you we are thinking of you at every moment and will provide you with all relevant support when needed.

Please remember 2 things:

*First, **take care of your safety** and stay away from the areas where large groups are gathering should you decide to take part in the upcoming referendum. I do understand how hard it is to remain* *calm and stay away when these political matters concern you, your families and the future of your country, but I ask you once again, remember that your safety comes first.*

Second, I am well aware of and share your concerns regarding your future as it might be impacted by the outcome of the referendum. I would like to assure you that whatever scenario comes into play, we have plans for all of them. **As a company we are ready to do our best** *to help you get through these challenging times.*

I want to repeat: we are with you in our thoughts and our hearts.

My warmest personal regards to you and your families,

Christos

* * *

We needed to adopt a new way to run the business. People have a tendency during a crisis to dwell on the extremes of negativity or, conversely, to believe that they've finally hit bottom and things can't possibly get any worse. As lightheartedly and humorously as possible, I tried to urge them to avoid despair and false optimism. I assured them that we would survive no matter what, but that they could not know yet how deep and dark the tunnel might turn out to be.

My own brain never stopped processing new information, playing out "What if" scenarios, calculating risk factors, and running through check-lists. I tried to infuse my team with this automatic "What if" thinking and attitude, too. We worked hard at imagining possible situations. With each new event or development, we learned to assess what it meant by asking, "What is it that we have in front of us, and what are the consequences of this change?" Out of that thought process, it became easier to imagine the options that were available to us and the actions we should take.

But we knew that in a living, breathing crisis, even those plans could quickly become pointless. So we practiced asking "What if" about those scenarios too, imagining everything that could possibly happen next. We crafted contingency plans for nearly every area of our business, and we identified trigger points that would indicate or predict a new escalation and propel us into action. So, for example, we knew what we would do if our factory, in close proximity to the fighting, was shut down. We knew what we would do if our phones were cut or our email service went out. We knew what we would do if we needed to evacuate our headquarters. And we kept these contingency plans as simple as possible. A page or a series of bullet points gave us more than enough information. That "What if" thinking became the new normal.

It was also important to make decisions quickly, move on them immediately and not become stuck worrying about perfection. Whenever possible, I gave my people the power to make their own decisions. I also assured them that as leader I was fully and totally responsible for the consequences when we failed, even as I gave them all the praise and credit when we scored a win. This helped reduce the pressure to make the "right" decision and kept us moving.

It would have been easy for us to make those decisions in secret, huddled up in our war room, safe from questions and demands. But even though we needed time to absorb new information, assess priorities, have candid conversations, and make big decisions, it was just as important for us to be out with the troops, experiencing the same reality as everyone else, and "leading from the front."

Instead of secrecy, we tried to communicate far more than normal. People were less confused and prone to panic, and more apt to make decisions in line with expectations when they understood clearly what was happening and how we felt about it. We didn't want anyone to think we were hoarding information or keeping bad news from them. It was important to be truthful about what was going on. It would have been easy to sugarcoat reality, sound too optimistic about the chances for success, or take the corporate line. If anything, I felt it helped to downplay expectations and assert our independence from the corporation, so people felt they were getting straight talk.

Put Purpose First

But the most important thing we did was to rely on a shared sense of purpose to steady us, motivate us, bind us together and keep us moving forward.

Our purpose in Ukraine was formed out of necessity. I'm not sure we had any choice. But we articulated it clearly and forcefully as a team and rallied around it. We decided that we needed to:

1. Keep our people as safe as possible despite the danger

2. Figure out how to continue business as usual, despite all the unpredictable disruptions and extraordinary barriers

3. Grow stronger as a team

Why those three things?

Well, the first is self-explanatory. There's nothing worse for a manager to lose a colleague or a report. We did not want to put anyone in harm's way for any reason. As I said, we took every possible measure to remove our people and their families from danger, especially those who were in the worst areas or who might have been targets.

Our second purpose felt important, too. During times of chaos, people—both our customers and our employees—get enormous reassurance from little signs of normalcy. Making sure that people could get the products they favored and that our employees had work to go to and paychecks to rely on seemed like things worth fighting for.

Finally, it was important to grow closer as a team. We needed to believe that we could rely on each other, that the hard work would pay off, and that together, through resilience, fortitude, creativity and luck, we could somehow survive and succeed.

It worked. Because of our shared sense of purpose, we never felt more alive during those months of geopolitical uncertainty and confusion. We were engaged at a deep level by our work and the problems before us. We didn't get tired, even when we barely slept for days on end. We were often afraid, but we didn't lose our ability to reason and make decisions. We were confronted by frustrating challenges and unexpected setbacks all the time, but we stayed resilient and creative and always found ways to make things work. We couldn't plan but we could improvise. Goals changed constantly. Success was measured by getting things done. We developed our professional capabilities as managers at an accelerated pace, learned how to delegate better, make decisions in the moment, act quickly and plan smart. We also grew as human beings. I felt that about myself—that I was really coming into my own—and I saw my colleagues rise above the responsibilities of their roles, and sort of take off their masks to show real empathy and understanding for others and to display insight and even wisdom on many occasions. We became closer as a team—we coordinated faster, collaborated easier, seemed to understand what each other were thinking without a lot of messing around. We formed real friendships across all the traditional barriers of age, level of experience, nationality, native language, and even political beliefs.

It could have been a disaster. We could have fallen apart as an organization, failed to meet our responsibilities, cowered in fear, become selfish and mean-spirited, and blamed each other for failures beyond our control. Instead, we survived and thrived. We somehow managed to keep everyone in our division safe. We achieved exceptional business and organizational results at a time when many companies had decided to "write off" Ukraine. We strengthened our focus, instead, and became more lean in our operations while maintaining our market and customer base.

We also served as a beacon of stability to our customers and the people of Ukraine during a difficult time. Anyone who has ever lived through a prolonged crisis or a war will appreciate how meaningful it is to be able to go to a nearby store and find a favorite product. It reinforces the value of ordinary life and provides reassurances that calm will one day return.

Because of the crisis, we discovered ourselves and became something bigger.

That's the power of purpose.

Every company can develop a vision, a mission, a strategic plan. But there's something missing without purpose. We were "lucky" enough to discover that need through a crisis no one would have wished to experience.

But because of that crisis we saw how purpose could motivate and inspire our people. We also saw how that sense of shared meaning and camaraderie sharpened our focus, resilience and stamina in a way that improved our organizational performance. We knew we were doing something bigger than just selling units and making money. A sense of purpose made everything seem possible.

I left Ukraine knowing I wanted to understand purpose better and figure out how to leverage it more deliberately and consciously in the future—with or without a crisis.

CHAPTER ONE RECAP

- Keep on your toes. We live in a time of constant crisis occurring in unexpected ways. You can't control it. You can't predict the future. You can develop plans for it, but that's not the real remedy.

- Organizations, teams and individuals are better equipped to survive a crisis when they develop or exist according to a higher purpose.

- During a crisis, the team navigates better with transparency, accountability, togetherness, agile decision-making and a common purpose.

- As a leader, if you have already experienced a crisis, you are lucky. Treat it as a gift. It has given you more skills, agility and courage. And for your team it is a reason to find meaning, purpose and wisdom to grow further.

Tools & Resources

My Crisis Management Checklist

This is what we did during the Ukraine crisis. When it happens to you, come back and check it out.

- Determine the role of the crisis team as a whole and each member.

- Determine routines and protocols for communication and briefings.

- Develop a mechanism for monitoring all events chronologically, such as a Log, Whiteboard, Digital Record, etc.

- Establish and equip a War Room—a place where the crisis team will meet.

- Engage in "What if" scenario planning to develop awareness, vigilance and agile thinking.

- Develop Signals & Triggers Map, a list of signals you're receiving from the field that assesses each event or trigger point by their likelihood to escalate.

- Determine who will be your Receivers & Doers—who will actively gather information and who will act upon new events or incidents.

- Establish a Master Book both digitally and on paper (this will include your assets, escape routes, meeting points, telephone lists, etc.). This is useful for all times, actually. The process of developing such a book can be beneficial on its own.

- Obtain Satellite Communications Hardware (satellite phones should cell phone reception fail), or if there is no physical threat in the immediate future, this might read as develop alternative channels of communications beyond the standard ones, just for the rainy days.

- Get your Go-Bags Ready—Emergency bags for the team and team members in case of evacuation, etc. As mentioned before, selecting what you keep with you in any severe crisis can put you in a position to really assess what is absolutely vital for the organization and your team.

Signals & Triggers Mapping

To monitor the events that would lead us toward specific actions helped us to better monitor the evolution of the crisis in Ukraine. We used the below template.

LEVELS OF ALERT APPLIED FOR THE SPECIFIC CRISIS HANDLING

- ALERT LEVEL 1 (DESCRIPTION)
- ALERT LEVEL 2 (DESCRIPTION)
- ALERT LEVEL 3 (DESCRIPTION)

ALERT LEVELS	DESCRIPTION OF LEVELS	INDICATORS/TRIGGERS TO ACTIVATE EACH LEVEL (POSSIBLE EVENTS)	DECISION MAKER NAME(S)

ACTION PLAN FOR EACH ALERT LEVEL			
ALERT LEVELS	ACTIONS (DESCRIPTIONS)	RESPONSIBLE NAME(S)	ACCOUNTABLE NAME(S)
LEVEL 1			
1			
2			
LEVEL 2			
1			
2			
LEVEL 3			
1			
2			

If you want to see a real-life example, visit my site www.christostsolkas.com

The House of Crisis

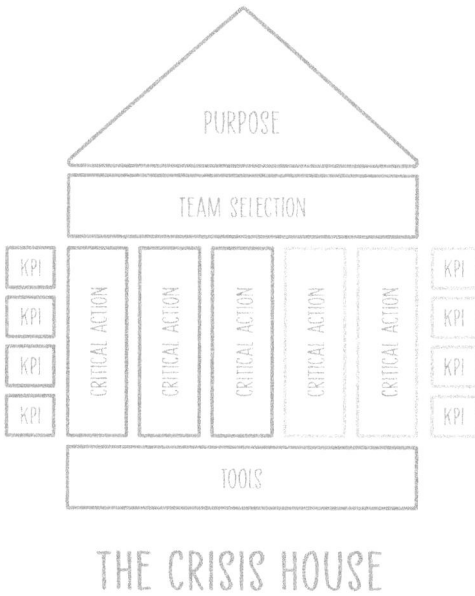

THE CRISIS HOUSE

- When a crisis starts, form and assemble your crisis team. Team selection is critical and depends on the crisis at hand.

- Define your purpose.

- Determine the critical actions required to deal with your situation and achieve your purpose.

- Build, assemble, or collect the skills needed to manage the situation effectively.

- Determine which tools (technological, systems, etc.) will help or are necessary.

- Decide on the Key Performance Indicators (KPIs) (one or two figures) by every critical action.

More info and guidelines on how to construct your Crisis House, you will find on my site www.christostsolkas.com

CHAPTER TWO

This Team Rocks

It was a beautiful summer evening on the beach in Panama City, Florida, in July 2017. Some people walked along the sand, others sunbathed, swam or body-surfed the waves. Then, a few people noticed that something was wrong.

Derek Simmons was picnicking with his family when he saw a crowd gathered at the edge of the water pointing out to sea. He walked over to find out what was going on, wondering if there had been a shark attack. What he discovered was just as horrible. An entire family was caught in a riptide. No one could rescue them. They were too far from shore, and the current was too strong to swim through. It was the most helpless feeling in the world.

Then Simmons got an idea. He turned to those next to him and said, "Let's try to get as many people as we can to form a human chain." He was thinking about ants and how they can come together during precarious situations.

At first people were reluctant. Probably they were afraid and worried about the distance. It wasn't their job to help rescue anyone, though the lifeguards were off-duty. Simmons' urgency shook off that passivity, and soon the group on the beach began hollering to others to join and help. New people ran over, immediately understood what was going on, and waded into the powerful current to take their place at the front of the growing line as it stretched out to sea, closer and closer to the stranded swimmers. A team formed one person at a time.

It took eighty strangers in the end. As the family of six and another couple (who'd swam out to help and gotten caught in the same riptide) struggled to stay above water, the human chain reached them. The people at the front grabbed the two children first, ages eight and eleven, and passed them along to the beach. The mother, close to drowning, was next, and so on.

It took an exhausting hour to get everyone to shore safely. The family's grandmother suffered a heart attack during the ordeal but survived. The crowd on the beach cheered and hugged and cried.

They knew they'd done something heroic and special by coming together. If they hadn't, eight people would have died. Then, that team dissolved and the eighty strangers, forever connected, went their separate ways.[1]

Teams Forming in Crisis

Eighty strangers on a beach is a large team. How about ten thousand? Among the countless heartwarming and heartbreaking stories from 9/11, here's one of the most amazing.

In 1925, Charles Lindbergh was the first person to pilot an airplane across the Atlantic, nonstop, taking 33½ hours in a single-engine plane to go from Long Island to Paris. In the early days of commercial air travel, however, it was difficult for larger planes to make the entire distance from New York City to London or Paris without refueling. Many commercial flights broke up the trip by landing in a remote northern Canadian town

[1] https://www.theguardian.com/us-news/2017/jul/11/80-people-form-human-chain-rescue-gulf-of-mexico-florida

called Gander. By the 1950s, Gander was the most important airport in the world. The Beatles landed in Gander on their way to New York City. The likes of Albert Einstein, Frank Sinatra, Marilyn Monroe, Elvis and Winston Churchill killed time at the airport bar or restaurant. The locals, who were ordinary, unpretentious people, took it all in stride.

By the 1960s, with the adoption of jet fuel, commercial airplanes became less common in Gander, and its importance receded. The airport was still in use, but its large capacity was a relic of a bygone era. Then with 9/11 that capacity came to the rescue. After two commercial aircraft struck the World Trade Center towers in New York City and a third hit the Pentagon outside Washington, D.C., air traffic over North America was grounded. This put cross-Atlantic flights in particularly desperate straits. With limited fuel and no way to turn back for Europe, where could all those flights land? Gander was one of the airports at the ready.

In all, thirty-eight commercial planes and four military planes were diverted to Gander that morning. The 6,600 civilian passengers and crew didn't know the real reason for the emergency diversion until they landed. Then, the passengers needed to remain on board until security teams could ensure that no terrorists or explosive devices were on board.

The world, horrified by the events in New York City and the Pentagon, had come to a stop. The passengers in Gander were stranded far from home and unable to return. All flights remained grounded for the next six days.

Six thousand, six hundred people represented 66 percent of the local population in Gander, an enormous influx even in this era of refugees pouring into Europe from Syria and Africa. The ten thousand citizens of Gander could have been excused for feeling overwhelmed. Instead, in a very coordinated fashion, they got to work. They filled gymnasiums and other open buildings with cots, and when the cots filled up, they found families to take the remaining passengers into their homes. Restaurants opened up to give free meals. The locals made sure passengers had access to showers and laundry machines to clean themselves up. They even cared for seventeen dogs and cats and two great apes. Most importantly, they helped comfort people who were far from home, in distress and worried about their loved ones and the future.[2, 3]

When passengers returned to their aircrafts almost a week later, they greeted each other like old friends and traded stories of what they'd been through. They hugged and exchanged phone numbers and email addresses. But mostly they remembered the people they'd met on the ground. As Flight Delta 15 filled up, a passenger asked the captain if he could use the PA system to make an announcement. Normally, this was not allowed, but the captain permitted it. The passenger talked about the amazing hospitality they had all received and said that he would like to set up a trust fund to provide college scholarships for the students of the local high school. He asked for donations of any amount from his fellow travelers. Many of the passengers bonded together, collected $14,000 on the spot, and helped the fund grow to over $1.5 million later.[4]

In a crisis, when chaos or confusion threatens to take over, human beings often reveal their best selves, usually by joining together in common cause. Daniel Aldritch, a political scientist at Perdue University in Indiana, saw this firsthand during Hurricane Katrina in 2005. Though flooding was imminent, officials had not yet ordered evacuation; but local communities, neighbors helping neighbors, immediately took up the task of telling people they should leave and helping those who needed help. Aldritch later conducted research at disasters all around the world and discovered it is almost always ad hoc teams of neighbors who do the most good after a calamity, saving and helping more people than paramedics, firefighters, police and soldiers. As Aldritch observed, "It's this passion for a local community and granular knowledge about who needs what that makes large-scale government interventions ineffective by comparison."[5]

2   https://www.nytimes.com/2005/03/20/travel/magazine/gander-airport-when-the-going-was-good.html

3   https://www.washingtonpost.com/local/on-sept-11-a-tiny-canadian-town opened its runways-and-heart-to-7000-stranded-travelers/2016/09/08/89d875da-75e5-11e6-8149-b8d05321db62_story.html?utm_term=.1d13762576a5

4   http://mytnnews.com/blog/2012/10/11/delta-flight-15-a-true-story-about-9-11/

5   https://www.npr.org/2011/07/04/137526401/the-key-to-disaster-survival-friends- and-neighbors

In her book, *A Paradise Built in Hell: The Extraordinary Communities that Arise in Disaster*, Rebecca Solnit tapped her experiences living through an earthquake in San Francisco in the late 1980s, and the research she later did at other sites of disaster. During such emergencies, she did not find greed, violence, fear or desperation, but extraordinary stories of teams of people coming together in community, collaboration and caring. As Solnit wrote,

> In the wake of an earthquake, a bombing or a major storm, most people are altruistic, urgently engaged in caring for themselves and those around them, strangers and neighbors as well as friends and loved ones. The image of the selfish, panicky or regressively savage human being in times of disaster has little truth to it. Decades of meticulous sociological research on behavior in disasters, from the bombings of World War II to floods, tornadoes, earthquakes and storms across the continent and around the world, have demonstrated this.... We need ties to survive, but they along with purposefulness, immediacy, and agency also give us joy—the startling, sharp joy I found over and over again in accounts of disaster.[6]

Even distance is no object. Today, in our global era of instant communication, collaborative teams can come together over any disaster. In 2010, when thirty-three Chilean miners got trapped 2,000 feet below ground, the situation appeared hopeless. Yet, teams formed instantly. The trapped miners organized themselves with an unusual level of collaboration, sharing space to stand or lie down, looking after each other's needs, taking shifts. Above ground, teams of engineers and aid workers formed to do what they could. The odds were long. Experts suggested a 2 percent chance that the miners could be dug out after four months. Because the technical capabilities were insufficient, the rescuers put out a call for help from anyone in the world who could assist. People sent important tools and support devices from all over the world. A small company in the U.S., learning about the crisis, offered a drilling rig that could do the necessary work in half the time. It arrived in Chile three days later. Two and a half months after the disaster, the miners were rescued—all alive. Without many teams all over the world coming together, it never would have happened.[7]

These spontanous teams make sense to us intuitively. People are willing to drop everything and help others, their neighbors, even strangers, even people on the other side of the world, when the need arises. Why?

Because there's no confusion—the purpose is crystal clear. How much more simple could it be? Some people are drowning—let's form a human chain. Thousands need shelter—let's open up our homes and coordinate meals. A group of miners are trapped—let's send our best experts and equipment.

The effect is powerful. Joined in common cause, the elation, camaraderie and collective power is something to behold. The people on a strong team are engaged and feel a deep and driving sense of shared purpose. No matter how traumatic the experience of an emergency or crisis might be, they don't seem paralyzed by anxiety or indecision. And afterwards, studies show, those people experience less grief and post-traumatic stress.

Lost Connections

Why do teams, organized around a clear purpose, make people feel so energized, engaged and alive? Because they get at a deep and often neglected human need. Let me explain.

Ordinary life—going to work, shopping for groceries, taking vacations—feels very different than the experience of being a team in a crisis. It should feel better, you would think, given the fact that our lives are not on the line on an average, ordinary day. But this is not always the case. In fact, our modern existence is often characterized by feelings that are in opposition to the feelings of being on a purpose-driven team. Instead of feeling engaged, energized, focused and powerful, many people often feel anxious, isolated or lonely and depressed. Although not a perfect correlation, more people than ever today rely on anti-depressant and anti-anxiety medication. In the

---

7   http://knowledge.wharton.upenn.edu/article/the-chilean-miner-rescue-a-lesson-in-global-teamwork/

U.S., 65 percent more Americans take such medications daily compared to fifteen years ago. Long-term reliance is also increasingly common.[8]

On a surface level, this development can seem bizarre or counter-intuitive. Everyone likes to complain that the "stress of modern living" is worse today than before. But unless you are living in a war zone, addicted to opioids, a refugee, incapacitated by illness, impoverished or unemployed long-term, chances are you are living a better, higher-quality life today than most humans who have ever been alive.

Still, loneliness and sense of isolation is up. Writers like Robert Putnam in *Bowling Alone* pointed out years ago that our social bonds are not as strong as they used to be. Once, most of us had large, sprawling families. Today, divorce rates are higher, and people tend to live at greater distances from their relatives than they did in the past.

Religious institutions have weakened, too. Attending a church, mosque or synagogue is still common in some countries or cultures but not as universal as it used to be. More people, especially here in Europe, question traditional religious values rather than embrace them whole-heartedly.

In the cities where most of us live, we can be surrounded by people and yet not know our neighbors. We don't have strong ties to our local communities even when we shop, because most neighborhood stores have been replaced by global chains, and the goods and services we consume have likely been produced far away because it's cheaper.

In our jobs, work is also typically no longer a local or community-based activity, but a global one. People move to new cities for their careers. Company headquarters may be in another country altogether. The people we work with on a daily basis on a project or in a department may not be the people we see every day. Virtual or remote teams are less the exception than the rule nowadays. We have fewer chances for casual, relationship-building exchanges.

Even our forms of entertainment and social engagement are oddly detached from the world we live in. Video games are extremely popular, especially among millennials, and massive multiplayer games do involve "gathering" large numbers of people into one universe. But those are usually

---

8   https://www.cbsnews.com/news/antidepressant-use-soars-65-percent-in-15-years/

not the same people we live, socialize and work with in the "real" world. Social media has the word "social" right in the name, but if you notice how many people are staring at their phones while they tweet, post or ping, you also see how little they are engaged in the world around them, how isolated from it they seem.

Are we happier, healthier, more satisfied with our modern lives? Fat chance.

My parents, who have always lived in Greece, had a very different experience of life than I have had—calm, consistent, almost uneventful. My father is eighty-nine years old now and very healthy and happy, thankfully. In his career, he was a public servant with a steady job, but he had very little responsibility and experienced almost no excitement. He didn't make much money, but he was very dedicated to being a good provider, and he was able to earn enough to support a family in a modest home. He wasn't a complete slave to his job. He had friends and hobbies. He occasionally wrote rhymes—he would not call them poems. His biggest priority was to raise his two sons at the highest ethical and educational standards possible. In spite of that "ordinary existence", he's been incredibly happy. In our family, we almost treat his happiness as a joke because it can be so annoying at times. My father laughs and jokes often. His mood is almost always optimistic and positive. Even my daughter finds it too much. She says, "Daddy, why is Grandpa always singing? I don't get it!"

Today, my parents live on an island that could be considered a kind of paradise. The climate is comfortable. There's little pollution. People have enough to eat and do. And they live exceptionally long, healthy and happy lives.

In fact, this island and others like it in Greece are famous as "Blue Zones." There are a number of other such areas around the world where there are many people over eighty years old and some even over a hundred who continue to live simple but healthy, happy and productive lives, even in a world that seems so stressful, dislocated and busy.[9] What's the secret of their happiness and longevity?

Most of the Blue Zone research focuses on diet and lifestyle. Having visited the island of Ikaria, which was profiled in the research, I can

9   https://www.nytimes.com/2012/10/28/magazine/the-island-where-people-forget-to-die.html

understand why. The island is incredibly beautiful and easy to live in. The food is wonderfully fresh and healthy and low in bad fat. The people live more on the "sun-clock" or the "stomach-clock" than the wristwatch. Shops are not open in the mornings, taverns serve you dinner with a smile whenever you want. You can wander to the main square at any time of the day or evening and find people to sit with and talk to. You get lots of exercise just by walking the hills, maybe doing some swimming. On festive occasions, there are fun things like folk dancing, which they proudly call "Ikariotiko".

The easy lifestyle, excellent food and frequent exercise are important for health and happiness. But the research has also emphasized the importance of the strong sense of social connection found in such Blue Zones. It is very easy to be social on an island like Ikaria—in fact, it is difficult not to be social. People are often playing games, dancing, talking. This seems trivial but it's not. Recent studies, especially among aged people, show that loneliness and social isolation is so bad for your health it's the equivalent of smoking two packs of cigarettes a day.

Why would being alone be so stressful and harmful to your health? The work of Johann Hari in his book *Lost Connections: Uncovering the Real Causes of Depression and the Unexpected Solutions* is helpful in understanding. As Hari puts it:

> The umbrella answer is that human beings have innate psychological needs just as we have physical needs. We need to feel we belong, that we have meaning and purpose, that people value us and that we have autonomy. We also live in a culture that's not meeting those psychological needs for most people. It does not manifest as full-blown depression and anxiety in most people; for some people it's just a feeling of unhappiness and a life less fulfilling than it could have been. We've built a society that has many great aspects, but it is not a good match for our human nature.[10]

---

10 https://www.theguardian.com/media/2018/jan/07/johann-hari-depression-brain-lost-connections-book-interview

Isolation and loneliness is a killer, Hari says, because we evolved as tribal animals. If you were isolated or exiled from a group in caveman days, that probably meant you were sick or in great danger and likely about to die. No wonder you would feel stressed, anxious, helpless and depressed.

Many people today work hard to avoid feeling unhappy and dissatisfied with life. They eat well, exercise more, go to occasional retreats for self-care or self-improvement like exercise boot camps, yoga, meditation, mindfulness and so on. Many are obsessed with maximizing everything—our time, our workouts, our brains. We engage in "life hacks" of one kind or another to be more efficient and get more out of our time.

But as Hari and others have pointed out, focusing predominantly on our own personal needs or desires does not necessarily mean we are living happier, more satisfying or meaningful lives. Instead, the real secret to happiness is not to get more but to give more. A study published at Harvard Business School, "Feel Good about Giving" noted the positive feedback loop of those who engaged in charitable or philanthropic activities: "Happier people give more and giving makes people happier ..."[11]

The effect is not only social, it's chemical. The more you do for others, the more serotonin is released into your brain. The recipient of that help gets

---

11   https://hbswk.hbs.edu/item/feeling-good-about-giving-the-benefits-and-costs-of-self-interested-charitable-behavior

a serotonin burst, too. The dynamic is remarkably win-win.[12] Hari points out that helping and supporting other people in any situation makes us feel less isolated, more engaged and more fulfilled. As he put it in an interview, "What heals human loneliness is not getting aid, it's engaging in a reciprocal relationship where someone is giving you something and somewhere down the line you'll give something back."[13]

I have seen this over and over again in my own life and career. In a positive team environment, people give and get all the time. They contribute and are supported in turn. This makes them feel less lonely and isolated and more engaged. When combined with a clear and compelling sense of shared purpose, such as during a crisis or important project, the team is even more powerful because it knows what to do and experiences less confusion or hesitation.

Over a period of time, these teams grow closer and more collaborative. Interestingly, the individuals of the team also grow as people and leaders.

We Better

As I mentioned, I first saw this in Greece when I took over my old home territory. Leading into the economic crisis, I was very eager to develop a strong management team for our business. We developed a vision, shared values and a strategic plan to improve important aspects of the business. The economic crisis hit, and our market collapsed overnight. Suddenly, all of our business plans were meaningless.

Our clear sense of purpose helped us make a lot of decisions. For example, when a downturn comes, the easiest thing in the world would be to let go as many employees as possible, narrow your brands portfolio to the bare minimum, close factories, sell assets, etc. On some occasions, these choices might even be the right ones. But we wanted to be in a better position after the crisis, so we did everything we could to maintain the

---

12   https://www.entrepreneur.com/video/287016

13   https://art19.com/shows/the-ezra-klein-show/episodes/
805c9dc7-ce7d-4238-9e1b-491f138e61e4

brands that would thrive and become our market leaders again and sustain as many employees as possible and keep open the factory that would need to be ready for a new production surge.

We also got closer as a team. Knowing this, when I transferred to Ukraine, I was even more deliberate in trying to develop the performance and closeness of my new team. Our "We Better" vision was a promise that all of our team development work benefit us in every way. By coming together as a team, we would improve our business, develop our careers and grow as individuals.

I wanted to track this growth and development very precisely, so I brought in my leadership coach who had very clear measures for team effectiveness across five critical performance areas. These were:

1. Capabilities and Infrastucture: Whether a team is set up for success by having the members, knowledge, processes and support it needs.

2. Goals and Purpose: Whether a team is focused on outputs and a shared purpose that energizes and gives them meaning.

3. Roles and Individual Expecations: Whether the members of the team are meeting their obligations and support each other in risk-taking and collaboration.

4. Interactions and Team Processes: Whether a team is aligned, efficient, communicates well and handles conflict productively.

5. Learning and Results: Whether a team is growing, developing capabilities and maturing over time.

Each of these five performance areas is divided into sub-factors, which are all measured by surveys of the team members and important stakeholders. The combined scores paint a multifaceted and highly nuanced picture of current team performance capability.

There are also strategies, of course, for developing weak areas over time. If a team doesn't score well on its capabilities and infrastructure, it might need to develop existing team members or recruit different people with the right capabilities to the team. If interactions and team processes score low, then new ways of communicating or holding meetings might be needed, or it might be important to develop team cohesion through intense team development workshops.

Over time, with much focused and precise work, a team can grow in performance capability. The goal is to become a Category One Team.

Category Four	Dysfunctional
Category Three	Adequate to good performance
Category Two	Very good performers but inconsistent or unreliable in sustaining top performance
Category One	Consistently excellent over a sustained period of time

In our first team effectiveness assessment, my management team achieved mostly Category Three level measures with some attributes in the Category Two range. As an ambitious and competitive person, I wanted us to become Category One. My coach told us that it would take two to three years under ordinary circumstances.

Fortunately, or unfortunately, our circumstances proved to be very unordinary. Crisis helped catalyze our development much more quickly.

Meet the Team

As I mentioned in the first chapter, when I came to Ukraine and got to know my team and my business, I discovered that our organization was not in great shape. We were losing market share, our people had no motivation, and my management team didn't have a winning attitude or a sense of urgency and was missing some critical leadership traits. I changed some people around and established a learning path so that we could become even more collaborative and successful in the future.

Individually, my management team was composed of eleven interesting people, each of whom had their own talents and personalities. Let me give you a sense of them by describing three who really stood out.

This is Tatiana

In many ways, Tatiana is a very characteristic Ukrainian woman. Ukraine, like many countries in Eastern Europe, is almost a matriarchal society. The women are highly educated, have strong personalities, and are often the breadwinners in the family. They have a tradition of being tough survivors.

Tatiana is no exception. When she was at school, she earned the opportunity to leave the former Soviet Union on a scholarship to the U.S., but she sacrificed her own advancement to stay home and look after her family.

In the company, Tatiana had already been recognized for her leadership potential and been given a number of challenging assignments abroad. She'd just returned to Ukraine when I arrived in 2012. I was really impressed by her experience and her level of engagement with work. She was in charge of our Corporate Affairs department, and the job was very much in her comfort zone. She loves politics and social issues. She's intelligent, and ambitious, and has strong people skills and a broad network of contacts. She's friendly and people like her.

I saw a lot of versatility in Tatiana and the potential to be a general manager one day, so I moved her into sales, an area she knew nothing about. I figured that experience running our field force would accelerate her development and raise her profile within the company. Like many performance-driven corporations, our company prizes people who can figure out ways to increase revenue and motivate a sales force. So this was a big opportunity for her.

Tatiana responded really well. As we got down to work, it was quickly apparent to me that she was one of the most reliable and hardworking people on my team. She would do whatever it took to get a job done, and she worked nonstop. On weekends, for example, it was almost impossible to get in touch with most people in the company by email or text when I had a question or a concern. Tatiana always replied within 30 minutes. After the crisis began, her response time was even faster. It didn't matter what time of day I checked in or what question I had, Tatiana got back to me almost immediately. I felt total trust in her commitment and her sense of responsibility.

This is Roman

Roman is also Ukrainian. He's young, only thirty-two when we worked together, and holds an MBA from the University of Chicago. He's extremely intelligent, a bit idiosyncratic at times, but impressive in person. He's very creative—the sort of lateral thinker who can be a great problem-solver on any team.

When I met Roman he was the CEO of a small local company. My predecessor had told me about him and suggested we get together. I quickly saw that Roman had skills and ambition we could use, so I recruited him to join our company. I didn't have a position for him at the time, so I sent him to corporate headquarters in Lausanne to do some projects as part of his onboarding process. He stayed there for a few months and then returned to Ukraine.

After I moved Tatiana into sales, I put Roman into her old position in corporate affairs. It was a good position for him to get a feel for the overall company.

Finally, this is Artem

Unlike Tatiana and Roman, Artem is Russian. He's from Saratov, a rather small-for-Russian standards provincial city. He's also one of the most intelligent people I've ever met. His brain is like a computer. He remembers numbers and can do complex calculations in his head.

From the outside, he looks tough. He's a man of few words, and has an unpolished way about him and sometimes comes across as rude in his demeanor. But I could tell a lot of that was due to inexperience and lack of sophistication. Over time, Artem showed that he actually had impressive leadership skills and a big heart. People found him intimidating at first but came to see him as endearing and charismatic the more they got to know him.

As every manager knows, a team is more than a group of talented individuals. It needs to come together as a unit and function at very high levels of collaboration, trust, determination with a compelling direction, clear guardrails and accountability for execution. Our coach kick-started the team-building process through which we started to gel. The exercises we did together were very interesting and incredibly helpful for what was to come. After I moved a few people like Tatiana and Roman into different positions with heavier responsibilities, we started to click through the normal course of doing business.

The team improved, performance got better. The Ukrainian crisis accelerated that progress dramatically.

Make the Team the Answer to as Many Problems as Possible

Leadership stories tend to focus on the leader, and leave the team as an afterthought. But the leader is not a superhero who can solve all problems independently. As much as possible, the leader should lead and not manage; but to make that judgment, the leader must assess the current capability of his or her team relative to the level or intensity of the crisis.

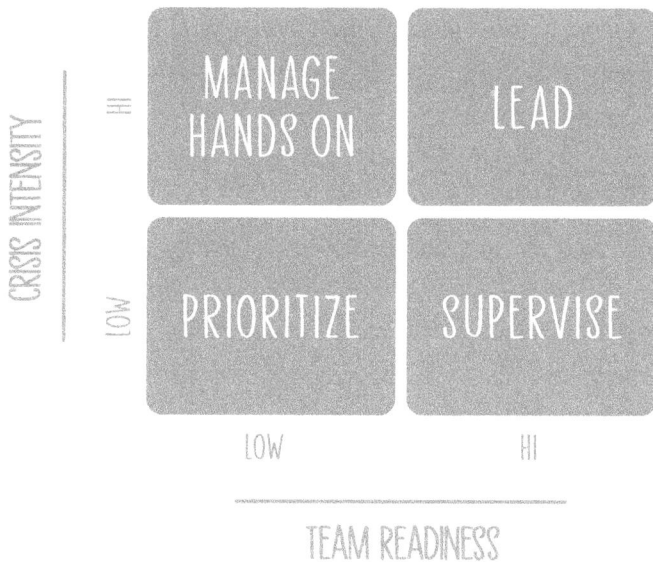

A 2x2 matrix. Vertical axis: CRISIS INTENSITY (HI at top, LOW at bottom). Horizontal axis: TEAM READINESS (LOW at left, HI at right). Quadrants: top-left MANAGE HANDS ON; top-right LEAD; bottom-left PRIORITIZE; bottom-right SUPERVISE.

If the crisis level is high but the team's readiness is low, the leader will need to be very hands-on, managing many functions and decisions. But if the readiness of the team is high, then the leader can be more of an orchestra conductor, directing the team appropriately while tapping their experience and expertise.

In Ukraine, each person on my team had different talents and skills, and they also handled their worries and responsibilities in different ways. Some were practical and logical. Others were skeptics who saw important faults in those plans. Some were great at being positive and keeping up morale through lighthearted jokes, stories, and relentless optimism. Others were sensitive and great at looking after those experiencing difficulty. Depending on the circumstances, different people were able to come to the forefront to lead. I never appreciated the diversity of a team more, and it helped immensely that I knew them well and was able to exploit their talents to the fullest.

Disagreements and debate were encouraged. We needed to have a variety of perspectives and opinions to come up with good ideas. We relied on the closeness of our team—fostered by our "tent time"—to have an environment that was safe for innovation and risk-taking.

As leader, I was also there to help the team, and I believed that to be my primary responsibility. I put the good of the team ahead of myself as well as any concerns about my own career and, at times, even the good of the company as a whole. I was there to be a key resource to the team, and to be useful in the most effective ways possible. Sometimes that meant I connected us to other parts of the company to tap critical information, approvals or resources. Sometimes my higher profile was needed to meet with key stakeholders or government officials. Other times my experience and expertise helped improve decisions that were particularly urgent and significant or gave the team the necessary authority. My team came to see that my attitude toward them was sincere, that I supported them in every way, and that I was there for them, not the other way around.

It also helped to have a vision. I think of a vision in a crisis as a belief in the future that goes beyond the immediate confusion and fear. It helped to calm, guide, and motivate the team. In Greece, our vision was openly debated, decided on, and articulated. We wanted to build a company that was better than before by taking advantage of the crisis as a moment to be aggressive in the market.

In Ukraine, perhaps because we were an even closer team, our vision was far less explicit, and yet I felt it was understood by everyone and even more powerful. We aimed to develop the emotional and intellectual experience of the team so that they would be capable of handling the crisis themselves, without me or any other leader. In other words, our vision was to become the leadership team of the future.

For many reasons, it was important to grow close as a team. We needed to believe that we could rely on each other, that the hard work would pay off, and that together, through resilience, fortitude, creativity and luck, we could somehow survive and succeed.

This sense of team camaraderie was critical. We could have fallen apart. Tatiana had a family to worry about, but we also needed her to look after a family of hundreds of salespeople in the field.

Like Tatiana, Roman was a mess watching the conflict tear his country apart. He could have easily left for safer and greener pastures. As a young, successful business person with a great education and a strong network in the U.S., he had half a mind to leave Ukraine and seek a fresh start. And the other half of him—the part of him that was a proud Ukrainian—wanted to join the army and fight. It meant a lot that in spite of this inner conflict he stayed with our organization and worked so hard for us.

Artem, on the other hand, was in a different and very challenging situation. As a native Russian, he basically represented the "enemy". It was hard on him personally to bear that burden. But the pressure didn't affect his work at all, except maybe to increase his dedication. He worked like a dog, practically sleeping in his office, and drinking Red Bull to keep himself going. And he always stayed levelheaded, rational and sympathetic, no matter what was happening. This had a calming effect on others. I watched him grow as a leader before my eyes.

The 10,000

I knew we'd grown a lot as a team in a very short period of time. When my coach assessed our progress at the end of the year period, he gave statistical evidence. From a team that was a Category Three to a Category Two level at the beginning, we had catapulted into becoming a Category One team in record time.

I'd seen this development with my own eyes. My people built rare characteristics and skills not normally called for in corporations, such as rapid decision-making, highly intuitive and analytical thinking, the ability to manage work and life in extreme stress, as well as courage, compassion, and resiliency. As I was preparing to move to Switzerland for a new role, I saw them conducting meetings without me, picking each other up when needed, and reacting to new trigger points with decisiveness.

This was illustrated most clearly one day when we visited our corporate HQ in Lausanne to present our new strategy to the senior leaders of the company. It was a nice break from the pressures of Ukraine, and we were excited to have the chance to review our performance numbers and get some direct recognition for work that had been done under incredibly difficult circumstances. However, in the middle of our presentation, news broke that a Malaysian airliner flying over Ukraine had crashed, killing 283 passengers and 15 crew members.

Almost immediately there were some crazy rumors and fears for the worst. Was it an accident, or had the plane been shot down by the Russians? What if the attackers were one of the anti-Ukrainian militias or the Ukrainian military itself? Did any of those possibilities signal a return to open military conflict or mark the beginning of an outright invasion? My team didn't wait, smartphones in hand, for Twitter to tell them what was going on. Instead, they huddled up and began to develop contingency plans based on various possible scenarios.

Our purpose remained the same. We needed to keep our people safe and achieve our normal business objectives if possible, but the team was a well-oiled machine. There was little fear or confusion and zero delay or hesitation. They knew what to do and how to do it. And they didn't need me to drive or even steer them anymore. They were a high-functioning team of leaders.

The experience of seeing them in action reminded me of a famous Greek story told by Xenephon, who was a student of Socrates and a contemporary of Plato and Aristotle.

Instead of focusing on philosophy, Xenephon wanted to experience the world, so he joined an army of Greek mercenaries that went to battle for a King in Persia that the Greeks admired. The Greeks fought well, but the Persian king was killed in battle. So the leaders of the Greek army met with the Persian leaders to discuss terms for a truce and safe passage back to Greece. During that negotiation, the Persians assasinated all of the Greek leaders. This left the Greek army of ten thousand mercenaries leaderless and stranded thousands of miles from home.

Xenephon was one of three officers elected by the troops to be part of the new leadership team. He made a speech to them that turned their fate around. Xenephon acknowledged that the Greek army had been tricked and deceived. The Persians hoped that by killing the Greek leaders, they would not have any direction, and the resulting confusion and anarchy would finish the job. With our leaders now gone, Xenephon said, we must all become leaders. The Persians will fear us because out of one leader, we will show them ten thousand.

The story of their long and arduous journey home, fighting through enemies and hardship at every step, is called the Anabasis, or the Uphill March, and Peter Drucker called it his favorite leadership story.

Xenephon understood the power of a team to come together by having all become leaders. This is what leadership is supposed to be about. If you are a leader, you are meant to develop the leadership capabilities of the people around you. You're not in a leadership role to ensure that you're indispensable and that your people will need to rely on you forever. Your most important objective and contribution to the organization is to make yourself obsolete.

So, in that sense, I was filled with pride as Tatiana, Artem, Roman and the others jumped into action and made fast decisions in the face of another crisis. Coming out of that ordeal, all three got better jobs. Artem was promoted to sales director in place of Tatiana. Despite being a Russian living in a Ukraine still in turmoil, he became supervisor for a group of five hundred Ukrainians, and is respected and appreciated for his leadership. My successor told me that he'd never taken over such a strong team before.

Crisis catalyzed our growth. Purpose made it possible.

CHAPTER TWO RECAP

- Do you have the right troops to fight a crisis? Strong teams are the secret weapon when things go wrong.

- Here are the five areas you need to work in order to build a Category One Team:

  1. Capabilities and Infrastructure

  2. Goals and Purpose

  3. Roles and Individual Expectations

  4. Interactions and Team Processes

  5. Learning and Results

- When dealing with crisis, the way a team works needs to adjust in order to meet the situational landscape. Then, it's all about capabilities and readiness.

- There is no higher responsibility for a leader than to recruit, prepare and develop a high-performance team.

Tools & Resources

Team Effectiveness Assessment

It can be helpful to objectively and quickly assess the capabilities of your current team.

The methodology we used was originally developed by Linkage, Inc.

With such an assessment, you can quickly fill gaps and give yourself specific and overall development goals. The whole methodology and roadmap we successfully followed to transform our team is illustrated on my site www.christostsolkas.com

The Appreciation Tool

During a time of crisis, when people are under great strain, "Appreciation" can be a very useful tool. Diana Chapman, an amazing psychologist and coach, helped me understand the art of appreciation. Here is a short video where Diana explains the secrets of Appreciation https://conscious.is/video/the-four-keys-to-mastering-the-art-of-appreciation.

The process we followed is illustrated on my site www.christostsolkas.com.

CHAPTER THREE

Leaders of Yesterday and Tomorrow

In 2006, a young American named Blake set out to see the world. A lot of young people get the travel bug at some point. Some long to what see what life is like outside their home country. Some want to find themselves. A few are looking for ways to do some good and make a difference. Blake was open to all three possibilities. He was friendly and curious. He wanted to travel at a relaxed pace and spend time in areas tourists don't usually bother to visit. And he was interested in figuring out how to make the world a better place.

In other ways, Blake was not a typical young traveler. He grew up in a middle-class family in Texas, but he was a highly driven person. During high school, he was an exceptional tennis player, and he got a partial scholarship to college until an injury ended his career. Instead of continuing his education, however, he dropped out and started a dry cleaning service for students. The company grew quickly. As soon as he sold the business, he started another company, an outdoor billboard business which promoted country music. He sold that to Clear Channel nine months after launch.

Looking for some fun, Blake and his sister next auditioned for the reality TV show *Survivor*. They didn't make the cut, but they did hear about a new show called the *Amazing Race*, which sent couples on a race around the world. On the show's second season, Blake and his sister missed the million-dollar prize by just four minutes.

Moving to Los Angeles, Blake started a cable company focused on reality TV. The idea was great but the business got squashed by Fox. Blake started two more companies in quick succession before his fateful vacation in 2006.

The decision to visit Argentina came directly out of his experience in the Amazing Race. Racing around the world for the show, Blake and his sister had barely seen the country. This time he would slow down. In a chance encounter, he met volunteers giving shoes to people in need. Traveling with them, he became deeply moved by the poverty he saw. The wheels in his brain started turning. Soon, he had a very big idea that would change his life and the lives of many others.

Today, Blake Mycoskie is famous as the founder of TOMS Shoes, the company that donates a pair of shoes to a needy person in the developing world whenever a customer buys shoes for themselves. This kind of "social entrepreneurialism" is becoming increasingly popular in business, especially among startups. The TOMS Shoes' business model is fundamentally purpose-driven, and Blake Mycoskie is a very new kind of leader.

The Evolution of Leadership

Around 10 million soldiers died in World War I. Two out of three died in combat; the rest from disease.[14] The loss of so many soldiers was largely a failure of leadership. World War I was the first "industrial" war. Weapons were more powerful than in previous wars. Battles were fought more intensely over small patches of land. As trench warfare set in, the kings, queens, generals and politicians in charge did not know how to change mindsets or tactics. They were stuck in a mindset that saw war as romantic and chivalrous. They overlooked the need for organization, clear tactics, risk assessment, and process. Ordinary people paid a horrible price.

14   https://www.historyonthenet.com/how-many-people-died-in-ww1

In business, a new breed of managers responded differently as the industrialization age took hold. Henry Ford led the pack. His factories were able to churn out millions of moderately priced cars—cheaply, efficiently and at high quality. Ford's approach to management helped improve society by giving ordinary people access to products that would once have only been affordable by the very rich.

The business leaders who followed Ford continued to refine processes and use resources as efficiently as possible to reduce costs and maximize outputs. Frederick Winslow Taylor studied this approach and how it could be best organized.[15] Taylor's famous "stop-watch" research showed how manufacturing or industrial work could be broken down into precise tasks (called jobs) with procedures that worked best when they were made as standardized as possible. Those jobs were filled with employees who were trained to meet very specific requirements. The jobs were good and well-paying. The overall system was managed by layers of administrators with ever-broader scope of supervisory responsibility, until the CEO at the top—the administrator of administrators.

This approach to leadership was not very different from the oldest hierarchies in history.

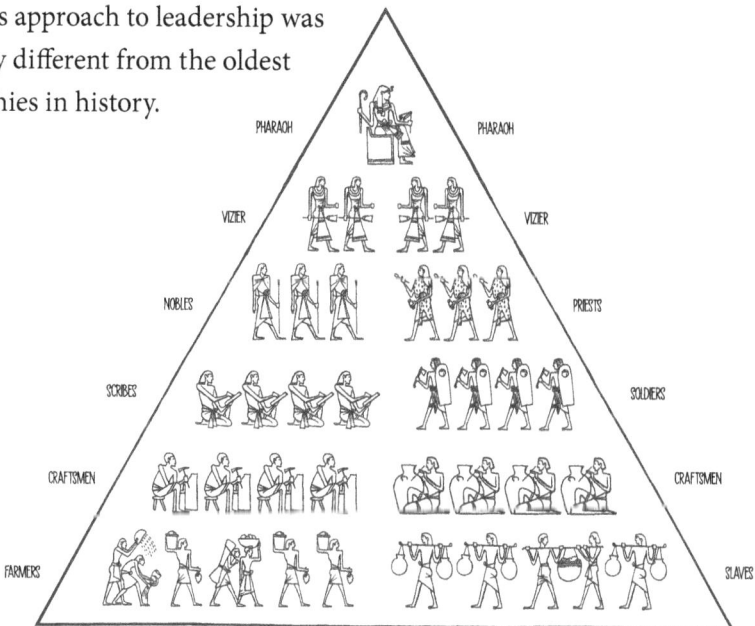

Such leadership was not glamorous, inspiring or romantic, but it did meet the needs of a rapidly industrializing world. Overnight, the world stopped being ruled by kings and queens and became ruled by men in gray flannel suits.

Managers were effective at getting things done. Society benefited. By the time World War II came around, pragmatic leaders were in charge. Logistics and organization were decisive factors in winning battles. Post-World War II, executives like Alfred Sloan, the CEO of General Motors, epitomized what good management looked like.[16] Researchers like Peter Drucker captured that evolution and articulated the modern theory of management.[17] They defined what good management looked like and showed how it created effective and efficient processes for generating quality, low-cost outputs. The American economy prospered—and most Americans shared in that growth. (Minorities are an obvious group who did not benefit as deeply or directly.)

The MBA, which formalized the study of the management sciences, was a profoundly American invention. Remember that MBA stands for Masters in Business Administration. That discipline focused originally on the core

---

16   https://en.wikipedia.org/wiki/Alfred_P._Sloan
17   https://hbr.org/1964/09/the-great-gm-mystery

processes of running a company which we think of now as functions, like finance, accounting, operations, marketing, and human resources. It had little to do with leadership as we think of it today.

Outside America, management followed a similar track in other countries post-World War II years. In Germany, business evolved from the traditions of medieval guilds, merchant associations, and chambers of commerce. German managers were very cognizant of the concerns of government and workers and yet were at the same time highly focused on the quality of products and the satisfaction of customers. As such, they became extremely efficient at processes. They were often engineers and scientists who turned their attention to the needs of the business.[18]

In France, managers are viewed as a separate and elite class of people defined by their intellect and their ability to solve complex problems.[19] As such, managers are highly networked among the other leaders of French society, including government and the military, and represent the "cream of the crop" of the ruling class. This shows the strong emphasis France puts on business management.

Japan was more like Germany in that it emphasized the improvement of industrial and organizational processes. Japan took the advances of productivity gurus like Edwards Deming[20] and put them on steroids, coming up with such approaches as Lean Production, just-in-time distribution, continuous improvement, Kaizen, and zero defects as ways to organize teams and workflow in order to minimize time, waste and cost while maximizing output and quality. Boosted by such techniques, Japanese manufacturers began to beat American manufacturers in terms of quality and price, most notably in the automobile industry, causing American business leaders to wonder how they had lost their special mojo.

---

18   http://www.photius.com/countries/germany/economy/germany_economy_the_culture_of_germa~1394.html

19   https://hbr.org/1991/07/the-making-of-a-french-manager

20   https://www.washingtonpost.com/archive/opinions/1993/12/23/japans-secret-w-edwards-deming/b69b8c00-4c5d-483a-b95e-4aeb1d94d2c6/?utm_term=.c48e2b1d9a78

MBA Meets *Mad Men*

John F. Kennedy was only forty-three years old when he was elected president of the United States. He won over Nixon, a very experienced former vice president, by bringing an unexpected skill. He understood style, image, personal brand and the medium of television like no candidate before him. Kennedy's prominence reflected a shift in a society looking for something more than just efficiency and practicality in leadership. That society also wanted inspiration, vision and style. This reflected a broader shift in the way people related to the products and services of business.

In the '50s, '60s, and '70s, as the U.S. and the world became more prosperous, a product's brand became almost as important as its function.

Efficient industrial manufacturing and the development of so many innovative new products generated tremendous economic growth and gave consumers more wealth and purchasing power as those goods also went down in price. At the same time, as more and more manufacturers competed with similar goods, the market became much more crowded. Businesses needed to distinguish themselves in the market to win over customers by convincing them why their products were different.

Branding is the art of differentiation. Iconic consumer products such as Coca-Cola, Campbell's Soup, and Marlboro Cigarettes became hugely successful because of marketing and sales. They made commodities appealing enough to sell widely at profitable prices.

Brands also represented an attempt at connecting with customers and employees through a sense of meaning and emotion. People were drawn to certain products and brands because they stood for something bigger or met certain emotional needs. The TV show *Mad Men* illustrated how effective this could be. Kodak's slide projector wheel, for example, got branded as a "carousel" because it reminded people of childhood memories of merry-go-rounds, which tied into a powerful nostalgia.

Leadership shifted accordingly, from its more "traditional" focus on process and efficiency to an emphasis on marketing and sales. Leaders had once been engineers, scientists or business administrators; increasingly, they were marketers who understood the power of brand. That sense of connection to brand also tied employees to their organizations. You were an IBM man or a GMC man—often loyal to a company for life.

Clarity, Credibility and Competence

By the early '70s, the tide was turning again. The Vietnam War had undermined confidence in American ideals. The oil shocks of the 1970s impeded economic growth. The Cold War intensified. Crime and unrest increased all over the world.

During this era of turmoil, people looked, understandably, for a new type of leader to follow. More than style or charisma, they wanted to be inspired by strength, certainty and simplicity; and they wanted to see results. President Ronald Reagan epitomized this quiet calm and inspiration. By the 1990s, corporations increasingly followed that lead. Jack Welch was the prototypical corporate leader of this era. No one doubted Welch's resolve, determination or follow-through. His clarity and simplicity was unambiguous. He declared that GE would be Number 1 or Number 2 in each of its markets or get out.[21] That was a measure of success everyone could judge and follow.

At the same time, the hierarchy of the organization was becoming flatter. Bosses increasingly had less authority and needed to become better at influencing. Communication and information became more important than ever. Women entered management and had different ways of relating and communicating. Relationships and networks became more important than command-and-control. Leadership got spread around.

Accordingly, good leadership became more sophisticated. A proliferation of leadership development training programs helped create "leaders at all levels" by emphasizing a balance of hard and soft skills. We still measured leadership on hard results, but we understood that those results were more achievable through persuasion, inspiration, charisma, trust, and so on.

---

21   https://hbr.org/1989/09/speed-simplicity-self-confidence-an-interview-with-jack-welch

The Era of Big Vision

The dot-com bubble of the late 1990s started to change our understanding of how to generate business growth and success. Managers who focused on efficiency and incremental improvement couldn't compete against leaders with vision for transformative change and massive growth. Suddenly, profits mattered less than potential, and small pioneers were stronger than established companies. This excitement for everything new and digital hit a wall with the dot-com crash of 2000, and yet the energy and ideas that were unleashed continue to have a lasting impact.

In this "break things and move fast" era, we are all about disruptive innovation. We even try to infuse a startup mentality in new and established businesses. Perhaps Peter Thiel, co-founder of PayPal and author of *Zero to One*, articulated these lessons best:

- It is better to risk boldness than triviality.

- A bad plan is better than no plan.

- Competitive markets destroy profits.

- Sales matters just as much as product.

Founder CEOs like Jeff Bezos and Larry Page do not think small, sweat failure or hesitate to enter new markets. They worry more about "global impact" and gaining and satisfying customers than about any product or profit.

The era of big vision is possible because of seven overarching trends that shape the paradigm of leadership of today.

Everything is Faster and More Connected

Today, the world is changing again, before our very eyes. Everything is interconnected, and information exchange is hyper-fast. Now any event or change can go global instantaneously. This has a profound impact on organizations and the type of leadership we need.

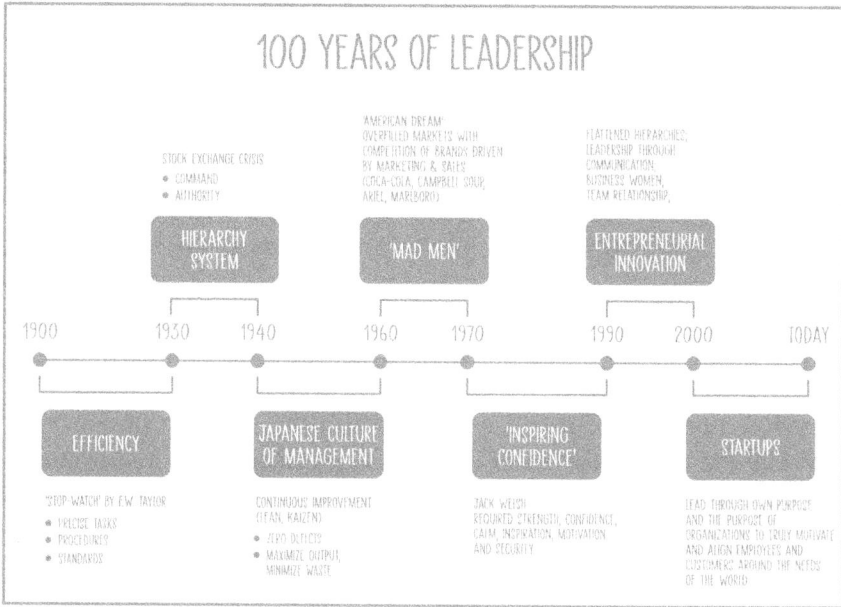

100 YEARS OF LEADERSHIP

Here's a story to illustrate how fast things can change and how quickly the impact of a crisis can spread. A friend of mine lives in St. Paul, Minnesota. One evening, a few blocks from his house, a police officer stopped a car. The African American driver explained that he had a permit for a gun and reached for his wallet in the glove compartment. The officer panicked and shot him seven times. The driver's girlfriend captured the aftermath of this deadly encounter on her phone and streamed it via Facebook Live as her partner lay dying and a police officer continued to shout at him. Millions watched and the tragic death of Philando Castile, a cafeteria worker at a local school, became an international phenomenon, almost the instant it happened.

In Chaos Theory, there is a famous metaphor that a butterfly flapping its wings in New Mexico can eventually cause a hurricane in China.[22] Today, that's not a metaphor any longer. Anything a company does, or even anything that happens to a customer, can have an overwhelming impact on a business, positive or negative.

---

22 https://fractalfoundation.org/resources/what-is-chaos-theory/

The World is More Transparent

The interconnectedness of information has brought transparency to an extreme. On an individual level, we've gotten used to broadcasting our most intimate thoughts, moments and life stories on social media. Our movements are easily tracked at all times, so long as we are carrying a cell phone or IoT device. As we drive a car, walk down a city street, or enter a public building, it's likely that cameras are watching us. In our homes, an assortment of devices like Amazon's Alexa collect data on our habits, activities, wants and even our moods. Meanwhile, our personal information and the private details of our lives—health records, credit ratings, family pictures—are vulnerable to hacks. The very idea of privacy has been demolished.

Many CEOs and senior leaders are already public figures and subject to intense scrutiny. Like anyone, their personal lives are vulnerable to exposure. Details about compensation and investments are easily discovered by anyone who wants to dig. The things they say or do on the job can be leaked by hackers, disgruntled employees, or colleagues with a political axe to grind.

Some loathe the lack of privacy, others embrace it. Intuit CEO Geoff Colvin is into radical transparency. He believes that transparency is good for business. He creates open platforms for any company, even a competitor, to build applications on Intuit products. And he shares sensitive information to employees as a way of increasing collaboration and trust. For example, every year Colvin emails his own unvarnished performance review to all employees.[23] Colvin gets that it's impossible to hide anything today!

The bottom line is this: Leaders are no longer just people who happen to run a company; they are more than public figures; they are political and cultural lightning rods.

---

23   http://fortune.com/2017/10/20/data-sheet-intuit-ceo-brad-smith/

People (Customers) Have More Freedom of Expression and Choice than Ever

As the Arab Spring, the EuroMaidan movement, and the 2018 March for Our Lives led by American teenagers shows, governments no longer control freedom of expression easily. Social media and smartphones make it possible for anyone to let their voice be heard.

While there are many positive aspects to freedom of expression and choice, there are also downsides. Many people lament the lack of civility on social media platforms. People can say whatever they want with little consequence. Opinions are also, increasingly, more powerful than facts. Recent studies show that fake news spreads faster than truth online.[24] Groups that think alike are more likely to stick together than intermingle with others.

In this Wild West of free expression, people are able to choose what they believe or don't believe. They are also quicker to align themselves more tightly with those they agree with. Where we live and who we see every day matters less and less compared to whose views we side with or what perspectives we consume. This makes a sense of purpose—a directional compass—more important than ever.

Young People Feel Entitled to Lead and are Quick to Assume Leadership

Every generation looks back and criticizes the generation that's coming up behind them. For my generation and older—baby boomers and Gen-Xers—the target of our criticism is millennials.

Millennials get accused of everything under the sun. They are too pampered, too lazy, not practical enough, lack focus or concentration, you name it.

For whatever reason, psychologists believe that millennials have a greater sense of entitlement than other generations. Perhaps they were raised to feel special or unique. Perhaps freedom of expression and choice allow them

---

24   https://www.nytimes.com/2018/03/08/technology/twitter-fake-news-research.html

to feel more powerful than the generation before them did. Whatever the case may be, millennials tend to disregard the rules and assume roles of leadership at an early and, some would say, inappropriate age.[25]

A good example comes from the students of Marjory Stoneman Douglas High School in Parkland, FL. After a shooter killed seventeen of their classmates on Valentine's Day in 2018, the students immediately took a political stance for more gun control. Pro-gun politicians, news organizations and the NRA criticized the students for expressing political opinions when they were so young and unsophisticated. The students cried "BS!" to that put-down, and made their voices even louder, demanding that legislative changes go into effect. Using social media tools they debated critics, pressured politicians and organized fellow students in a march on Washington.

Once upon a time, most people waited to be "senior" enough or experienced enough to assume a position and voice of leadership. A generation of young people today see no reason to wait and no reason why they shoudn't lead. Like all younger generations, they also tend to be more idealistic and "purposeful" than those who are older.

Teams Matter More than Ever

Leonardo da Vinci was a painter, sculptor, inventor, military expert, anatomist and scientist. He did it all, and that's why they called him a Renaissance Man.

That myth of the Renaissance Man lives on but, in reality, they were far from the norm. Most people in the Renaissance were specialists—farmers, soldiers, craftsmen, priests, monks. They specialized in one particular thing. In fact, groups of specialists often banded together to increase their security and power in guilds, monasteries and unions. Early companies were very specialized, too. They manufactured one thing, provided one service or focused on one market.

25 https://www.indy100.com/article/young-people-entitlement-disappointed-narcissism-psychology-research-7867961

This continues today. We train and hire for specialization and expertise. We can also access expertise instantly and cheaply. Ivy League schools broadcast lectures on podcasts. Great teachers provide in-depth tutorials on Khan Academy or MasterClass. Anyone who needs to do anything can find a YouTube video explaining how.

As expertise matters less, we increasingly need people from different specialties and areas of expertise to come together on one task, project or cause. They must somehow communicate and collaborate effectively.

Leadership must align teams around a shared sense of energy, direction, cohesion, resilience and creativity.

Value Chains Are Expanding

When a company comes up with some innovative new product or service, it strives to get it to the market quickly so as to enjoy dominant market share as long as possible before competitors come in with a similar product, win customers and cause prices to drop. Everyone knows that product life cycle is now faster than ever.

I had the good fortune and opportunity to study this at Stanford University. Major innovations often occur when companies change previously dependent attributes. For example, the traditional taxi business has a number of dependent attributes which are necessary for customers and drivers to do business. Uber disrupted that process by radically changing existing or adding new attributes. Traditionally, customers call or hail a cab to get a ride, which is an unpredictable and often time-consuming experience. Uber lets you do so by app, instantly, and you can even follow the progress of your taxi on your phone. Traditionally, taxi drivers needed to be licensed and cars needed to be registered. Uber removes those barriers, allowing anyone and any vehicle to participate. Traditionally, when the ride is over you pay with cash or credit card. With Uber you hop out because your ride is already paid for. If you want, you can even rate your driver, too. The driver has the same functionality.

Value chains also change the nature of competiion. Markets used to move up and down verticals within distinct zones of influence. For example, Ford made cars and sold them through dealers. IBM made computers and sold them. In contrast, some new businesses engage with consumers in multiple aspects of their lives. A company like Uber, collecting massive amounts of customer data, knows where you live and many other habits, such as, possibly, how you commute, where you like to go for entertainment and how late you come home. This can lead to a whole range of ancillary services. Uber could get into the tour business or deliver meals or transport patients. In fact, it's doing all those things.

Today, your competitor is not just your competitor. Your competitor may also be your supplier, your customer and even your employee. Customers, partners and service providers can be in collaboration or competition with one another at the same time. The most sophisticated components of any process today can be outsourced, offshored, made and delivered from places that you don't know, and you don't need to know. The goal is the purpose and the customer.

Trust in Leadership Is Down

Even as leaders with giant visions took over industry after industry, another countervailing force influenced our society. For the first time since the 1960s, people have stopped trusting traditional leaders and the establishment.

Even people in the leadership development business don't think leadership is working anymore. A 2018 memo by McKinsey noted:

> The almost insatiable demand for leadership studies is a natural outgrowth of the all-too-frequent leadership failures in government, business, and nonprofits. Few people trust their leaders, according to the Edelman Trust Barometer surveys, among others. Gallup data show low levels of employee engagement worldwide, while the Conference Board finds job satisfaction at a low ebb and executive tenures decreasing. Other research consistently indicates that companies give their

own leadership-development efforts low marks. Leaders aren't doing a good job for themselves or their workplaces, and things don't seem to be improving.[26]

I believe trust in leadership shifted because of the very failures the McKinsey author describes. Think of the chaos we've experienced in the past twenty years. Enron. The dot-com crash. 9-11. The Iraq War. The mortgage crisis and Great Recession of 2008. Financial turmoil in the EU. The collapse of the Middle East. Protests against the 1 percent. Skyrocketing CEO pay. Unemployment and stress. Stagnant wages and wealth growth. Terrorism. The Syrian refugee crisis. Brexit. Fake News. Russia-Gate. Cambridge Analytica hack.

Lack of faith in traditional leadership has intensified as a result of this turmoil and confusion. Leaders were supposed to be our guardian angels, but many turned out to be ineffective at best or villains at worst. All the old attributes of leadership—expertise, experience, practical know-how and charisma—seem less and less believable with each failure or scandal.

As we've lost faith in leaders, we've begun to look for something different. Many are seeking values and principles they can believe in, embodied in leaders who seem to live those values in a pure way. We're looking for leaders with clarity of purpose.

Riding the Wave of Change

Today's old-school leaders are professional managers hired for their competence and rewarded for their results. Their ability to inspire is, at best, a secondary consideration. Most sound artificial, bland and inauthentic.

A new era of business leaders has gained in prominence over the past few years. A generation of CEO/founders is creating movements as much as they are building companies. They are driven by needs beyond business. They put at least some of their focus on "What the world needs" instead.

---

26 https://www.mckinsey.com/featured-insights/leadership/getting-beyond-the-bs-of-leadership-literature

A leader like Blake Mycoskie manages to integrate business objectives with a passion for having an impact on the world's problems.

His journey to this end started like a kind of quest. Exploring the world, he collected raw data about needs and problems. Tapping the experiences of others, he turned this data into information and eventually knowledge. Seeing the desperate need for shoes among the poor in developed countries, Mycoskie decided to figure out how to alleviate that need. His first thought was a charity, but his entrepreneurial experience and brain sent him down another tract. Donations could always run out, and charities constantly scramble just to fulfill their mission. But a for-profit business, properly leveraged, could become a shoe-donation machine.

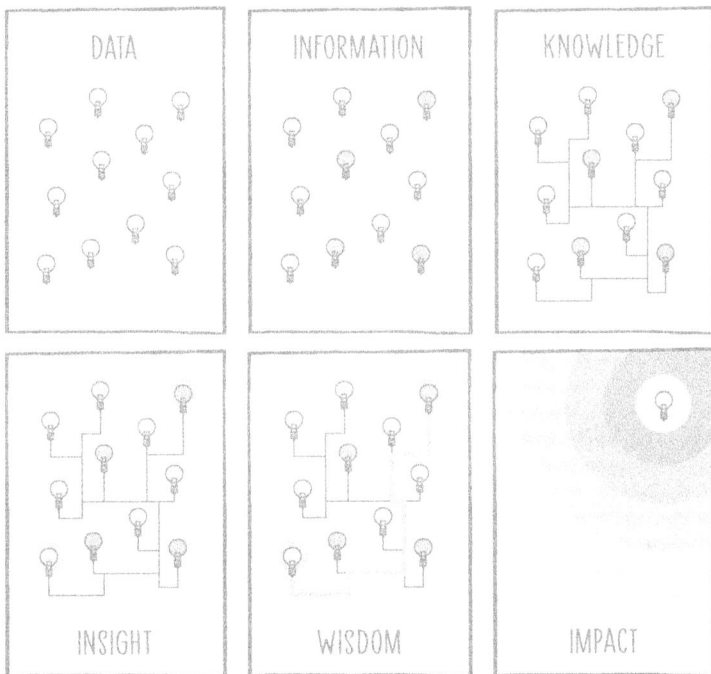

This was Mycoskie's critical insight. He describes the idea as, "Sell a pair of shoes today, give a pair of shoes tomorrow." His wisdom came from understanding human behavior. Mycoskie understood that customers who wanted to help make the world a better place would also be motivated to buy TOMS shoes.

This vision gave Mycoskie even more energy and focus than his previous endeavors. He entered a business he knew little about, solved all problems that came his way, and sold friends, investors and an industry on the power of that story. TOMS shoes grew fast and customers loved that they could help others in need simply by buying something. TOMS continues to expand its "one for one" business model with a new product each year.

This model is not without its critics. Some say that the approach undermines local producers by making foreign goods available. It doesn't have to be that way, and regardless, many companies have followed TOMS with their own "one for one" models. Warby Parker sells and distributes eyeglasses; Roma Boots sells and gives away boots; Nouri Bar donates a meal for a hungry child for every nutritional bar it sells; Sir Richard's sells and donates condoms; KNO Clothing gives away clothes and donates to homeless shelters; Soapbox Soaps donates a month of water, a bar of soap, or a year of vitamins for each soap product it sells, and so on.[27]

Other companies have adopted a variation of this model called the 1 percent pledge. In this approach, companies offer a percentage of their executive time, products, and so on, to those in need.[28] Salesforce, Altasian and YELP are among the pioneers of this movement. But my personal view is that a 1 percent philanthropic gift is less sustainable and less organizationally empowering because the approach is not tied into the business model and success of the company. It's an add-on or a nice-to-have that can also go away.

The model of the new purpose leader is still evolving. But here are some of the attributes that are important.

1. A purpose leader stands for something

Few people would ask a traditional CEO what he or she stands for socially and politically. The answer would barely be relevant. But ask a leader of purpose what he or she stands for and you will get a clear answer.

---

27 https://knowledge.wharton.upenn.edu/article/one-one-business-model-social-impact-avoiding-unintended-consequences/

28 https://pledge1percent.org/

Jane Chen, the co-founder of Embrace, developed a product to help millions of poor premature babies.

Elon Musk wants to reduce the planet's consumption of fossil fuels.

Muhammad Yunus believes in economic opportunity for the poor and developed a microlending bank to help them become business entrepreneurs.

2. A purpose leader has background and personality

Traditional leaders struggle to tell us something about themselves that stands out. They are more about what they do than who they are. In fact, we are suspicious when their backgrounds are too colorful. Purpose leaders have very clear stories with compelling backgrounds. Who they are is part of what attracts and inspires people.

3. A purpose leader tells a story

Today, there's so much noise and confusion that normal messages and brands can't get through. Purpose connects to people by telling stories. Bullet points, details, and even facts are far less important than story. People don't want to listen with their ears and brains, they listen with their bodies. I'm not suggesting that purpose leaders do not have any experience or practical know-how. Far from it. They can be very effective and strategic, but they must also be something more. No era starts with a blank slate. Every new era builds from a foundation of what came before it.

Even though leadership became about marketing in the *Mad Men* era, it still required leaders who could manage processes and operations.

Leaders in the '80s and '90s were a combination of managerial abilities and salesmanship. That's how they motivated and inspired while also running their organizations effectively.

While the idea of servant leadership originated in the early 1970s, it has only really become a popular concept in the past ten years, as leaders began to recognize that their most effective role as leaders was not to serve themselves but to make the people around them successful.

The purpose leader of today retains all of those phases and capabilities while also connecting to people in a much more meaningful and authentic way.

This is becoming essential for success in our modern era. People, especially young idealistic millennials, are very suspicious of inauthenticity and greed. They are no longer seeking employment just for the money but want to contribute to something bigger than themselves, often by helping to make the world a better place. They are looking, in other words, for purpose.

Customers, too, are increasingly looking for something more than just low prices and high quality. They want goods and services that have been ethically made with a sense of environmental stewardship and social responsibility. They want to connect to the brands and businesses they support—not just through the product itself but through the sense of shared purpose aligned with that company and product.

The successful leaders of the future will be different from the past, in that they will not need to craft or design their "authentic purpose" but will have developed and shaped it as a matter of living. They will embody that purpose with integrity. They will not need to try and tie purpose to their business or career but will start or lead their business or cause to make their purpose have broader impact.

The fundamental nature of leadership has changed. It's no longer about competence. Now, it's about purpose. People are looking for meaning, significance, impact and strong emotional connection.

Purpose is the new leadership.

CHAPTER THREE RECAP

- Today many talk about purpose. That purpose reflects and communicates the impact of our work, our business operations, and the essence of our company to others. Purpose-Driven Leadership means we do business while doing good for the world (not only our customers but also non-users of our product or service offering).

- Over the past one hundred years, leadership has gone through different stages—these are the ancestors of today's Leadership model.

- Today's Leadership model is driven by: speed and hyper-connectivity, the need for transparency, the increased freedom of expression and choice, a sense of entitlement (especially of the young), the heightened importance of teams, a change in competition from linear to multidimensional value chains, the lack of strong ideological narratives and the loss of trust in institutions.

- Essentially the new Leadership paradigm transforms the nature and model of business itself.

Tools & Resources

Storytelling

I am a strong believer that stories help us understand organizations and teams, deliver important messages, and help build your leadership persona. Dr. Jennifer Aaker from Stanford University opened my eyes to the power of stories. I recommend spending a few minutes watching one of her videos (on my site www.christostsolkas.com you can see all references).

Generational Changes and Leadership Entitlement

As a Gen-X leader, I need to stay in tune with the attitudes, beliefs and wants and needs of younger employees. Millennials and Gen-Zs, for example, feel a strong sense that they have a leadership role to play, especially when it comes to Level One problems, regardless of their position in the hierarchy or tenure in the organization. This is a major driver in this new era of leadership.

Simon Sinek refers to this as leadership "entitlement". On my site www.christostsolkas.com you can find the link of his revealing talk which helped me understand the whole dynamic.

The Critical Importance of Teams

Teams seem to be more important than ever today. My favorite book about teams describes how teams can achieve success by being fluid, versatile and trust-based. I encourage you to read it.

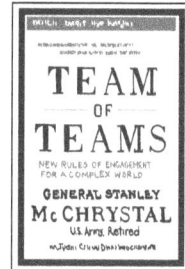

CHAPTER FOUR

Purpose Drives Growth—Discovering Your Truth

CEOs are highly motivated individuals. But their big job is to motivate other people, sometimes tens of thousands of them, to perform better and ultimately drive company growth. The most powerful means of motivation is purpose. Here's an example.

From its launch in 1975, Microsoft grew like crazy. By 1998, it was the largest company in the world, but by 2000 co-founder Bill Gates was ready to transition out of the CEO role. This is a difficult shift for any company, especially one as successful as Microsoft.

For his replacement, Gates chose Steve Ballmer. Ballmer was an interesting and understandable pick. He was the thirtieth employee ever hired by the company, and obviously knew its business and culture inside and out. He had been a successful salesman, driving some of Microsoft's biggest product wins. He was also highly driven and passionate. His motivational style was legendary, however, and not for the right reasons. His speeches to employees, in which he bounded onto the stage, flung his body around and screamed about how much he loved the company, attracted attention for all the wrong reasons. Videos of his performances went viral.

Still, Ballmer lasted fourteen years as CEO, four years longer than corporate America's average. By many measures, his tenure was a success. He moved Microsoft away from computers and toward services, networks and solutions. He acquired or developed a number of very interesting businesses (though others failed spectacularly). Significantly, Microsoft's revenues also kept growing. The company returned, in 2014, to the very lofty position of world's second most valuable company in terms of market capitalization, behind only ExxonMobil.

Yet, most people view Ballmer's leadership at Microsoft as mixed or even a failure. The main reason was hard to measure yet impossible not to feel. During his reign, Microsoft lost relevancy as a company. Over that fourteen-year period, dynamic competitors like Google, Apple and Amazon rocked the world by creating and then dominating entirely new markets. In the process, they had an enormous impact, changing the way billions of consumers work, live and even think. In comparison, Microsoft was well-run and its business units made lots of money. But the company didn't seem to stand for anything besides revenue growth and operational efficiency. It wasn't an organization that people thought about when they were looking for an answer to some unmet need. It was just Microsoft—too big to be forgotten but not particularly worth thinking about.

Satya Nadella, Microsoft's current CEO, couldn't be more different than Ballmer. An unlikely success story, he grew up in India, got rejected by India's version of MIT and was far more interested in cricket than computers. In America, he studied at a run-of-the-mill college in Wisconsin, not a Harvard, Stanford or USC. Perhaps this background explains Nadella's humble and highly open approach to leadership. As the new CEO of Microsoft, he started by asking some very basic questions: "What is it that we should do? What's the sensibility that would be lost if we should disappear?" Technology trends come and go, but Microsoft needed to stand for something eternal.

One of the answers came out of a difficult personal experience. He and his wife have a child with cerebral palsy. Nadella has spent many nights in hospital emergency rooms as a result. On one of those nights, Nadella looked around at the equipment in his son's room and realized that everything was powered by Microsoft. Suddenly, he felt a deeper sense of meaning in the company's work that went beyond just devices and services. Microsoft was actually changing and improving people's lives. This realization informed his beliefs about the difference the company could and should make in the world. In a very real sense, Nadella discovered (or rediscovered) Microsoft's purpose and made it real for others.

For example, as CEO, Nadella made "accessibility" a big part of Microsoft's new focus. This manifested in inclusion programs for employees with disabilities like blindness and autism. But it also figured into Microsoft's drive for innovation. Artificial intelligence, for example, "completely changes the game around accessibility," Nadella says. Windows 10 is built with gaze-tracking capabilities that can help people who are paralyzed. Microsoft's "Seeing AI" app helps identify objects for the visually impaired. The company's work in virtual reality and holograms supports their video game products, but it has also been applied to tools and services for medical doctors to operate on cancerous tumors and for medical students to learn anatomy. AI and VR, in Nadella's words, can "empower humans to do more, achieve more."

There's no question in Nadella's mind that he developed this sense of empathy for the vulnerable and less fortunate because of his child's serious physical and medical needs. Nadella insists that empathy is not just a nice human quality, however; it's a source of innovation. Most companies listen to customers to figure out how to sell them more stuff. Empathy helps you listen to customers and figure out what they really need to improve their lives.

Today, Microsoft is in business to "empower every person and every organization on the planet to achieve more." To make that happen, Nadella has fostered a very collaborative and open culture that values continual learning and a growth mindset. As a result, Microsoft is doing a better job attracting talent motivated by this purpose, building strategic partnerships and listening to customers. Microsoft is now a growth stock once more, its share price doubling under Nadella's watch, after a long period of stagnation with Ballmer.

Purpose has fueled its innovation and growth.

Searching for Urgency

In Ukraine, I experienced how crisis could ignite a sense of purpose which helped us develop as a team and improve performance. After I left Ukraine,

I wondered how that sense of urgency and energy could be replicated when crisis was missing. Was crisis necessary for purpose? If so, were there different kinds of crises than the one I experienced?

This became a very personal question. When I rotated back to our corporate HQ in Lausanne, all that urgency and energy I felt leading a team left me, and I experienced a lack of purpose in my own life. Like a professional athlete after the season ends or a musician after a concert, I crashed emotionally after my adrenaline rush was over. I had also just tuned fifty and was wondering what to do with my life—a difficult personal combination! If I wasn't sure how to find my own purpose, I also didn't know how to instill it in my new team.

Ukraine was the Wild West. Anything could happen at any time. Lausanne, in comparison, is a peaceful utopia. As I write this book, I'm still living here and I love it. Switzerland is one of the most beautiful, prosperous and progressive countries in the world. Stunning mountains. Beautiful lakes. Healthy people. Vibrant economy. The citizens of Switzerland believe in their country and feel a strong sense of connection and commitment to their society. They work hard, play hard, and live well. What's not to appreciate, respect and love about that?

But my new life was also a little boring at first, and I felt isolated from my old colleagues and out of touch. My change in role was particularly tough. In Ukraine, I'd been a line manager who literally put his life on the line. I loved having a big diverse territory encompassing four different countries with many direct reports, a factory and a large sales force. I got excited by ambitious performance targets and the opportunity to test new strategies and innovations in operations and marketing, knowing that ultimately the success or failure of those initiatives was mine. I appreciated how the pressure of the crisis in Ukraine tested our mental and physical resiliency. I enjoyed the camaraderie of a team in "battle" together, and even the emotional roller-coaster of the unpredictable ups and downs.

Then it ended. In Switzerland, all that responsibility and excitement was gone. My company gave me an impressive title—I was named head of sales strategy for the global sales organization—but there was little substance to the job. Officially, I was now responsible for coordinating and developing strategy, and tasked with creating a new vision for the company in the sales space. My team was there to help develop and deliver those services to our internal customers—the various sales organizations in territories around the world. But we had no authority over those affiliates and only acted in an advisory role as consultants. Suddenly, I went from managing a territory with a significant budget, lots of people and ambitious sales goals to working from a small office at the end of a quiet corridor with a small team, no territory, and no real numbers to hit.

I started wondering, theoretically, how any team could capture or replicate the feelings we'd had during the Ukrainian crisis under more normal business conditions.

This seems particularly challenging in a big company. Although there's always lots of pressure to perform in an established corporate environment, the system tends to dampen strong feelings, excitement and drama. Even when bold ideas or convictions emerge, they often seem to dissipate or become diminished by the bureaucratic processes of the organization. The new marketing strategy gets its sharp edges smoothed off by the lawyers or the middle managers. The customer-first declaration of the CEO gets effectively ignored because the finance function demands that quarterly results need to be hit, no matter what customers really need. It makes me understand why someone like Steve Ballmer might feel the urge to scream and throw himself around the stage: He's trying to cut through the layers of complacency and stir up some passion.

High-performing organizations are very good at doing what they have always done. Producing products. Delivering services. Growing market share. Improving processes incrementally. For many years of my career, this is exactly what I helped do. The game was clear. Our leaders set goals that pushed us hard. We needed to plan, strategize, think, convince, manage, inspire, lead—and some of the things we did felt like "change" because they were slightly different than before. But they weren't fundamentally or radically different, and I don't think their emotional impact was all that powerful—we didn't feel like our lives changed as a result; we weren't inseparable as a team; we didn't grow incredibly quickly as people and leaders.

When I thought about that and looked around at all the different companies I knew, I realized something interesting. Absent a crisis, the closest example of the environment we'd experienced in Ukraine was at startups. Accordingly, I started studying startup culture wherever I could find it, from small companies in Europe to exciting ventures in Silicon Valley. What I learned supported my instincts.

Project Startup

The best startups have an "us against the world" mentality. The people in them work incredibly hard, sometimes for very little reward, and bond very closely, much like my teams in Ukraine and Greece had bonded during our "tent time." People develop rapidly in a startup environment, too. They need to make decisions quickly with little data, so they just go ahead and make them. In the process of shouldering that responsibility and learning from failure and mistakes, they grow as leaders. There's also very little bureaucratic administration in startups to dampen exciting ideas or slow down decisions. On the other hand, there's usually little financial runway to last long if you make mistakes. This ensures that startups, in a sense, are always in crisis mode. The business idea may be great, but the company, for any number of financial, operational, competitive or personal reasons, can fall apart at any moment.

Finally, there's another thing I noticed that startups do well. They're incredible attuned to the outside world. In a big corporation, it's easier to basically ignore the outside world and listen and respond to your own organizational voices instead. Everyone talks about how important the customer is to a business, but most people in big companies are more concerned about meeting internal priorities and demands. In a startup, the customer is everything. You have to figure out what the customer wants, how the customer thinks, what the customer needs in order to have a chance with them. Then you try out whatever service or product idea you come up with and see if it meets those needs. When it doesn't, you ask more questions, get more data, and try again. You become, to paraphrase Nadella, an empathy machine.

This helped me frame a purpose for my Global Sales-Strategy team.

When it came to sales, my view was that our larger company's biggest need was to give more autonomy and decision-making power to people on the front line. Like entrepreneurs in their own company, those people needed to feel a sense of ownership and urgency to be more innovative, make meaningful decisions, and help advance the organization's vision and strategic goals in a much more dynamic consumer world.

I'd seen how that sense of empowerment helped my team in Ukraine. During our crisis, we learned how to take complete ownership over a situation and make fast decisions in line with our vision and goals. We had no sense of "it's not my problem." We were focused externally, on the changing world, rather than internally on our bureaucratic processes and priorities. So that's the spirit I decided we should instill in our global sales team. The question was, how?

Ironically, like a startup, I had few resources at my disposal. I also couldn't tell people what to do or how they needed to change. I could explain why they should change and I could try to persuade them through meetings and presentations, but I didn't have any illusions that this would lead to a meaningful impact. Even if some people were sort of inspired by my talks and wanted to change, they wouldn't be equipped to think differently or adopt new approaches.

What I really needed to do was create a mind shift, and not just in one person or even in the managing directors all over the world, but in many people. In other words, I needed to inspire a culture change in which people would act and think more like the people who work in startups.

How could my team and I infuse that "startup culture" in the global sales force without any resources, authority or mandate? We were just a very small group of strategists occupying an ordinary corridor. The global sales force was the enormous "empire," a huge machine doing what it has done for decades. But, it's also true that startups overturn industries all the time. No one expected Apple and Microsoft to become bigger than IBM, or Airbnb to challenge the hotel industry, or Walmart to overthrow Sears.

Startups start small and change the world. So, I decided to turn my little group into a startup and figure out how to drive that mindset and culture into our larger organization.

Inside the Corridor

I told our team we could have an outsized influence on the whole organization by influencing the culture of the global sales force. Our company needed to change because the world was changing. Outside forces beyond our control were affecting our business. We could serve as a model for how the company should operate and spread that way of working like a virus. Here are the steps we took to make that happen:

Step 1: Adopt the mindset of a founder

The first step was personal. Though our organization is very hierarchical, I needed to act like a founder of a startup to establish a culture that was different than our larger company. I made very practical changes to my leadership priorities as a result.

For example, corporate executives usually want corner offices, big budgets and lots of direct reports. Startup founders don't care about any of that stuff. They have minimal resources, staff and time. They'd rather test ideas with a "minimal viable product" than develop and launch a brand from A to Z.

This can be a difficult shift in mindset for any corporate executive, and requires new ways of thinking about success and progress, but it's also very freeing.

Step 2: Focus less on execution and more on the type of people you want

At a startup, you want creative, empowered people who come up with new solutions on their own initiative. You're creating an ecosystem in which people thrive on hard work, bonding and fun. To recruit talent for my team, I focused on millennials because, according to Gallup, they are particularly inspired by an organization that has a strong sense of purpose they can believe in and that makes them feel their job matters.[29] I also believed millennials would respond better to a looser hierarchy and a more collaborative culture. I tried to encourage my people to think laterally, not linearly, about problems. My motto was, "Think like an artist, not an engineer!"

Step 3: Build the right space

At Lausanne HQ, we built a space where people would enjoy hanging out, using as little budget as possible. We bought IKEA furniture and put in more couches and coffee tables than desks and chairs, and got a cheap foosball table and a stereo. This really changed the way people worked and interacted, and made our office more inviting. We were a lot more social and traded ideas all the time and got up and moved around when we talked, and we encouraged others to come hang out as a way of winning converts with a sign that said, "Coffee & Friends!" People who came for meetings didn't want to go back to their own offices. When team members were transferred out, they didn't want to leave!

---

29   http://news.gallup.com/businessjournal/197486/millennials-not-connecting-company-mission.aspx

Workspace changes the way you think and relate to others.[30] Every time I visit Silicon Valley, I enjoy seeing the different ways American companies help people be more creative, interactive and productive at work.

Step 4: Figure out what customers need

Established companies struggle with innovation because they focus on incremental improvements to existing processes and products. At startups, you start with customer needs first and reverse engineer an approach to deliver those needs. Our customers were the internal sales teams around the organization. We spent a lot of time talking to them. Most of the conversations boiled down to the "5 Whys Technique"[31] which I'll discuss in more detail in Chapter Six. The goal is to start with a problem and follow a chain of questions to determine its ultimate source.

When that doesn't work, I find it helpful to get the customer to tell you a story of a crisis they've experienced, such as a customer relationship gone wrong, a supply problem, a financial scandal, etc. This way, you discover what is important to the customer, and help identify their purpose.

From a corridor to an ant colony

Turning our little team into a sort of startup energized us all and rejuvenated me personally. It gave our team a feeling of power and optimism about the impact a small group can have on a much bigger organization.

Our focus wasn't on a product, but on culture and the way of thinking. Our goal was to be a source of creative disruption to ordinary approaches inside the company. We knew we couldn't order anyone to follow our suggestions, so we had to learn how to market and sell our ideas. This was challenging for me, personally. At times, I was anxious and pushed boundaries by overselling our ideas and plans. Now, I believe that introducing innovation in a big corporation requires timing. Moving too quickly is as

---

30   https://www.economist.com/news/business/21721423-their-eccentric-buildings-offer-clues-about-how-people-will-work-technology-firms-and-office

31   https://www.huffingtonpost.com/mitch-ditkoff/why-you-need-to-ask-why_b_2681958.html

big a mistake as offering up the wrong idea. Startup founders struggle with those things, too. They need to effectively pitch their ideas and passion to investors, suppliers, people and customers in order to have an impact.

Our investors and stakeholders were the people in other departments and geographies. We tried to pass on our message by being an example of what a startup culture feels like and how it thinks, and we also learned how to talk to them about what we were up to at every opportunity, from formal presentations to elevator pitches. We wanted to win "mindshare" to win market share. So, we networked a lot, and in the process our single corridor became connected to other parts of the company, like an ant colony, carrying ideas and people back and forth, and helping to bring change everywhere.

We made real progress.

We created a signature event that helped us reach our sales groups around the world with some simple core messages.

We brought together business thinkers, founders, strategists, academics and specialists on digital and retail strategies as well as automation and robotics. For the first time, our large global organization opened its doors to startups and encountered ideas like Design Thinking, 10X Growth, and Lean innovation. We created a lot of enthusiasm, planned more global events and got great commitment from many groups. We created traction for our existing business model while helping advance a more forward-looking perspective.

There was only one thing we were missing. Our purpose was to change the mindset and behaviors of our global sales force. But this wasn't meaningful enough to really drive innovation and growth. We needed to think bigger. So, in 2016, I asked my team to start researching how purpose can spur innovation and drive growth.

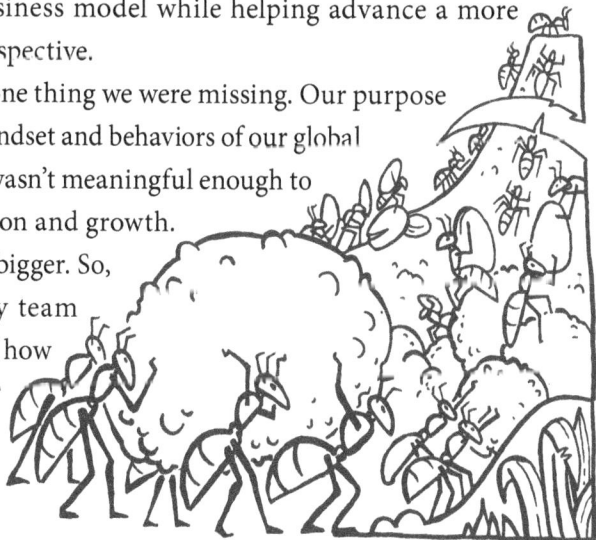

Studying Purpose

To analyze the link between purpose and innovation and growth, we decided to look at a wide range of companies over the past fifteen years, assessing whether their purpose had an impact on their success or growth.

We only looked at companies in the Fortune 500 because we believed it would be easier to verify performance. We started in one sector, Food & Beverage, and then broadened out across eight other sectors ranging from High Tech to Motor Vehicles and Telecoms, focusing on the top three to five companies in each sector. These ranged from established companies to recent startups.

We were looking, in particular, for companies that seemed to have a strong, emotionally resonant sense of purpose internally, as well as a well-developed external focus on the deeper needs of their customers and the world. We analyzed mission statements and the way these companies focused on problems or needs that were linked with their purpose. We also assessed how clearly their business models were aligned with creating impact on their sector, on society or on the world.

The Food & Beverage sector may not strike you as exciting compared to high-growth tech companies like Amazon, Google or Apple. Nevertheless, it was interesting to see that the five largest global companies in that sector, Danone, PepsiCo, Nestle, Unilever, and Mondelez, have deliberately shifted the way they do business to align their purpose more closely with their growth algorithm and strategy.

Paris-based Danone is at the forefront of this change. It has linked itself to health and nutrition from its founding in 1919 with a mission to achieve "health through food" by encouraging healthier eating habits and sourcing practices. Since 1972, Danone has been deliberately applying that ideal to shape its approach to doing business. Specifically, Danone develops, markets and sells products in collaboration with local stakeholders and in consideration of local needs, cultures, and economic circumstances. This helps Danone advance its purpose to reduce world hunger and improve nutrition and sourcing while also achieving growth and market share.

The approach still plays out decades later. In 2006, Grameen Bank founder, Muhammad Yunus, partnered with Danone to develop a Bangladesh-based enterprise, Grameen Danone, launched to develop nutritious yogurt that local populations could afford. The company leveraged local saleswomen to sell an inexpensive product on commission and build interest before developing local production facilities to meet demand. That strategy aligned purpose (reduce malnutrition and poverty) with practice (a workable business model that helped Danone enter and establish growth in a new market). As a result, Grameen Danone developed new products and approaches that are hard for other companies to compete with or copy. The pursuit of purpose, in other words, has helped the company develop and scale an appealing product that not only meets the market need for taste and affordability and improves health and nutrition, but also boxes out competitors.

Danone isn't alone in this. Unilever, a company that shuns short-term profitability over long-term growth objectives, especially in emerging markets, tries to develop brands linked to distinct social causes. It has found that those brands grow at twice the speed of brands without a clear purpose. Putting its money where its mouth is, Unilever also promises to pull its ads from social media platforms that proliferate toxic content.[32]

Nestle has organized its business around thirty-nine commitments to social value, in areas such as nutrition (e.g., reduce salt and sugar in products), rural development (e.g., implement responsible sourcing), water (e.g., increase efficient use and sustainability), the environment (e.g., improve packaging), and human rights (e.g., eliminate child labor). Rather than limit themselves to one purpose, this approach aligns them to many different purposes that impact the world.

PepsiCo has shaped its growth strategy around its "Performance with Purpose" outlook, and is investing in sustainable agriculture and environmental practices that serve their purpose and profitability goals. An example is its LIFEWTR product line and the introduction of Bubly sparkling water.

---

32   https://www.businessinsider.com/unilever-threatens-to-reduce-digital-ad-spend-2018-2?r=US&IR=T

One of Pepsi's goals is to ensure that by 2025 two-thirds of its global beverage portfolio volume will have 100 calories or fewer.[33]

Mondelez, reliant on innovation and talent to win market share in a highly competitive environment, has essentially outsourced its innovation function to a network of startups and retailers to develop new consumer offerings, linking those products more closely to customer needs.

Seeing how clearly these companies leverage purpose in their business, I wondered whether corporations in the Food & Beverage sector focus on socially productive issues because they are vulnerable to consumer and environmental criticism, and closely linked to health, nutrition, and sourcing issues.

Nevertheless, these companies weren't just ticking boxes on a public-relations-oriented CSR effort. They were actively leveraging purpose to motivate employees, meet deep customer needs AND achieve growth, profitability, and competitive advantage.

Purpose and Business Model Together

This was an exciting discovery for us! We realized that companies with a clear purpose not only connect their employees and their customers to something meaningful, they also integrate that with their business model. This outward focus helps them see the world, society and the marketplace differently. It gives them an ability to spot problems and opportunities more clearly, and it actually drives them to become more innovative than ordinary competitors in filling those needs or gaps with urgency. This, in turn, drives higher levels of performance and growth.

Not all companies were equally idealistic, as the examples from the Food & Beverage industry also show. Some companies are very global and altruistic in focus. They openly strive to "make the world a better place." Others are more concerned with immediate customers and market pressures. They want to satisfy customers with better products or lower prices or more efficient processes. This does not indicate a defect or flaw in one purpose

---

33   https://www.bevindustry.com/articles/90919-pepsico-launches-bubly-sparkling-water

or a virtue or strength in another. Instead, the difference is an indication of where that company is strategically focused.

This analysis, which I'll explore in more detail in Chapters Five and Six, helped me resolve some long-unanswered questions. Like many people, I have had "mixed feelings" about corporate purpose for years. What is its function or value? At times I have believed in purpose as a driver of culture, strategy and collaboration. At other times, I have felt downright cynical about the idea, seeing it as little more than a vehicle for public relations or even propaganda, inside and outside the company.

HBR's 2015 report, "The Business Case for Purpose," indicated that such sentiments are widely shared, even among business leaders. That survey of 474 executives found that more than 80 percent of executives believe corporate purpose is important to many key measures of a business, such as employee engagement, success in transformation efforts, customer loyalty, and product quality. Seventy percent also believe it is important to integrate purpose into core business functions. Less than half, however, believe that their organization has a shared sense of purpose or aligns its strategy to its purpose. Fewer than 38 percent say that employees are clear on purpose or that the business model and operations are well-aligned with their purpose. In other words, few leaders know how to think about purpose in a clear and focused way or how to use it to help their people act differently and their companies be more successful.

By dictionary definition, a purpose is an aim or a goal. But corporations already have a concept for that, commonly known as Vision. Vision statements are designed to provide a company with something to strive for, and they also help focus, organize and motivate employees.

Strategy is how you get there. It's the best or smartest path forward. You make decisions about resources, markets, talent, capital, etc., to achieve the vision in accordance with the challenges, competition and opportunities the organization faces. Operations is how you execute and perform. Values are your basic beliefs about "right" versus "wrong", and they strongly influence how you behave.

So where does purpose fit in? It's not the "direction" of the organization, because that's the Vision. It's not the principles of the company, because that's the Values. It's not the culture, strategy or operations, either.

Some people call the purpose of an organization its "reason to exist." Simon Sinek, one of the most influential thinkers in this area, calls it the organization's "Why." Why is the organization in business? What's it for? Satya Nadella touched on this when he asked existential questions about Microsoft.

Legendary business thinker Peter Drucker argued, however, that "The purpose of a business is to create a customer." The clarity of this is powerful. Companies are in business to get customers to buy their products or services. This is how they earn revenue, which is their lifeblood, and it's also how they grow and gain market share. There's a lot of variety in how different companies accomplish such a thing. Some companies build better widgets, others sell them more cheaply. But shouldn't purpose *really* matter? Shouldn't it matter more than *just* business?

Rather than a simple why, as Simon Sinek says, a better question might be "Why is my company in business?" Drucker points to the customer. Others point to the world. A number of fast-growing high-tech companies in recent years declare this very thing. They're in business to "change the world" rather than simply make money. A few, such as Google and Groupon, famously included founder's letters in their IPO prospectuses to declare their focus on long-term purpose over short-term profit. Customers matter to these people, but the world matters more. Or, to put it another way, they're in business not just to sell to customers, but to make their customers' lives better. To them, purpose is not a CSR effort, and it's not a business measure; it's a unique combination of both.

In her book *Becoming a Conscious Leader: How to Lead Successfully in a World That's Waking Up*, Gina Hayden talks about different companies that publicly dismiss the pursuit of profits. As Apple CEO Tim Cook said, "When we work on making our devices accessible by the blind, I don't consider the bloody ROI." They believe that profits come when an organization solves a big problem and makes the world a better place. In other words,

Profits + Purpose = Growth. Moreover, they think this is the moral way for a company to behave. Businesses need to do well by doing good.

In our research, we discovered numerous organizations, often category leaders, that use purpose in a very distinct but deliberate way. First, they define purpose as their company's unique ability to have an impact on meaningful challenges faced by customers in their market or within society or even globally. Second, they leverage that sense of purpose as a core driver of their business rather than as a merely altruistic exercise.

Using purpose in this way shifts their orientation from internal concerns and problems to urgent, emerging or future challenges and needs of customers, society, or the world. The pursuit of that purpose helps them drive innovations that improve or disrupt products, services and strategies and either change the game in existing markets or create entirely new markets. As a result, these companies engage more directly and meaningfully with customers, achieve growth that is directed toward filling more significant or meaningful needs, and distinguish themselves from competitors in a way that is difficult to emulate.

Many startups understand this formula inherently. A sense of purpose is at their core because they were built to serve some need in the world.

To us this was very, very exciting.

Purpose is not just about organizing, motivating or inspiring people to achieve better for the company, it's about innovating to fill some need and make the world just a little bit better. In other words, purpose and innovation are linked. In the following chapters, I will describe how such a connection works.

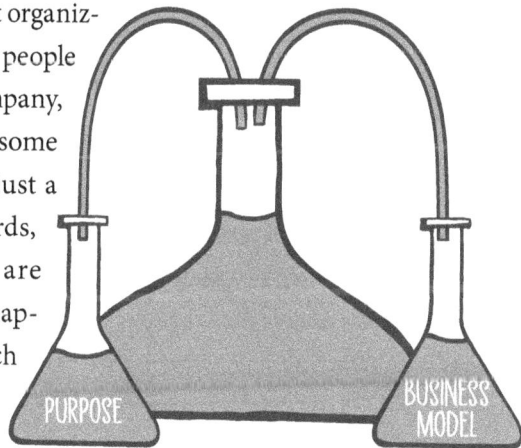

CHAPTER FOUR RECAP

- Evidence from success stories suggests that a clear purpose facilitates innovation and growth.

- Learning from the startup world can pollinate big corporations in the following ways:

  1. Establish a founder's mindset.

  2. Reduce "leadership" and "execution" while tuning-up purpose, team bonding and hard work.

  3. Transform your working environment into a creative playroom.

  4. Connect with real customers in everyday life.

  5. Wait for the right wave to come.

- Companies integrating purpose into their business model create great operational results and increase employee/stakeholder's engagement. Innovation and purpose are inherently connected.

Tools & Resources

The Enemies/Supporters List

This exercise can help broaden your perspective. Usually, companies look only to their customers for feedback and direction. But looking to your "haters" can be invaluable, especially during times of turmoil.

Enemies

  1. List your "haters".

     Select an adequate number of them, ideally from different areas.

2. Ask them one-on-one "What are the three top reasons why you don't like our company?"

3. List and group the most frequently given answers.

Supporters

4. Select a few fans of the company (users and nonusers of your product and service).

5. Ask them "What makes our company unique, best in class?" They, especially the nonusers, will likely mention more reputational aspects of your company.

Lessons

6. List and group all the answers.

   Then ask the same audience, the Supporters, a contra question, "What can we do, about it?"

7. List proposed solutions.

This can become a crucial repository of ideas that will help you design your purpose. Remember: Purpose is Impact on Others.

More detailed guidelines of how to do this exercise you will find on my site www.christostsolkas.com.

Determine Your Real Brand Value

During your journey to identify your brand or company purpose, you might be aided by the following visual exercise, tweaked from the original idea of Milan Semelak at http://createvalue.com/.

The real value of your product or service proposition is a combination of three factors. In my view, you don't necessarily need to pick just one. The functional performance or benefits of your company,

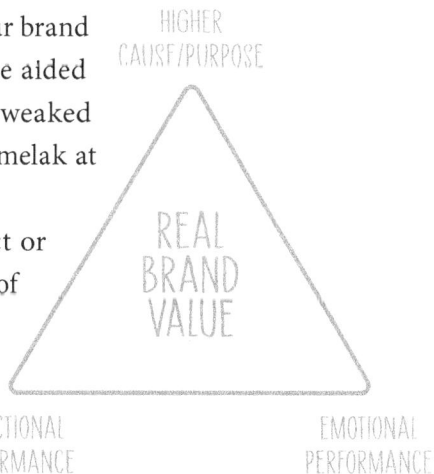

HIGHER CAUSE/PURPOSE

REAL BRAND VALUE

FUNCTIONAL PERFORMANCE

EMOTIONAL PERFORMANCE

the emotional content and context, and finally the impact you have on the world, measured by others. Patagonia, for example, might look like 60 percent on Purpose, 30 percent on Emotional Performance and only 10 percent on Functional Performance of its product range. This approach is simple, can be quantified using research and can be benchmarked with your competition. Spend some time with your team thinking about this triangle.

CHAPTER FIVE

Competing on Purpose Inside and Outside the Box

Mature markets are tough. Dominated by long-established players, competition is fierce. In some sectors, products are so similar there's little to distinguish one company's offering from a competitor's. How does ExxonMobil's oil differ from Shell's? Both come out of the ground and get refined through highly technical processes to achieve standards of quality that today's modern engines demand. At the pump, where prices are approximately the same, the big oil companies try to convince consumers that their oil has special attributes. Yet, no car driver could ever tell the difference.

In mature markets, innovation is usually incremental. It's rare for one established company to come out with a new product or a new twist on an old product that is different or compelling enough to leave competitors in the dust. This doesn't mean companies don't try. Many invest a lot into research and development, but it's difficult to build a better mousetrap when the mousetrap industry has been around for a long time. If one company comes up with a tweak to their mousetrap, everyone else copies it pretty quickly anyway.

Michael Porter explained these dynamics in his monumental 1985 book, *Competitive Advantage*. To Porter, companies achieve competitive advantage based on costs, differentiation or focus. This has influenced the operations and positioning of many organizations over the years. Once a strategy mix becomes successful, incumbents build walls around their approach to protect it. Competitors engage in trench warfare to take that fortress on. They chip away at advantage through incremental innovations or improvements.[34]

Yet, it's hard to compete on price or quality when commodity products are similar. Accordingly, companies typically engage in a battle to reduce costs and enhance service. The best ones are highly efficient. They try to execute flawlessly and work to constantly improve operations. This focus on process innovation helps them drive costs down and deliver on their promises to customers. That discipline can become a source of competitive advantage, though it's rarely game-changing and can be difficult to sustain long-term.

Companies in mature markets also spend a lot of money on marketing, for obvious reasons. Customers may value reliable service, but when products are relatively interchangeable, they need additional incentives to continue buying. Companies work hard to develop a distinct brand that encourages customer loyalty. Differentiation is critical. Advertisements, product placement, reward programs and discounts are among the tools companies have long used to encourage people to buy. Today, companies also deploy technology tools and platforms such as apps and social media strategies to engage with customers, collect and leverage data, keep a brand top of mind, and make a product more convenient or easy to buy.

Everything makes a difference. No stone is left unturned. Competition in a mature market is a tough slog and a battle of attrition. Companies in such markets need leaders with a clear strategy, managers with the ability to make the trains run on time, employees who are equipped and able to perform. And if those companies do all these things well—operate efficiently, constantly improve processes, keep costs low, maximize revenues, differentiate from others, satisfy customers—then they will likely be rewarded with more market share and the approval of Wall Street. But for how long? Somebody who has absolutely nothing to lose will disrupt you.

---

34   https://www.thebalance.com/what-is-competitive-advantage-3-strategies-that-work-3305930

Think of how Dollar Shave Club disrupted Gillette. Starting with a single-branded offering and viral marketing, Dollar Shave won over Gillette's target customers with a sense of humor and an acknowledgement of their pain points and built itself into a billion-dollar company. Competing in mature markets is getting harder and harder in a world where purpose also matters.

When Brand and Efficiency Was King

McDonald's is one of the most powerful brands of the past century. Once the company was incredibly innovative. Today, although still enormously successful, its growth path has been challenged by a changing world.

When the McDonald's brothers launched their first restaurant in California in the 1940s, they sold all kinds of barbeque-cooked foods, including hamburgers, and operated like a traditional "carhop" restaurant, delivering meals to car windows. Seeing that hamburgers were their most profitable food item and costs could be further reduced through efficiencies, they reduced their menu selection, switched from car service to self-service, and developed assembly-line processes.

Over the next few years, they continued to hone and refine the McDonald's concept we know today. They developed a restaurant design that was sleek, clean and eye-catching with gleaming stainless steel counters, red chairs and the famous "golden arches." They didn't make the restaurant too comfortable, however, because they wanted people to eat quickly, giving birth to the idea of "fast food." Customers liked the approach, the taste and the prices.

Success breeds success. Realizing their fast-food concept could be replicated systematically, the McDonald's brothers began to sell franchises. They required new franchisees to follow very strict "rules" for how a restaurant could be designed and operated—understanding implicitly that "brand experience" was critical. A milkshake machine salesman named Ray Kroc, impressed by the volume of sales the California restaurants generated, secured a deal to develop franchises across the country. The numbers started small but began to grow. Kroc, who understood the power of advertising, began to leverage the golden arches and distinctive look of the restaurants to draw in customers. Over the next few decades, as franchises were opened in all fifty states and billions of hamburgers were sold, McDonald's constantly tweaked processes and continued to innovate its menu offerings—pre-sliced buns, breakfast meals, drive-through service—generating almost unimaginable growth.

McDonald's was a pioneering company in many ways. In 1961, it opened "Hamburger University" to train franchisees and executives. To give back, the company launched Ronald McDonald House in 1974, providing families a place to stay when their children required extended hospital treatment. The business expanded internationally in 1976, starting in New Zealand. From 1990, the company committed to using recycled materials and reducing waste. In the mid-1990s, it began to include Disney and Pixar toys with Happy Meals. Each innovation seemed in tune with McDonald's promise to its customers. McDonald's was the epitome of fast, convenient, tasty food at family-friendly prices.

The McDonald's formula allowed the company to thrive in a maturing market, despite intense competition, many challenges and occasional ups-and-downs. Over the past decade, however, McDonald's seems increasingly out of sorts with a changing world. Today, customers often spend entire days at a Starbucks, working, taking meetings, seeing friends. Unlike McDonalds, Starbucks encourages customers to think of it as their "Third place."[35] In an environment in which companies are increasingly criticized for not providing a living wage for employees, McDonald's is a target. But most importantly, customers are far more health-conscious today than they have ever been throughout McDonald's long history.[36] McDonald's has tried to respond with healthier offerings, such as fresh beef,[37] but its signature kale salad has more calories and fat than a Big Mac when the dressing is applied.[38]

Today, McDonald's is back on a growth track, thanks to its new strategy, expanded delivery options and apps. Yet its path seems incremental rather than revolutionary.[39] Its "Velocity Growth Plan" involves serving more customers, more often—something that doesn't seem very inspiring, connecting or meaningful in a world that increasingly values purpose.[40] Meanwhile, companies like Pret a Manger (or simply Pret) are gaining market share by focusing on healthy, organic "fast-food" meals and drinks that customers love.[41]

What would McDonalds have to do or change to become a force of purpose-driven innovation again? The company no longer seems to be shaping or leading the world so much as navigating it.

---

35   https://www.fastcompany.com/887990/starbucks-third-place-and-creating-ultimate-customer-experience

36   http://fortune.com/2015/05/15/mcdonalds-anniversary/

37   https://www.eater.com/2018/3/8/17097078/mcdonalds-fresh-beef-quarter-pounders-rollout-operational-changes

38   https://www.cbc.ca/news/business/mcdonalds-kale-calorie-questions-1.3423938

39   https://www.forbes.com/sites/andriacheng/2018/01/31/mcdonalds-is-lovin-it-well-almost/#779d96f75a50

40   https://corporate.mcdonalds.com/corpmcd/about-us/our-growth-strategy.html

41   https://www.ukessays.com/essays/marketing/the-corporate-analysis-pret-a-manger-marketing-essay.php

Performance with Purpose

In contrast, PepsiCo is a company that has taken a more active and deliberate approach to purpose and innovation.

Pepsi was invented around the same time as Coke, another syrupy soft drink that promised to perk you up and boost your health. Pepsi competed with its soft drink rivals on price, but lagged in sales because it lacked Coca-Cola's innovations in bottling, marketing and distribution.[42] In the 1930s, after making a bad bet on sugar futures, the company went bankrupt and changed hands several times, slowly regaining popularity.

Interestingly, in the late 1940s, Pepsi began marketing to the underserved African American population with positive advertising and intensive sales team efforts. As a result, Pepsi achieved dominant market share in that niche. However, those efforts were abandoned following a leadership change in 1950.[43]

In 1975, Pepsi introduced the Pepsi Challenge campaign, which involved blind taste tests to compare preference for Pepsi over Coke. This was the first cannon shot in the intensely competitive Cola Wars. While Coca-Cola's brand identity was stronger than Pepsi's, consumers generally preferred the taste of Pepsi. As a result, in 1985, Coca-Cola launched New Coke, a formula with a sweeter taste closer to Pepsi. This scandalized Coke customers and allowed Pepsi to declare victory in its battle. However, Coca-Cola, realizing its mistake quickly, relaunched its old formula as Coke Classic and regained brand dominance.

Yet, today, PepsiCo, which includes Frito-Lay, Quaker Oats

42 https://www.businessinsider.com/coca-cola-vs-pepsi-timeline-2013-1#coke-developed-its-iconic-contour-bottle-got-big-name-endorsements-and-expanded-to-europe-meanwhile-pepsi-went-bankrupt-because-of-wwi-4

43 https://www.wsj.com/articles/SB116831396726171042

and Gatorade, is currently the world's third-largest food and beverage conglomerate, while Coca-Cola recorded one of the largest-ever falls on the Global 2000 list.[44] It's easy to pinpoint the shift as starting in 2006 with the leadership of former PepsiCo CEO, Indra Nooyi. One of the most notable decisions Nooyi made early in her tenure was to reclassify Pepsi products into three categories: "fun for you" (traditional junk food), "better for you" (low fat, low sugar alternatives), and "good for you" (healthy snacks, foods and drinks like oatmeal, hummus and Naked Juice). She also endeavored to improve the nutrition of products in the fun category.

Nooyi viewed innovation as solving a customer need, in this case, healthier alternatives to junk food and drinks. PepsiCo has also been a leader in environmental sustainability. Nooyi, as a native of India, was very conscious of water issues and strove to make operations as conservationally focused and environmentally friendly as possible.

In 2015, PepsiCo launched its new growth strategy based on its "Performance with Purpose 2025 Agenda." To this end, PepsiCo focuses on three purpose-driven areas—Products, Planet and People—which it sees as not just "good to do" but essential for success, profitability and growth as a business.

To improve products, PepsiCo is reducing sugar, fat and salt while shifting its portfolio toward healthier offerings. One of Pepsi's goals is to ensure that by 2025 two-thirds of its global beverage portfolio volume will have 100 calories or fewer.[45]

To improve the planet, PepsiCo is working to replenish water, especially in high-risk watersheds, while also striving to provide more people with safe water access.

To help people, PepsiCo is working with local farmers to improve agricultural practices because half of all people on the planet work on farms. It's investing in training and education of women and girls in local communities because most of those farmers and community leaders are women.

---

44   https://www.forbes.com/sites/maggiemcgrath/2018/06/06/worlds-largest-food-and-beverage-companies-2018-anheuser-busch-nestle-and-pepsi-top-the-list/#feea4ce1b08d

45   https://www.bevindustry.com/articles/90919-pepsico-launches-bubly-sparkling-water

And it's increasing female representation among corporate management because diversity of perspective and experience is essential for long-term business success.[46]

Likewise, Coca-Cola has taken similar measures. They use their market clout to connect with developing societies. For example, their RAIN initiative is helping African communities get access to water. This is an effective program. Like a number of other major multinationals, Coca-Cola has also launched a plastics recycling project to help sustainability.[47] [48]

In my view, however, when such initiatives remain isolated from the primary business of the company, their impact is limited and ephemeral. After all, it's not likely that mega companies engaged in charitable operations can or will sustain such activities when the financial going gets tough. At the first sign of trouble, big companies find it all too easy to pull the plug on philanthropic business. In contrast, if ethical activities make the company money, you can bet they will be sustained.

Fortune Favors the Purposeful

PepsiCo is succeeding today through a strategy of diversification and a purpose-centered approach to innovation. PepsiCo leadership believes that Performance with a Purpose goes well beyond a CSR program and actually fortifies the company through hard times while giving it the capability to compete more successfully in the future by drawing committed talent and aligning the company's offerings and values more closely with customers and partners.[49]

Even successful and long-established companies are incredibly vulnerable, however. A bad economic cycle, an unexpected scandal or an aggressive

46   https://www.fastcompany.com/3066378/how-pepsico-ceo-indra-nooyi-is-steering-the-company-tva

47   https://www.coca-colacompany.com/stories/the-replenish-africa-initiative

48   https://www.beveragedaily.com/Article/2019/03/26/Diageo-Unilever-Coca-Cola-Nestle-launch-Africa-Plastics-Recycling-Alliance

49   https://www.forbes.com/sites/csr/2011/04/07/pepsi-takes-performance-with-purpose-to-heart/#7e09424340b4

new competitor can put a business on life support overnight. Amazon, for example, has decimated many retail businesses such as Borders Books, Sears, and more. But its formidable strength has been in distribution, not Amazon label products. In 2009, it launched its own battery to compete with Duracell and Energizer, instantly taking one-third of the traditional competitors' market share. Duracell and Energizer thought they were just fighting each other; it turns out, Amazon was an even more daunting enemy.[50] Now, Amazon is releasing hundreds of private label products and it has the advertising, distribution and data might to destroy established competitors in those mature markets.

When a company stands for more than just profit and market share, it has more resilience and determination to overcome tough challenges. Its people and customers are more dedicated and committed. Its brand has more stickiness. But the new realization of purpose is that it also helps a company innovate. Purpose brings a business closer to the needs and values of the customer.

When Apple was founded, it basically invented the personal computer market. Then, competitors quickly got into the game and sold machines that were almost as good at much cheaper prices. Apple lost revenue and market share rapidly, and co-founder Steve Jobs was fired. When Jobs returned in 1996, the company was on life-support. Jobs, however, infused the business with a renewed sense of purpose. Apple was not really in the business of building pretty boxes (though it did that very well); instead, it was in the business of helping customers "think different".[51] That sense of purpose permeated and reinvigorated the organization, making Apple a mission-driven and very different computer company.

For sure, Apple also became a very sophisticated company able to combine design, marketing, technology, production, distribution, retail and finance in integrated ways to enable profitability while helping recapture market share. But it was the sense of purpose, embodied in "think different", which gave the company the direction and capability to innovate in bold new ways.

50 https://www.nytimes.com/2018/06/23/business/amazon-the-brand-buster.html
51 https://www.youtube.com/watch?v=4HsGAc0_Y5c

Few could have imagined the company Apple would soon become. Although Apple still competes in the laptop market, its innovations, first with the iPod and then the iPhone, allowed it to create and dominate two entirely new sectors, portable music and smartphones. These innovations drove Apple to incredible levels of profitability, making it one of the largest and most successful companies in the world, in only a few short years. Afterwards, computer and cell phone handset companies that once mocked Apple either copied them or became largely irrelevant.

Whether Apple can sustain that level of relevance and innovation going forward remains to be seen. But it rose from the ashes, achieved greatness as a business and changed the world because it focused on "purpose" and leveraged that deep sense of meaning to innovate and grow.

Redefining the Market

If you can't beat them, change the game you're playing. In today's global economy, one way to do that is to expand your appeal in a traditional market by going beyond the product to meet bigger, more universal concerns.

Unilever, the world's largest consumer goods company, operates explicitly in a purpose-driven way. The British-Dutch company was founded in 1930 when a margarine maker and a soap maker merged. Since its founding, the company has grown largely through acquisitions, accumulating over four hundred brands.

Unilever ties its most popular or famous brands to a specific social cause, linking them to environmental, societal or community issues. The company shuns short-term profitability over long-term growth objectives, especially in emerging markets. It also refuses to push ads on social media platforms that proliferate toxic content.[52] Ex CEO Paul Polman believed this adherence to a sense of purpose is critical on several levels.

First, it gives employees and customers a shared sense of meaning that goes way beyond a particular product. For example, Dove focuses on

52   https://www.businessinsider.com/unilever-threatens-to-reduce-digital-ad-spend-2018-2?IR=T

women's self-esteem with its "Campaign for Beauty" ads, while the ice cream Ben & Jerry's amplifies social justice issues. Other brands in Unilever's sustainable-living portfolio overtly tie environmental concerns to challenges around mass production, packaging and consumption.

Second, those brands outperform Unilever's brands that are not tied directly to purpose. The company discovered in 2016 that its sustainable-living products generated 60 percent of the company's growth. In general, the company's purpose-oriented brands grow twice as fast as its ordinary brands. In other words, purpose can generate growth and profitability.[53]

Unilever researched this in its landmark study "Make Purpose Pay", which looked at how twenty thousand people around the world made purchasing decisions.[54] Unilever discovered that people interested in sustainability as an issue really do buy products that offer more sustainable choices when offered. When they don't do so it is because they either believe that the claims of sustainability are not genuine, or they worry that the cost is higher. By building up its credibility as an authentically purpose-driven company and keeping its prices competitive, Unilever is able to grow profitability and market share by doing good. This also reinforces the sense of engagement that employees feel for their company and work.

Unilever is so faithful to the importance of its sense of purpose that it resisted and withstood an unwanted merger offer by 3G, a South American company under the Berkshire Hathaway umbrella. Despite the hit to its share price, Unilever worried that its acquirer would not see value in Unilever's purpose-driven innovation focus and might.

Seizing the High Ground and Competitive Advantage

Most established companies compete on operational efficiency and incremental innovation in an existing market space. This makes them vulnerable to competitors that adopt a more global approach to purpose and meaning.

---

53 http://fortune.com/2017/02/17/unilever-paul-polman-responsibility-growth/

54 https://www.unilever.com/Images/making-purpose-pay-inspiring-sustainable-living-170515_tcm244-506419_en.pdf

Such companies simply engage with consumers and employees on a different level. They also seem to be able to innovate and respond to new societal or market issues faster than traditional companies focused more exclusively on profit and share price.

Most companies in the world operate or try to operate like P&G or McDonald's or ExxonMobile. Valuing operational excellence and discipline, they stick to their lanes by focusing on the essential uses of the products they make and sell and striving to meet the basic needs of their customers. They believe that understanding the customer's basic needs allows them to make the sorts of changes and tweaks that will keep their products necessary and appealing.

Today, that mode creates several problems. It prevents companies from being sensitive to big swings in society or strong movements or concerns. A company reliant on a strong brand that it incrementally innovates year after year will be extremely reluctant and risk-averse to changing that brand in a big way when societal expectations or markets change. In contrast, a company that is concerned about more than profit may forego short-term profitability for a larger sense of purpose. But in the process, it sets itself for longer-term and more sustainable growth. Its products will be less static and "packaged" than competitors.

P&G, a formidable, high-quality, strong-performing company for almost two hundred years, is starting to learn that lesson. As former CEO Bob McDonald once noted, "There needs to be an emotional component [to innovation] as well—a source of inspiration that motivates people."[55] In 2004, the company took steps in that direction with its Children's Safe Drinking Water Program, which provides clean drinking water in developing nations. Its water purifier product is specifically tied into this effort and bears the P&G brand name, rather than a specific product brand name.

Also in 2004, the company tried to alleviate issues related to global disasters with that safe drinking program, developing purification sachets to kill bacteria, viruses and parasites in water that may be unsafe due to

---

55   https://www.chegg.com/homework-help/questions-and-answers/p-g-tripled-innovation-success-rate-hbr-case-strategies-innovation-b-bac-k-2000-prospects--q16231705

disasters. The company also developed a fleet of mobile laundromats to do the laundry of people affected by global disasters, an effort welcomed by anyone who has experienced a calamity.

In 2013, the company finally began to address the environmental sustainability challenge by reducing its use of water and expelling of pollutants. Additionally, the company has begun to produce and market other environmentally friendly products like recyclable shampoo bottles made partially from recycled beach plastic. In 2015, the company took an unusually bold step in tying its brand to consciousness-raising issues around "girl power," while tying those issues specifically to feminine products that girls need to buy.

All of those actions count, but they aren't intrinsically part of P&G's business model or growth plan. If it dropped those efforts and returned to the old way of doing things, P&G's operations wouldn't change. In contrast, companies like Unilever focus on global appeal in their innovations, and often outperform competitors that focus more purely on basic operational challenges. When purpose is part of the business model, it gives companies like Unilever something a little extra in the hearts and minds of customers and employees.

As I mentioned in the previous chapter, this research began with a small exercise that my team initiated and established. Together, we looked at eight robust sectors ranging from Food & Beverage to Motor Vehicles and Telecoms, and selected the top three to five representatives of those sectors according to the *Fortune Global 500*. We analyzed their mission statements and purpose to see how clearly they articulated recognition of and service toward some larger societal or global need. Then we analyzed their business model to assess potential impact on those needs. Basically, we were looking for alignment between purpose and business activity.

Then, for comparison, we also looked at a number of small or emergent startups with particularly clear or compelling purpose-orientation.

Existing market spaces were the easiest to define. We found companies clustered into two categories. Some of those companies had a strong operational focus. By way of a hypothetical example, one company we worked with believed that "our role in the world is to become the total food company, satisfying shareholders, customers and employees."

Group A

- AT&T
- China Mobile
- Volkswagen
- GM
- Daimler
- L'Oreal
- P&G
- Exor
- Christian Dior
- Toyota
- Verizon
- Pepsico (marginally)

Other companies focused on broader needs that are more societal (i.e., they improve economic inequality or injustice) or global in nature (they focus on world hunger or environmental sustainability).

Group B

- Unilever
- Nestle
- TOMS Shoes
- Danone
- Warby Parker
- Mondelez

The high-value zone, in my view, is on the second grouping. When products and services are lifted above their most utilitarian elements, they can be tied to a stronger, more resonant sense of meaning. This, in turn, gives those companies a compelling advantage with customers and employees who believe in those values.

But how can a company set itself up for exponential growth and disruptive change of an industry? Is purpose the most important ingredient of that recipe? Instinctively, we assumed that "innovation" would comprise the other parameter. So we started digging into each one of the companies in our sample to see whether they try to achieve differentiation via incremental or disruptive innovation, in existing or completely new spaces. We grouped them accordingly and started plotting the two axes to place our results.

Below you'll see the X/Y axis and where we were headed.

But before we go further, I want to tell you about the two other groups of companies we identified.

CHAPTER FIVE RECAP

■ Operating in mature, fragmented markets is tough. Every decimal point of growth takes sweat and blood. By default, any attempt at innovation is incremental. So are the results.

■ Companies try to satisfy consumers, stakeholders and shareholders by traditional means. They rarely focus on purpose or global impact.

■ Some incumbents try to escape this deadly loop by establishing a broader operational scope and attempting to define a larger purpose. These companies tend to be more successful and impactful.

Tools & Resources

- Collective consciousness helps you understand that you are not in business only for business. A talk by Dr. Deepak Chopra helped me see this. I started a hashtag after watching this video #dobusiness_dogood. Follow it and also don't miss Chopra's video talking about purpose (visit my site www.christostsolkas.com to see the link).

- Read this book by Rita Gunter McGrath to better understand how quickly traditional strategies and competitive advantage can become obsolete and what you need to do to stay alive and win.

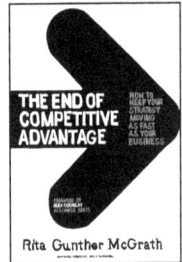

CHAPTER SIX

Going for the Unthinkable

In the 1920s, two brothers, Adolf and Rudolph Dassler, began making athletic shoes in Germany. Track runners had long used spiked shoes to gain better traction when racing. The Dassler brothers figured out a way to make those shoes lighter using canvas and rubber. In 1936, they convinced American track star Jesse Owens to wear their shoes in the Berlin Olympics. Owens won four gold medals, and the Dassler brand became synonymous with Olympic glory. Soon the brothers were selling two hundred thousand shoes a year. Their product was so famous that U.S. forces didn't destroy their factory during World War II, even though it had been producing tanks. When the Allied occupation began, all the soldiers of the American army wanted Dassler shoes.

How does a product stand out from the ranks of other, similar products to catalyze the rapid growth of a company? Innovation is obviously key. But innovation, on its own, is not enough. If it were, then any company could spur rapid growth by tweaking or improving existing products. In reality, people don't want something that is merely better than other products on the market. They want something that is "different" in some new and special way. The Dassler brothers, it turned out, were not just selling shoes. They were selling elite athletic performance.

After the war, the Dassler brothers conflicted as business partners and went their separate ways. Adolph Dassler, known as "Adi", formed a new shoe company he called "Adi-das." Rudolph Dassler started "Ru-da", which later became "Puma." For decades, Adidas and Puma dominated the athletic shoe market globally, along with a number of others like America's Converse and the UK's Reebok. Then came a company called Blue Ribbon Sports launched in 1964 in Beaverton, Oregon.

The founders of Blue Ribbon Sports were an odd couple. Bill Bowerman was a coach at the University of Oregon who made track shoes as a hobby. Phil Knight had been one of Bowerman's athletes. Knight was working as an accountant when he realized that his real passion was for entrepreneurship. He saw Bowerman's shoes as a product he could sell. Bowerman's passion was for making better athletic shoes. He couldn't believe the industry still hadn't figured out how to do it right. He kept experimenting with different designs and materials on the theory that the slightest reduction in weight would produce a substantial advantage in speed. For seven years he made incremental improvements; then came his Eureka moment.

The track at the University of Oregon was changing to a new artificial surface. That was the future. Maybe spikes, which were the heaviest part of a shoe, were not necessary when the track was no longer made of dirt, grass or wood chips. But what to replace them with? Bowerman tried all kinds of different ideas until inspiration struck. One Sunday, making brunch for his wife, he stared at the waffle iron. The grooves produced on a waffle looked like a surface that could provide traction. What if Bowerman made a similar pattern out of rubber and attached that to the bottom of a shoe? The rubber tread might function like spikes on an artificial surface, but the shoe would weigh considerably less. Bowerman abandoned his breakfast and heated up some rubber instead, sacrificing the family's waffle iron to create the first rubber-treaded sole which he cut to shape and sewed on to a canvas shoe. The tread worked!

That was 1971. Invigorated by Bowerman's innovation, the company changed its name to Nike, after the Greek goddess of speed, strength and victory, and Knight got to work selling shoes that were unique on the market. They called the first of this new line the Waffle Trainer. Knight drove around the Pacific Northwest and sold Waffle Trainers out of the back of his car to amateur track athletes.

Like Dassler, Nike needed its own Jesse Owens. One of the first converts to the Waffle Trainer was a local track star named Steve Prefontaine. Highly recruited as a high school athlete, Prefontaine chose University of Oregon because Bill Bowerman was the coach. Prefontaine liked Bowerman's innovative approach to training and racing. Bowerman got Prefontaine ready for the 1972 Munich Olympics.

Fans loved Prefontaine's style of running. He was an aggressive competitor, and liked to come out hard, take the lead and stay out front at a time when most runners adopted more "wait and see" tactics. He also was a rebel who seemed disdainful of old rules and traditions. Constantly promoting Nike shoes to other athletes and organizations, Prefontaine became the face of the company and helped make the swoosh logo famous through his racing style. As he put it, "Some people create with words or with music or with a brush and paints. I like to make something beautiful when I run. I like to make people stop and say, 'I've never seen anyone run like that before.'" Then tragedy struck. Prefontaine was killed in a car accident just before the 1976 Montreal Olympics. America and the running world mourned.

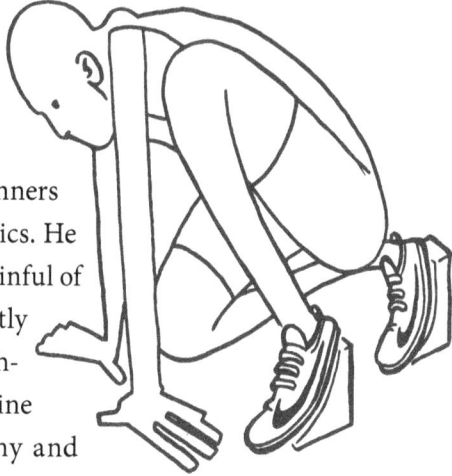

Those two legends seemed to embody Nike—the waffle iron and the heroic young runner who fought the establishment and the odds. Innovation meets guts. The Nike culture was one of constant innovation (always trying to make the shoes a little bit better) and a scrappy, highly competitive approach to the market. But what set Nike apart? It did the same things as any other athletic shoe company—designed shoes for performance, reduced costs as much as possible through efficient manufacturing and distribution, and marketed like crazy. It may have been better at marketing than most, and its shoes did seem to offer improvements more often, so is that how

Nike came out of nowhere to become the biggest athletic shoe and apparel company in the world today?

Not quite.

Constantly improved shoe designs, solid business operations, intensive marketing and celebrity endorsements were enough to allow Nike to play the game with the world's global athletic shoe companies like Adidas, Puma, Reebok and Converse. But though the company grew revenues and market share at an exceptional pace, it still struggled to differentiate itself playing by those rules. For instance, in the 1984 Los Angeles Olympics, American Carl Lewis, wearing Nike shoes, equaled Jesse Owens' achievement of winning four gold medals, but Nike did not receive any noticeable surge in shoe sales as a result. People expected athletic shoes to improve athletic performance. That was the old game.

Nike won by playing a new game—shifting the athletic shoe business into a different space. Phil Knight had come to believe that Nike wasn't in the shoe business, but the entertainment business.[56] This changed the way the company viewed products, innovation, marketing and celebrity endorsements.

That vision came to realization in 1985. A University of North Carolina basketball player by the name of Michael Jordan started playing for the Chicago Bulls. Drafted third overall, Jordan was electrifying and looked like he had the potential to be a generational player. His ability to leap and dunk seemed to defy gravity. Fans became very excited. The media attention overwhelmed teammates. At the All-Star game, the other players, resenting Jordan's fame, froze him out and refused to pass to him. Jordan kept breaking records in response.

Here's how Nike came into the picture. Jordan's favorite shoes were Adidas, and he wanted a shoe deal that could keep him wearing them. But Adidas was in management turmoil after the death of founder Adi Dassler. During a meeting with the Adidas leadership team, Jordan's agent asked what sort of innovations in shoes or marketing Adidas had planned. Adidas had no answer. Reluctantly, Jordan and his agent met with Nike.

56   http://www.espn.com/blog/playbook/dollars/post/_/id/2918/how-nike-landed-michael-jordan

THE GIFT OF CRISIS | 119

Jordan didn't like Nike basketball shoes, but he was quickly swayed by the company's drive to try innovative approaches to product and marketing. For its part, Nike viewed Jordan's entertaining playing style and charismatic personality as something that would transcend basketball and shoes. So Nike told Michael Jordan they would let him design his own shoe line, and they would build a very different sort of advertising campaign around him that would capitalize on Jordan's personal appeal and excitement.

Michael Jordan's playing career far exceeded expectations. He was perhaps the greatest to ever play in the NBA. As Nike envisioned, he also became a cultural icon whose personal brand went way beyond sports. The shoe marketing deal with Jordan helped launch Nike into a new stage of growth and helped make Jordan very rich. As Nike grew, the company continued to focus on athletic performance, but the energy of the brand focused on fashion and entertainment. Other famous personalities like Tiger Woods, Lance Armstrong, LeBron James and Kanye West helped lift the shoes beyond sports to something bigger—fame, success, revolution. As a result of this premium, Nike could produce more varieties of shoes and sell them at higher prices. Other companies, like Adidas, attempted to follow Nike into the fashion business, but Nike was first and better at it for a long time.

Today, Nike is the largest supplier of athletic shoes and apparel in the world with one of the most iconic brands and slogans of all time. The Nike swoosh and "Just Do It" slogan are strongly linked with quality shoes, competitive athletics and celebrity fashion.

Blue Oceans vs Red Oceans

In existing spaces, competition is fierce. Long-established players fight over every inch of market share through incremental innovation and an obsessive focus on efficiency, cost reduction and margins. In their book, *Blue Ocean Strategy: How to Create Uncontested Market Space and Make the Competition Irrelevant*, authors Chan Kim and Renee Mauborgne describe established markets as Red Oceans because competitors act like sharks tearing each other apart. In contrast, Blue Oceans are new market spaces, free of competitors, waiting to be explored. In those Blue Oceans, pioneering companies grow like crazy.

According to the authors, companies discover Blue Oceans by focusing on new value innovation in products or services while still keeping operations lean and low cost. Companies like Nike differentiate their products or services substantially to create a new game while still maintaining the operational discipline of the old game. In this way, they turbocharge their growth. That's how Nike did it: It shifted its focus from "shoes" to "fashion" while still leveraging its prowess at production, distribution and marketing.

How do Blue Ocean companies figure out which new markets to move into? That magic formula is harder to crack. If it were easy, businesses would do it all the time. According to the authors, Blue Ocean companies get their new ideas by looking across the traditional boundaries of competition. Instead of focusing on current rivals and maximizing the profit of existing products and services, they scan complementary industries with similar products and services where they can apply their expertise and know-how with new customers. Instead of focusing on current trends, they try to shape future trends. Instead of focusing on marginal price competition, they seek products and services that can be priced at a premium because they have an emotional impact with consumers.

Apple is one of the easiest to see that approach come into play. Apple was launched by looking at one industry—mainframe business computers—and seeing how that concept and technology could be adapted for individual consumers: personal computers. They brought ideas and modes from creative industries and embedded them in a highly technical engineering industry. They didn't follow the trends of an industry in development, they constantly tried to get ahead of trends—in computing, digital music, smartphones, watches, etc.—in order to shape or create markets in which they could dominate. Apple's iPhones are produced with incredible operational discipline and designed and marketed exceptionally well, but they can also be priced higher than anything in the market because customers value what they mean.

This is because Apple, like Nike, looks for ways to meet customers' deeper needs and emotional wants, the ones people don't even know exist. Computers and smartphones are not just devices or commodities for Apple, they are ways to help people be more versatile, flexible, productive and creative in their work, life and hobbies without being impeded by cumbersome operating systems or complicated technology. In the process, Apple enables many new markets to flourish, from music, photography and graphic design to advertising, publishing, education, film, and so on.

Note that Apple and Nike are very pragmatic, customer-focused companies. They may have lofty views of their products, but they are still selling commodities. In other words, though both Nike and Apple like to describe themselves as "rebels" or "revolutionaries", they are not trying to change society or the world in a sweeping or transformative way. Instead, very much in the tradition of products throughout the 20th century, like laundry detergent, cars, refrigerators, etc., their purpose is to meet individual consumer needs in a deeper, more satisfying and engaging way.

Netflix is another classic example of a company meeting individual consumer needs in new ways that made it a market buster and category leader.

Throughout much of the twentieth century, people watched movies at theaters or on TV when reruns were broadcast by network television channels. After videotape cassettes came out in the mid-1970s, the entertainment industry started to change. Home video machines began to drop in price, and retail stores were created that let people rent movies and bring them home for a day or two.

By the mid-1980s, there were around fifteen thousand video rental stores in the U.S. Most were "mom and pop" stores or regional businesses. Sometimes these stores specialized by offering different kinds of movies— ranging from more popular titles to more art-house or foreign movies—but generally they all operated the same. Customers applied for a membership card which gave them the right to rent a video and bring it home while making them liable for lost, stolen or damaged videos.

Rentals were not too expensive, a few dollars at most. But the secret to profitability was late fees. When customers were even an hour late returning a movie, they could be charged an extra day. Sometimes customers forgot to bring a movie back for weeks and the fees piled up. Video stores counted on this to make money.

An industry with so many bit players is ripe for consolidation. Blockbuster Video, which originated with one store in Dallas, Texas, in 1985, eventually became that beast. With a solid store concept and lots of financing behind it, Blockbuster began expanding and buying up other regional competitors. By 2004, Blockbuster had nine thousand stores in the U.S.

But Blockbuster's end was already in motion. In 1997, a new movie recording technology, Digital Video Disc or DVD, came out that was less liable to break, cheaper to make and smaller. Soon, DVDs were being rented in video stores alongside VHS cassettes.

To a couple of upstart companies, Redbox and Netflix, DVDs had another advantage. They were small, cheap and light enough to store in a vending machine or send through the mail. No doubt, Blockbuster looked at these competitors in the same way Adidas once looked at Nike: Who cares? When a company completely dominates the market , an upstart competitor with a new approach is just an irritant. But Blockbuster didn't realize the "need" or "want" that Netflix, in particular, was meeting in customers who liked renting videos. Blockbuster thought nobody really wanted to order a video online and wait for days to get it in the mail. Netflix customers liked being able to line up their future movie selections on the computer and avoid spending hours in stores, scanning the shelves. Even more importantly, Netflix customers HATED paying for late fees. Famously, founder and CEO Reed Hoffman launched the company after he was forced to pay $40 in late fees for a movie he'd forgotten to return to Blockbuster. With Netflix mail-delivered DVDs, customers could keep a movie as long as they liked.

Netflix's subscription model was a less obvious innovation that helped the company grow. Stable, growing, monthly revenue is a terrific way to fuel profitability. Slowly, Netflix began to creep up on Blockbuster, and

Blockbuster began to take notice. At one point, the two companies discussed the idea of Blockbuster buying Netflix. Netflix would serve as Blockbuster's online arm. But just as those plans looked like they might go through, the Blockbuster board fired their CEO and rehired their previous CEO, a former 7 Eleven convenience store executive, who dismissed online businesses as fads and doubled down on brick-and-mortar retail stores. Within a few years, Blockbuster had peaked, but Netflix kept surging by focusing on a traditional product in a new market space and meeting deeper customer needs in the process.

The Netflix story would be interesting if that's all there was to it, but Netflix has been remarkable for its drive to stay on top by continuing to move into new Blue Ocean spaces. Recognizing that its mail-delivery model would be made obsolete by streaming video, Netflix went "all in" on streaming video earlier than any other big player. This met deeper customer needs for convenience and ease while reinforcing and growing Netflix's subscription revenue model. At one point, Netflix's streaming movies represented 40 percent of all Internet traffic in the U.S.

Then, knowing that other well-funded competitors were going to eat away at Netflix's streaming service advantage, the company innovated again by getting into producing original content. Their productions of original TV shows and movies met customer insatiable demands for high-quality programming and entertainment. Netflix's competitors, especially Hulu and Amazon, quickly followed suit. Netflix keeps moving into new spaces and competing with existing competitors in new ways. It will be interesting to see if Netflix can continue to do so.

New-Space Machines

A new breed of company has emerged in the past few years that takes Blue Ocean/new-space strategies to the extreme. These companies describe themselves as being "intensely customer-driven" and relentlessly innovation-focused. They demonstrate the power of seeking new spaces constantly, wherever they can be found.

Amazon is the example that most of us know well. Famously, Amazon started as an online distributor of books at a time when "dot-com" businesses were the stock market's darlings, and businesses like Pets.com were valued higher than General Motors. When that speculative market crashed, many dot-com businesses disappeared and a few kept going, Amazon among them.

Amazon's book distribution business, like Netflix's DVD mail order business, met customer needs in new-space ways. Customers like bookstores but they also like the convenience of ordering online, especially when the book costs less. Amazon's distribution model was so profitable, it began to put most brick-and-mortar competitors out of business. From the beginning, however, Amazon wasn't really in the book distribution business. Instead, it was actually a "distribution" company. Starting with books, Amazon quickly moved into other products that could be distributed through its growing system of warehouses and suppliers.

Amazon didn't stop there. Recognizing that discovering "new space" customer needs was critical for fueling growth, the company kept upping the ante. Deliveries got super-fast, from a week or more, down to two days. Today, Amazon has a network of suppliers in most cities that can deliver most things customers order within a few hours. Unlike most companies, Amazon didn't want to charge more for those deliveries, it wanted to charge less. So, it offered a yearly subscription fee model called Amazon Prime, which eliminated delivery fees. Customers loved this and signed up in droves.

Through Amazon Prime, Amazon continued to offer new services that met new needs. Restaurant delivery. Music. Movies and TV shows. Groceries. Shoes. In the process, it entered hundreds of traditional markets but offered new levels of service, convenience, variety and prices that competitors couldn't beat. Whenever Amazon met roadblocks in that service orientation, it quickly adapted and developed new business lines. For example, one Christmas, Amazon's famous two-day delivery service hit a snafu when its distribution partners (USPS, UPS, FedEx) couldn't handle the volume. Rather than see this as a defeat, Amazon just developed its own delivery services and partnered with new delivery partners like Uber.

Amazon's success fueled its growth into new markets that were so outside Amazon's core expertise that observers were surprised. For example, rather than stick with online sales, Amazon bought Whole Foods groceries because it recognized this link between distribution, local convenience and Amazon Prime membership benefits as another leverage point with customers. Needing to build its own server farms to house vast amounts of data, Amazon built AWS services and sold them to other businesses with similar needs, including competitors. Today, that division is responsible for most of Amazon's pure profitability. Not all of Amazon's innovations have worked out. For example, its smartphone, the Amazon Fire, failed to turn customers on. But another moon-shot product, Amazon's Alexa, its in-home voice-activated service, started off slow but now is making great inroads with customers, integrating Amazon services deeper into customers' lives in ways that they value.

Amazon may seem like a one-of-a-kind company, but it is not alone. Its biggest global competitor is a company built very much in the same relentlessly customer-driven innovation-focused model, though it has attacked different traditional markets in different ways. I'm talking about Alibaba.

Alibaba is an "everything" company, almost as if you combined Amazon, Facebook, Yahoo, Google, PayPal, eBay, IBM, Tesla, Orbitz, Sony, Microsoft, Salesforce and so on, into one entity. The company was founded in 1999 as an online marketplace. Its first "new space" angle was the untapped market in China. Basically, it brought online commerce and business services to a market of consumers who desperately wanted them. It was a Blue Ocean rather than a Red Ocean because the big American players were locked out by the Chinese government.

Alibaba didn't stand still on that advantage, however. It kept expanding services from e-commerce to e-shopping to e-banking with consumer-to-consumer and business-to-consumer portals. The focus on innovation is real. Today, Alibaba makes and sells cars that work like computers or robots. It uses facial recognition software to complete transactions that rely on customer smiles. It delivers pharmaceuticals to markets that lack access. It also moved out of China and into two hundred countries worldwide.

In the process, Alibaba has become the largest e-commerce company in the world.

The future of hyper-growth is companies like Amazon and Alibaba. With platforms built to generate customer satisfaction, their purpose is to discover new spaces that meet customer needs. It doesn't matter what the product, service or market might be. These companies will go there to win. In the process, they grow and grow and grow.

Coming back to our exercise as described in the previous chapter, we grouped the companies innovating outside their box/space, operating in a unique way, as listed below:

Group C

- Alibaba
- Amazon
- PayPal

- Facebook
- Netflix
- Nike

- Salesforce
- Airbnb

Hyper-Disruption

Hyper-disruption companies are not for the faint of heart. Because they break the rules and strive for a purpose that's far bigger than business, they can also seem irrational, grandiose, unrealistic, improbable, and even faintly ridiculous. It can take a special type of leader to conceive of and drive such a company successfully. It was said of Steve Jobs that he created his own "reality distortion field."[57] Perhaps Elon Musk is the leader and visionary who comes closest to that characterization today. This is not entirely complementary. Just as Jobs crashed and burned at Apple in the 1980s, so Musk may be on his way to doing the same today. Yet, it's inarguable that both men have had an outsized impact on their industries and the world. Let's look at Musk, an unusual person, from that perspective.

---

57 https://www.theatlantic.com/technology/archive/2012/02/the-steve-jobs-reality-distortion-field-even-makes-it-into-his-fbi-file/252832/

In July 2016, Musk wrote an unusual memo to the employees and shareholders of Tesla Motors. He called it "Master Plan Part Deux." In it, he explained the underlying rationale for Tesla's strategic decisions. The implication was that Tesla's strategic decisions could seem random or counter-productive without an understanding of the bigger picture—the purpose of Tesla Motors.

Unlike most companies, Tesla is not in business to make money or satisfy customers, but to save the planet. Electric cars, Musk implied, are just a "vehicle," so to speak, for accomplishing that goal. This mindset makes Tesla representative of a new breed of company, conceived and operated to achieve something far beyond the scope of traditional business.

Musk started Tesla with a problem to solve. When he was in college, he famously outlined five areas of science he believed would have the most influence on the future of the human species:

1. the Internet

2. sustainable energy

3. space exploration

4. artificial intelligence

5. human genetics

With Tesla and a related company, SolarCity, Musk focused on sustainable energy. He recognized that modern civilization's reliance on fossil fuels puts the future of humanity in peril.

Most people who are worried about climate change or sustainability do very little about it except worry—they see it as a daunting social and economic problem. Most business leaders who care view it as something outside their responsibilities to customers and shareholders. Musk viewed the planetary threat of fossil fuel reliance as a business problem. How do we shift the global economy to a new alternative fuel source? He ultimately came up with a solution that combined engineering and marketing. This was the thinking he outlined in Master Plan Part Deux.

Fossil fuels power our modern world and have done so since the dawn of the Industrial Revolution. Our addiction to them is incredibly strong. Before the Industrial Revolution, wind power, water power, wood and coal (the main fossil fuel of the bunch) were the primary sources of energy we used for transportation, agriculture, heat, etc. After the Industrial Revolution, the need for reliable, cheap fuel grew exponentially—and oil fit the bill because it is relatively inexpensive, easy to find, transportable, storable, refined and adaptable to many different purposes.

Some people have long argued that wind and solar power are cheaper (free, they insist) and more available. But they actually present complex problems as fuel sources. They are not as reliable, easy to store, transportable or adaptable. And until recently, the cost of solar panels and wind turbines was prohibitive. Those costs are finally going down as the adoption of the technologies scale. Weaning off fossil fuels is more possible than ever today but still extremely challenging.

As an engineer, Musk knew that most of our fossil fuels (up to 60 percent) are used in vehicles, especially personal vehicles and transport trucks. And the world has billions of them. This is why, to help convert the world to greater sustainable energy use, he decided to focus on manufacturing electric vehicles. Thus, Tesla was born.

Electric vehicles are not a solution unto themselves, however. They present a number of very difficult problems in any grand effort to increase the use of alternative solar power. Here are some big obstacles:

- **Fuel storage**

   Crude oil, once refined and converted to gasoline, can be stored in tanks. A car can carry its own fuel as it travels, burning that fuel along the way.

   Solar energy can't be carried in a tank but must be stored in a battery. Until recently, batteries for electric vehicles presented a formidable engineering problem. They were extremely expensive and poor performing, offering limited power and range at high cost. Tesla and other car makers helped advance battery technology significantly in the past decade, enabling vehicles with more power and range.

Nevertheless, other problems remained. When a gas-powered car gets low on fuel, it can stop at a convenient gas station and get more fuel, quickly and cheaply. This network of gas stations did not arise overnight but developed and expanded over a century. Such a network is not easy to replicate quickly, especially when the customer base for electric energy is so small.

This is where Musk's other company, SolarCity, came in. SolarCity, an electric solar panel manufacturing and installation company, developed products that would not only power homes and buildings, but electric vehicles, too. Today, SolarCity (founded by two of Musk's cousins but based on his idea) is a subsidiary of Tesla. The vision of cheap, reliable solar power requires a network of solar panels generating electricity, batteries that can store that electricity, and homes and vehicles that use the electricity. Such a network is necessary to convert more of humanity to sustainable energy.

■ Cost and Market Appeal

Cost is another hurdle to widescale adoption and success. There's a reason why the world has so few car manufacturers. Most were formed seventy-five to one hundred years ago. Producing new vehicles is extremely expensive. It takes years of sales to achieve the production scale to reduce costs and compete with other, established manufacturers.

Tesla made their first electric vehicles as cheap as possible, but they knew that would still be far too expensive for most car buyers. So Tesla decided to appeal to early, wealthy adopters, accustomed to fast, smart-looking cars. The first Teslas were stylish high-performance vehicles with distinctive features, like winged doors. They were exciting to drive.

This approach to product development is counter to the strategies of most new market entrants. When cracking established markets, new entrants typically release a cheaper version first. Early cars, radios or TVs made in Japan, for example, were shoddy products but so cheap that people saw them as attractive alternatives. Only later, after achieving market share, did Japanese manufacturers improve their products and raise their prices to match the levels of performance of the established competition. In our own day, new entrants in the smartphone market, like Android, started with cheaper alternatives to the expensive iPhone.

After gaining market awareness and revenue from its costly high-end vehicles, Tesla began to produce and release more affordable mass-market vehicles. This worked as a business strategy and an adoption strategy.

With more car sales, the use of sustainable energy began to grow.

- **Scale and Impact**

Still, car sales are just a drop in the bucket. Musk knows that adoption must gain scale to have an impact.

Accordingly, Tesla plans to develop affordable fleets of trucks and buses to begin to supplant existing gas- or diesel-powered transportation vehicles.

It also knows that the market for electric vehicles will only grow if other manufacturers follow Tesla's lead. In line with that view, Tesla did something that no "normal" business would do—it released all its patents. By making the plans for Tesla vehicles and batteries open source and available to all, Tesla is encouraging competitors and adoption.

- **Other Innovations**

Tesla has also been focused on developing driverless technology. This is not just to make Tesla vehicles more cool or even to save lives lost in accidents, but to solve significant problems in fuel consumption.

Traffic jams exacerbate fuel waste. Driverless technology, when present in numerous vehicles, allows those vehicles to coordinate their movements and improve traffic flow.

Driverless cars also allow drivers to do other things while driving, like work, read or communicate, improving productivity.

By turning the car into what is essentially a mobile computer on wheels, Tesla's driverless technology also helps convert cars into data nodes. Car operations and behaviors can be monitored constantly by artificial intelligence. Car performance can be optimized by sending cars new instructions in real time. Cars essentially become nodes in a larger network.

Perhaps this can even reduce the need for cars. Cars can be shared or rented more easily, and arrive when and where you need them, if they are operated by an intelligent network.

These are not normal business strategies. They are the priorities of a business whose purpose is to save the world. Most CEOs would get fired for such audacious plans. Even leaders who might want to save the world would likely keep those grandiose thoughts to themselves. Not Musk. As he put it, Master Plan Part Deux:

> By definition, we must at some point achieve a sustainable energy economy or we will run out of fossil fuels to burn and civilization will collapse. Given that we must get off fossil fuels anyway and that virtually all scientists agree that dramatically increasing atmospheric and oceanic carbon levels is insane, the faster we achieve sustainability, the better.
>
> Here is what we plan to do to make that day come sooner:

- *Create stunning solar roofs with seamlessly integrated battery storage*
- *Expand the electric vehicle product line to address all major segments*
- *Develop a self-driving capability that is 10X safer than manual via massive fleet learning*
- *Enable your car to make money for you when you aren't using it*

A New Approach to Innovation

Purpose can seem so intangible or idealistic that some leaders might find it difficult to imagine how they can leverage purpose to actually innovate and solve business challenges. The key is to start with a meaningful purpose and work backwards through the practical challenges (business, technological, market) that stand in the way, while leveraging innovative solutions and business approaches to overcome them. In this way, purpose and innovation become tightly woven with strategy and business model.

As a purpose-driven leader, Elon Musk thinks of business as a means to an end, a tool for solving big, global problems. When Musk identifies problems with critical needs, they seem beyond the scope of individuals or even organizations to solve. So Musk reverse engineers those problems to come up with practical solutions, breaking challenges down into manageable tasks and solving each one in turn. Often this requires lots of money and talent to accomplish. A corporate structure enables Musk to attract investors, hire people, build products, sell them in the market, and move the needle on the global problem he wants to solve.

The process is very similar to the 5 Whys Technique"[58] I alluded to in Chapter Four in which you identify a problem at one level and follow a chain of questions to determine the ultimate source of that problem. Here's how it goes:

- Name a problem you're having

- Ask why it's happening

---

58   https://www.huffingtonpost.com/mitch-ditkoff/why-you-need-to-ask-why_b_2681958.html

- Get an answer

- Then ask why about that

- Get an answer

- Then ask why about that—and so on, five times

When you "reach the bottom", you usually unpack the essence of the problem, the opportunity, the real point.

Musk starts his own version of the 5 Whys Technique with Purpose—the ultimate why. Then he gets to a viable product that will succeed in the market while still helping to achieve his original goal. His analysis looks like this:

- **Purpose (global)**—to reduce CO_2 emission levels and help save the planet

- **How**—by (replacing) transitioning energy use from fossil fuels to solar power

- **Through**—increasing use of electric vehicles and making it easier to use solar power in homes

  - **Obstacle**—widespread reliance on fossil-fuel powered automobiles
  - **Solution**—build high-performance electric vehicle

  - **Obstacle**—current battery performance levels poor
  - **Solution**—bring in the best engineers to substantially build a better battery

  - **Obstacle**—customers don't see electric vehicles as appealing
  - **Solution**—focus on speed, style, and brand to increase high-end demand

  - **Obstacle**—to scale and achieve mass consumption, lower-cost models are required
  - **Solution**—build successively cheaper versions and cut out middle-men (dealers) to reduce costs

- **Obstacle**—need competition to spur demand for electric vehicles and associated services. Need open platform to scale
- **Solution**—release all patents for electric-vehicle technology

- **Obstacle**—need to stimulate broad demand for solar power
- **Solution**—build battery pack for home use to allow solar power customers to store and efficiently use that energy

Musk has pressed on through many obstacles and maintained focus on the fundamental problem because of the importance of the purpose in his sights.

PURPOSE-DRIVEN INNOVATION IN FIVE STEPS

| WHY-WHAT-HOW | DISRUPTIVE BUSINESS MODEL | SCALE | CORPORATE AND SOCIAL MERIT |

The same thinking and approach applies to Musk's other major company, SpaceX.

Space exploration is one of the five areas of science that Musk believed in college would affect the future of humanity. But space exploration for its own sake is not the point. Rather, Musk believes space exploration is necessary to preserve the viability of the human species. After all, if climate change does make life inhospitable for humans or some other extinction event (like a planet-killing meteor) does occur, then the human species will only survive if it can migrate to another planet.

This may seem like an outlandish and even ridiculous reason to build a company, but Musk has taken a very practical path. Once again, he reverse-engineers the big problem to identify the key challenges in the way and then builds businesses to solve those challenges. In this case, one of the major barriers to interplanetary travel is the cost of rocket technology. Every time NASA sent a space capsule into space, it threw away a giant rocket (essentially a fuel tank). This limited space flights and impeded the kind of delivery of people and resources necessary to build and establish a colony on another planet, such as Mars.

There is, however, a viable market for sending satellites into space. As of 2017, there were 4,635 artificial satellites orbiting the Earth.[59] Most are commercial devices. Musk saw an opportunity to supplant government-funded space programs like NASA by developing cheaper, reusable rocket technology for delivering satellites and materials to space and the International Space Station.

This is a very new way of looking at purpose and business. It's not for every leader, but at a time when leaders (especially young leaders) are more idealistic and purpose-driven than ever, it is becoming a more common way to build, fund, staff and run a viable business.

Such companies are focused on global needs in areas that are not being served by businesses or with technologies and approaches that are not being applied to those problems. They are disruptive in the sense that they are driving innovations that haven't been seen before while also bringing benefits beyond the boundaries of their sectors or markets. A mix of startups and established companies occupy this space; though, typically, the more established companies had internal startup engines driving their innovations. Success for these companies is measured through disruptive growth that also helps improve global problems.

Here are some other examples:

Grameen Bank/Kiva

Muhammad Yunus, mentioned in the Grameen Danone example, was a banker who wanted to alleviate poverty in Bangladesh (a purpose with global need). Yunus observed the impact that small loans could have on helping launch and support small businesses. He decided the most effective solution would be to offer microloans to female entrepreneurs specifically because that gender is under-employed, highly motivated to support their families, and lacking in access to capital. Yunus' Grameen Bank hit multiple

---

59   https://www.pixalytics.com/sats-orbiting-earth-2017/

objectives: It funded new business growth, alleviated family poverty, and saw a return on its investment.

Inspired by Yunus, Matt Flannery and Jessica Jackley launched Kiva Microfunds which enables people to give money to entrepreneurs in developing countries via a network of field partners. This brings the power of microfinance to greater scale with more expansive reach. Like Grameen, most of Kiva's loans go to female entrepreneurs. Loans are also made to enable students to attend higher education or to support refugees.[60]

BIONIC/G-Star Raw

G-Star Raw is an environmentally focused Dutch designer-jeans manufacturer founded in 1989.[61] Initially, G-Star specialized in using raw denim, which means that the cotton is unwashed and untreated by harmful chemicals. In addition, G-Star Raw sourced organic cotton, grown sustainably, for its clothing.

This would have been another example of a business competing in an established space with a higher purpose by adopting more sustainable practices. In 2014, however, the company joined forces with BIONIC, a company co-owned by musician and producer Pharrell Williams.[62] BIONIC is a raw material manufacturing company, launched on the principle that "a company can successfully marry purpose with profit." BIONIC focused on using plastic pollution recovered from the oceans and coastlines as the source of its fabrics and materials for any number of applications, from clothing to furniture and cars and industrial uses. The goal is to alleviate the massive problem of plastic pollution—an island of plastic the size of Texas floats in the Pacific Ocean. G-Star Raw made the decision to use BIONIC recycled materials in its jeans.[63] This required the company to completely

---

60   https://www.bizjournals.com/columbus/news/2018/07/26/social-entrepreneur-kiva-expanding-access-to.html

61   https://www.inverse.com/article/15182-for-g-star-raw-the-hottest-fashion-trend-is-recycled-plastic

62   http://bionic.is

63   https://www.forbes.com/sites/zackomalleygreenburg/2014/02/10/from-blue-to-green-inside-pharrells-latest-fashion-venture/#57570d5754e4

overhaul its sourcing strategy and adopt its factories. The new product has helped G-Star Raw enhance its brand with many celebrity endorsements and good press while expanding its market with new stores around the world.

Impossible Foods

Impossible Foods, founded by Stanford biochemistry professor, Patrick Brown, is one of a host of companies trying to alleviate global reliance on CO_2-producing cows by converting meat- and cheese-eaters to delicious plant-based substitutes. Approximately 30 percent of arable land is devoted to farming animals. Brown claims that Impossible Foods' technology uses 95 percent less land and 75 percent less water than beef. He notes that, if the world switches away from animal-based meat and cheese and to plant-based meat and cheese, the impact on the planet's plant biomass will be "easily visible from outer space."[64] Impossible Foods also has numerous celebrity endorsements and is gaining traction in grocery stores and restaurants, including fast-food franchises.

Uncharted Power

Uncharted Play was launched by Harvard grad and Nigerian-American dual citizen, Jessica O. Matthews, to help bring electric power to underserved communities around the world. The first product was a soccer ball called the Soccket that generated electric charge as children played with it. The ball could then be used to power lights.

The idea was inspiring, the objective admirable, but the business faltered. The balls themselves did not last long and distribution problems impeded sales. As a top executive of Coca-Cola told Matthews, "you have to become a business so people can do business with you."[65]

So, Uncharted Play pivoted. They realized they were not a maker of soccer balls or jump ropes but of a technology that enables microgenerators to harvest energy. Partner companies could make the devices for those

64   https://www.bloomberg.com/news/articles/2018-04-20/impossible-foods-quest-to-save-planet-draws-environmentalist-ire
65   https://medium.com/@jessicaomatthews/unchartedpower-dfd781a2f19

microgenerators. This helped Uncharted Play broaden the scope of its ventures beyond "play" objects. In 2016, its technology was used to generate power through vehicular traffic. The company soon changed its name to Uncharted Power.[66]

This shows the centrality of purpose to Matthews and her company. It might have been easy with praise and funding to pivot in a more purely commercial direction, but the company stayed true to its goal to democratize the availability of power.

Khan Academy/Udacity/Coursera

Nonprofit organizations can also disrupt existing industries while endeavoring to solve global problems. Education is one of the great disparities between the well-off and economically deprived people as well as people from developing countries. Access to quality education can significantly impact the prospects of any individual. MOOCs, or Massive Open Online Courses, threaten the exclusivity of expensive academic institutions but democratize learning at unprecedented scale.

Organizations like Khan Academy, Udacity and Coursera were launched as ambitious, world-changing initiatives. Though each has narrowed its focus to specific market niches, these companies are still striving to make advanced education and learning available at global scale.

We thought that this new breed of companies that both innovate in completely new spaces while addressing global issues belong to a separate category, and this is how we grouped them:

Group D

- Uber
- Tesla
- GE
- Uncharted Play
- Khan Academy
- G-Star Raw
- Impossible Foods
- Space X
- Google
- Grameen Bank
- Embrace

66   https://medium.com/@jessicaomatthews/unchartedpower-dfd781a2f19

Beneath the Bottom Line

Purpose-driven businesses enhance their appeal by focusing on problems or issues that their employees and the customers of their products and services care about. The "loftiness" of their purpose dictates the space in which they play.

Plotting these ideas on an innovation vs purpose context diagram (the X/Y chart described in Chapter Five) we ended up with the below picture:

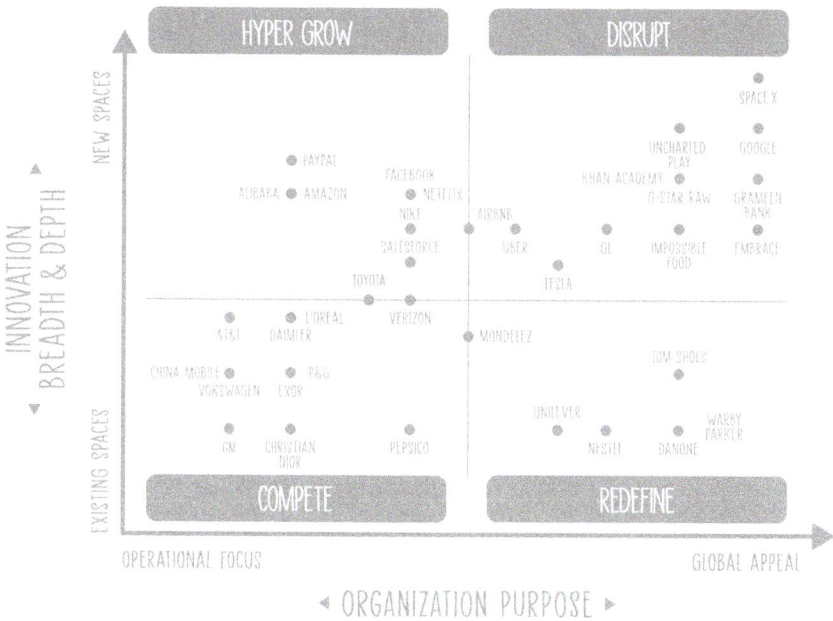

Companies with an operational focus in an existing space (Compete) are focused on delivering service, price, and/or experience their customers value. Their fundamental goal is to satisfy customers while serving as a good corporate citizen—fortifying communities, enhancing diversity, operating ethically. This is Quadrant 1.

Companies that compete in existing spaces with global appeal deliver the same kinds of products and services, but they are also cognizant of larger needs their products can help fill. They recognize that businesses use and may even exploit resources, labor and economically undeveloped areas, for example, and strive to operate in such a way that the world (not just the customer) is better off because of their business, rather diminished by it. They sit in Quadrant 2.

Companies with an operational focus in a new space (Hyper-Growth) want to delight customers, rather than merely satisfy them, by meeting their needs in ways that exceed traditional expectations for service, experience, convenience, price, etc. They believe the customer is the highest good and the focus of all innovation, and will sacrifice short-term profit to meet customer needs. Most probably revenue and scale is their primary focus, and they are located in Quadrant 3.

Companies that focus on global concerns in a new space are more idealistic and ambitious than traditional businesses. They are trying to save the world by leveraging the structure, operations, funding and revenue models of traditional businesses in service of some great cause. This is clearly Quadrant 4.

All purpose-driven companies attempt to live by a higher standard or code than mere bottom-line concerns like maximizing profit or growing market share. The degree to which they strive for higher aims depends on their quadrant. Does this approach to business make a positive difference? We've tried to show that it does, because purpose-driven companies typically outperform traditional competitors. Purpose can be linked to more discretionary effort on behalf of employees and more intense brand loyalty from customers. It may not be top of mind all the time but it's there, beneath the bottom line. Purpose also provides direction and focus for innovation. The performance of such companies shows that purpose supports profits.

Purpose-driven companies are also more resilient over time. During moments of crisis, scandal or failure, a strong and clear purpose reinforces commitment to the company and helps leaders guide people through choppy waters. In effect, it gives companies extra credibility and latitude with customers and employees. No one expects those companies to lose money deliberately or to not operate fundamentally like normal businesses. But the companies stand for something more, and they have relatively clear values or moral lines.

Indeed, companies cross these lines or violate their customers' and employees' expectations at their peril. It's one thing for a finance company like Wells Fargo to rip off customers with extra accounts, service charges and improper foreclosures—Wells Fargo does not have a sincere reputation as a purpose-driven company. However, when purpose-driven companies or purpose-focused leaders seem to violate a lofty reputation, the public repercussions can be severe.

For example, in 2018, cracks began to show in Elon Musk's glowing reputation. With investors (especially analysts and short-sellers) and others, Musk revealed erratic and occasionally vindictive behavior unbecoming of a planetary savior. However, the true believers of Telsa (customers, employees and investors) are holding on, perhaps because Musk's overall purpose remains strong, and he has yet to violate the values they want to see in him.

There are advantages to being a purpose-driven business today, but there are hazards, too. Authenticity and integrity must be demonstrated. Purpose-driven companies and leaders must speak and live their truth.

CHAPTER SIX RECAP

- Innovating in unchartered territories that are new to the industry and new to the world is an alternative way to overcome incrementalism and achieve hyper-growth. The stories of Nike, Apple, Netflix, Amazon prove it.

- The secret is to discover and address the needs of your customers that they do not even know they have.

- To achieve hyper-growth, innovation alone does not suffice.

- Disruptive companies do not just break the existing rules, they expand the business to address global societal needs and do it in an organized, step-by-step approach.

- A purpose-driven innovation model embraces the goal of exponential and disruptive growth.

- The innovation-purpose matrix can help you define your strategic pursuit of growth.

Tools & Resources

- Read the continuous innovation article by Ash Maurya. It nicely illustrates how the innovation process has changed over the years, until today when it is intrinsic to every company's continuously evolving business model. Visit my site www.christostsolkas.com to check out the link.

- Get familiar with the innovation process through the use of Ideation Templates. It is an innovation process enabler developed by one of my favorite teachers at Stanford, Dr. Jonathan Levav. Here are the titles of his five templates:

  - Subtraction—useful for complex products or to control costs

- Task unification—when aiming to control costs

- Division—for simple quantitative improvements

- Multiplication—for simple quantitative improvements

- Attribute dependency—useful generally, but hard

Visit my site www.christostsolkas.com to watch the video where Jonathan explains the theory with examples.

- Similary, Business Model Innovation (BMI) is very nicely presented and taught at St. Gallen University. The thinking is based on the underlying assumption that all business models are consisted of distinguishable patterns. Innovation, therefore, comes when these patterns are creatively reassembled in different combination.

  Visit my site www.christostsolkas.com to read a very comprehensive paper of BMI.

CHAPTER SEVEN

Pick a Global Problem, Any Problem

On December 7, 1972, the Apollo 17 spaceship was launched. For a few hours, the space capsule orbited the Earth's atmosphere, then its third-stage rocket was ignited to break the spaceship away from Earth and establish its trajectory to the moon. Almost two hours after departing from orbit, astronaut Jack Schmitt did something that the spaceflight's tight schedule did not authorize him to do. He pointed a camera at Earth, lined up his shot and took a picture.

That photograph was the first to capture the whole planet in a single, non-composite image from outer space. To the astronauts on board and the countless millions who've admired it since, the image is awe-inspiring. The Earth looks like a beautiful "Blue Marble" afloat in a black and infinite sea.

Many had longed for such an image for some time. A counterculture leader named Stewart Brand had lobbied NASA through the 1960s to release a picture of the Earth from space because he believed it would inspire a more planetary consciousness. Brand had used a composite image of the moon on the very first edition of a new magazine he published in 1968 called *The Whole Earth Catalog*. He used other images of the moon for the covers of subsequent editions. *Whole Earth* was an eclectic collection of essays, articles and product reviews which aimed to promote a view of the Earth as a single planet, not a collection of different countries and people. Brand and his readers believed that global challenges such as environmental pollution, overpopulation and the threat of nuclear destruction could only be tackled if more people understood the holistic, shared nature of the Earth. As futurist architect and scientist Buckminster Fuller put it at the time, "people perceived the earth as flat and infinite, and that that was the root of all their misbehavior."

Apollo 17 was the last manned spaceflight to leave the Earth's atmosphere. Five years later, in September 1977, NASA launched an unmanned robotic spacecraft called Voyager 1 to study the solar system. It was a bold goal with unlikely chances of success. Even if Voyager 1 reached Jupiter or Saturn, it was very possible human beings would lose contact with the spaceship and never know what had happened to it.

In 1980, Voyager 1 achieved its primary objective by reaching Saturn and viewing the planet and its moons from perspectives never before seen by humans. Then, in accordance with its original flight plan, Voyager 1 built up enough velocity to escape Saturn's orbit and set off for interstellar space. This would take it farther than the engineers and scientists who built Voyager 1 ever dreamed.

Although Voyager 1 was on a mission to explore the universe, Carl Sagan insisted that Earth should not be forgotten. He pushed hard for the NASA team to turn the spaceship's camera around one last time and take a picture of Earth from the far reaches of the solar system. Despite the technical challenges and the possible danger to Voyager 1's systems from the sun's powerful radiation, Sagan was successful in his argument. On February 14, 1990, the spaceship rotated and took a photograph of Earth.

From such a great distance, Earth was no beautiful Blue Marble filling up the image. Instead, it was a pale Blue Dot in a sea of indistinguishable stars.

After that, Voyager 1's cameras were powered down, and the spaceship continued its journey into the beyond. It still travels through space today, over forty years later.

In 1994, in a speech at Cornell University, Sagan said,

Our planet is a lonely speck in the great enveloping cosmic dark. In our obscurity—in all this vastness—there is no hint that help will come from elsewhere to save us from ourselves. It is up to us. It's been said that astronomy is a humbling, and I might add, a character-building experience. To my mind, there is perhaps no better demonstration of the folly of human conceits than this distant image of our tiny world. To me, it underscores our responsibility to deal more kindly and compassionately with one another and to preserve and cherish that pale blue dot, the only home we've ever known.

The idea that there are global problems to solve is a relatively new concept for human beings. The possibility that businesses are the best tool for solving those problems is newer still.

Global problems threaten existence or quality of life. I define them as Level One problems because they are both urgent and almost too massive to conceive of resolving. Ironically, they also offer the greatest opportunity for business growth. Any company that points itself toward a Level One problem and delivers a viable market solution that can be brought to scale is likely to achieve exponential growth.

It's a very new thing, however, for a Level One problem to be tackled by business. For most of our history, when human beings have managed to face such a threat, they have done so through the vehicle of government. How can a business leader identify a global or Level One problem and develop a solution or a market approach that can galvanize a company (including shareholders) and be successful with customers?

Addressing Global Problems—the Institutional Approach

World War I, known then as the Great War, created such horrendous suffering at such scale that many wished or believed it would be forever known as the "war to end all wars." The savagery of war, the fear of disease, even injustice did not stay within one country's borders. Problems in one country affected other countries, too. People of all nations, we now understood, shared a common enemy.

Crisis motivates purpose and channels energy. The new thinking around ending war evolved quickly in the lead-up to the peace treaty negotiations. U.S. President Woodrow Wilson, in preparation for the negotiations, developed a list of "Fourteen Points" that envisioned how a more peaceful and just world could be secured. Wilson's plan included the establishment of a general association of nations guaranteeing the security and political independence of each state.

By 1920, a League of Nations had been formed. Its goals were to prevent wars and settle international disputes through negotiation while also addressing issues like labor conditions, mistreatment of native peoples and minorities, and global health problems. The League failed to gain a hold over world affairs as many nations, especially the United States, did not join. "America First" became a slogan among the nationalists in the U.S. who did not want to get involved in other countries' problems. Thinking of today's political ambient, it sounds ironical but also scary. Fascism began to emerge in Germany, Italy and Spain.

In opposition to the ultranationalist trend, however, stood the communist movement. Centered in the new Soviet Union, universal communism held that all workers, regardless of national origin, belonged together in common cause against the ruling and capitalist classes. It was a very purpose-driven view of the world, close to religion. Yet, like most religions, it was also highly conflict oriented and saw those with contrary views as enemies.

World War II brought global conflict back again. All nations and regions of the world were affected. The League of Nations was dissolved in 1943 and replaced with a new United Nations, in the hope that some day the world could begin to strive for peace and problem-solving again. The development of the atomic bomb made such a global perspective all the more urgent. Suddenly, the total destruction of the world was possible. Other problems like pollution, explosive population growth and famine were almost as threatening. These sorts of challenges and crises could not be addressed by single nations or even alliances because they crossed many borders and regions. They were global problems.

This gave even more energy and sense of purpose to global organizations like the United Nations and the World Bank. Though somewhat independent of nations, these are essentially political organizations that reflect the values, strategies and priorities of their member states. As such, the solutions they offer to global problems are often ineffective or hampered by political disagreements or alliances. For example, a war in the Middle East might threaten global peace, but attempts to intervene could be blocked by Security Council members that don't want to upset a client state or a delicate strategic balance.

To address global problems and crises more directly, non-governmental organizations (NGOs) like UNICEF, the International Red Cross, Doctors without Borders and so on, have arisen. These organizations are less hampered by politics but also less powerful because they are not backed by a government or nation. Instead, they rely on donations, expertise and political skill to achieve their goals. Typically, they focus on a specific type of global problem—like disaster relief, hunger, education, urgent care, blindness, malaria, etc.

For example, when the dreaded Ebola virus broke out in the Congo, both the Congolese government and the international community were unable to respond effectively to the crisis, perhaps due to the fear of the virus spreading. The international NGO Doctors without Borders/Medicine sans Frontiers went anyway. An emergency care team flew into the capital. Helicopters were unavailable, so they rented cars and drove three days into the jungle to the grass hut town where the virus had shown up. The DWB's team built an isolation ward within 24 hours and began testing the villagers for the virus. They had to overcome the reluctance of people who feared being tested. When they learned of deaths in nearby villages, they went to those bodies immediately, isolated them, disinfected everything and transported the bodies back to their base. Battling Ebola is a race against time. DWB care teams were willing to do whatever it took to help people in need.

NGOs have advantages. They are built to provide a solution that fills a deep need in the world, and their employees and donors are more likely to care passionately about that cause. This can make the purpose-driven organizations. Since they are not affiliated with a particular government, they can address cross-border or global problems more easily. Unfortunately, they often lack clout or resources as a result. They are frustratingly limited in their ability to solve the causes of problems, and instead tend to focus on alleviating the effects.

Can business possibly hope to tackle global problems more effectively given the limits of market capitalism and its focus on profit?

Enter technology.

Technology Speeds Up Globalization

Technology has always played a huge role in giving people a more global perspective. The printing press made the mass production of books and newspapers possible and launched the international circulation of information and ideas. The steam engine launched the Industrial Revolution, creating great opportunities for manufacturing, necessitating global trade, increasing the speed of transportation, and enabling the expansion of nations and businesses around the world—for good and bad.

Electronic communication increased the speed of globalization and deepened global ties. The telegraph, the telephone, the radio and then the television began to eliminate the distance between peoples, and facilitated more sharing of ideas, news, information, culture, events and, yes, problems, too.

Airplane travel made physical distances smaller. When Charles Lindbergh crossed the Atlantic by plane, he opened up the possibility that people could move about the planet more freely and conveniently. When the Soviet Union launched the Sputnik space satellite, it galvanized America to develop its own space program. Speaking to a crowd in Texas, the American President John F. Kennedy gave one of his most famous and inspiring speeches which focused on the sense of purpose a mission to the moon would bring.

We choose to go to the Moon... because that goal will serve to organize and measure the best of our energies and skills, because that challenge

is one that we are willing to accept, one we are unwilling to postpone,
and one we intend to win...

And on the last of those Apollo moon missions, an astronaut aimed his camera at Earth and took a picture.

When the *Whole Earth Catalog* put the photograph of the Earth taken from outer space on its cover, it captured the minds of many global young visionaries at the time. Steve Jobs noticed. In his famous 2005 commencement speech at Stanford University, Jobs described the *Whole Earth Catalog* as the first Google because it introduced curious people of his generation to ideas and possibilities they could find nowhere else. *Whole Earth Catalog* founder Stewart Brand seemed to have that vision in mind when he founded the WELL (Whole Earth 'Lectronic Link), one of the world's first virtual communities. WELL started as an electronic Bulletin Board System (BBS) before the development of Internet browsers, then became one of the first ISPs when commercial traffic on the Internet was permitted. In the WELL, topics of conversation were divided into sub-categories, much like REDDIT today.

The Internet changed everything, of course. The emergence of giant companies like Amazon and, especially Google, enabled globalization to take a quantum leap. Devices like smartphones gave mobility to computer power and the Internet. Use of the Internet expanded from idea exchange to business exchange. Even small businesses have become global in our technology-enabled world. Users have become customers, and those customers can be found everywhere.

Now, as a result of technology, people and businesses can influence events in other parts of the world and be influenced by them in turn.

The Business of Business Is Changing

Today, for the first time in history, organizations are stepping up to meet the challenges that governments and international organizations can't seem to resolve. Until recently, corporations put little focus on problems not related directly to their business. Shareholders and even customers insisted that corporations concentrate not on social problems but on making desirable products and services as cheaply and efficiently as possible. Any attention paid to global problems should occur through philanthropic funding and activity.

That's changing for the reasons I described in Chapter Three. If a customer buys a shirt in America today, they want it to be inexpensive, but they are also concerned that it be manufactured under humane labor conditions. Likewise, a company producing a refreshing drink or a smartphone had better deliver that product as cheaply and conveniently as possible, while also not exacerbating any environmental problems around the world. Companies can no longer outsource or offshore their bad behaviors.

Today's new generation of founders and CEOs take that sense of corporate responsibility even further. They believe in the power of business to do good while also doing well, and they know this can be channeled to help propel their businesses to greater success.

They understand how purpose can motivate, satisfy and align people like few other sources of meaning.

Some companies seek to do good by dramatically improving business operations in line with a sense of purpose or mission. These are the companies in Quadrant 3. Often they do this by increasing efficiency and access while reducing prices and friction. Amazon, Nike and Netflix took traditional business models and turbocharged them on behalf of customers, scaling their offerings to another level compared to competitors. This enables them to reach more customers, provide better service and earn more revenue which gets fed back into customer service and efficiency. The result is a dramatic enhancement of value, operational efficiency, access to global markets and improvement in customer satisfaction and experience.

Some companies seek to do good by leveraging their business models and processes in a more purpose-driven way to benefit individuals, communities and the world. These are the companies in Quadrant 2. Danone, TOMS Shoes and Patagonia are among the companies that provide traditional goods and services but tweak their business models to improve people's lives, often beyond their customer base. Danone helps improve the sustainability of farming and water. TOMS Shoes delivers footwear to those who are too poor to afford it. Patagonia is trying to improve sourcing practices and help the environment. No analyst would say these efforts are "good for business" or the bottom line; and yet, when such companies live by a sense of purpose, they create goodwill, commitment and enthusiasm among employees, customers and communities, that pays significant dividends.

For companies that wish to be purpose-driven, Quadrants 2 and 3 offer clear paths forward. Such companies are offering products and services aligned with commercial demand.

If there is a problem with Quadrants 2 and 3, it is this: Those arenas of innovation are getting increasingly crowded. Twenty years ago, with the dawn of the popular Internet, a great wave of startups strove to "dot-com" existing business models. Amazon transformed brick-and-mortar bookstores with its digital platform and then moved on to overwhelm every other retail product distributor. Netflix out-competed brick-and-mortar video stores and later attacked traditional cable channels. Nike elevated the brand of a shoe and linked it to the passion for athletics and competition. Today, creating room in this space with a new company or a new twist on an existing sector is daunting. There is limited Blue Ocean to explore.

Same goes for Quadrant 2 companies. Given the success of Patagonia, Danone and TOMS Shoes, more companies will increasingly integrate their philanthropic or corporate social responsibility initiatives into their business models. To the extent that they are sincere about improving lives, communities and the world, this trend will be a good thing. The planet can use all the help it can get. But it will be increasingly difficult to differentiate companies that leverage their business models to do good and achieve greater ends. Perhaps, however, it will also become the norm.

The area with the most Blue Ocean or white space is Quadrant 4, where organizations are specifically built and directed toward solving a global problem or meeting a global need. Traditionally, this has been outside the interests of for-profit business. NGOs and global organizations, supported by governments and donors, have been able to provide services without the need for profits. In recent years, for-profit enterprises have begun to move into that space, but most are either very small or their transition to profitability remains far off.

Yet, in the future, this is where the action will be. The potential scale and need is enormous. This is the new realm for massive growth. The question is: What crisis will you focus on? What urgent global need will your business seek to fill? And in that sense, what is the use case you are working on?

Identifying Level One Problems

In his book, *The Better Angels of Our Nature*, Steven Pinker says we are living in the most peaceful period in the history of humankind. Our likelihood of being murdered, dying in a war or losing a child to a fatal disease is lower than ever. Compared to previous eras, millions more people than ever live above subsistence levels and are able to afford luxury items like electronic goods and vehicles. Access to education has never been more widespread. Intolerance and systematic repression is less prevalent, despite the attention such problems receive in the media. By most normal standards, life today is very good, even though many people may not feel that way.

The irony is that we are also living in one of the most dangerous periods in human history. Much of that danger is a direct byproduct of our technological progress, economic development and the social institutions and systems that seem at a breaking point. Nuclear war. Climate change. Social media platforms that manipulate the public. Algorithms that restrict choice. Authoritarian governments with high-tech monitoring capabilities. The social injustice of unfair financial or voting systems enabled by digital technology. The list of potential threats is long, complex and varied.

How should we define Level One global problems and crises that can or should be tackled by business? I examined many different lists put forward by many thoughtful groups. There were plenty of commonalities and some interesting differences. For example, almost every list noted climate change and war. This is understandable since we are experiencing great disruption from storms, weather patterns, conflicts in the Middle East and the migration of refugees. But millennial survey respondents, unlike other demographic groups or populations, focused almost as heavily on social justice, government accountability and economic opportunity.[67] No doubt this is because millennials worry a lot about the challenges of making their way in a world where they are not yet established in their careers, and worry less about the challenges of growing old or sick. The U.N.'s list was more comprehensive, covering many issues, from water and food to refugees, international justice and the status of women.[68] However, that list was excessively long and was more random in terms of its categories.

Finding less overlap than I expected, I decided to identify my own short list of significant problems. I made the categories as broad as possible (Level One problems) so that I could include other, secondary problems as outgrowths or consequences. Here is my Top Three:

1. The Destruction of the Planet

The human impact on the global environment is profound. We see this through the many manifestations of climate change and the devastation due to waste and pollution.

Destructive forces that afflict the environment also threaten communities, safety, security, agriculture, livelihoods, health, etc. Rising sea levels. Arctic melting. Severe drought. Intense flooding. Hurricanes. Wildfires. The spread of disease-bearing insects. A surge in allergies. Oceans filled with plastic and human waste. Lakes and reservoirs poisoned by farm runoff.

Environmental degradation can even be linked to war, displacement and political upheaval. Scientists believe that rising temperatures, for example, contributed to the number of Syrian

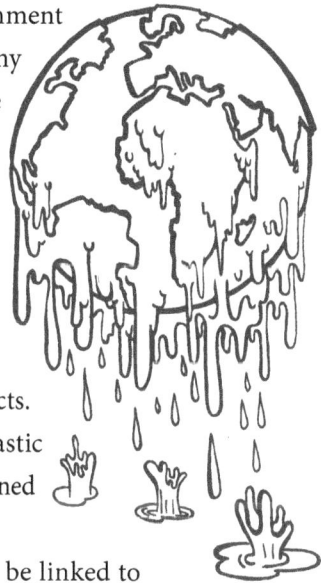

---

67   https://www.businessinsider.com/world-problems-most-serious-according-to-millennials-2017-8/#10-lack-of-economic-opportunity-and-employment-121-1

68   http://www.un.org/en/sections/issues-depth/global-issues-overview/

refugees fleeing that war-torn region for the EU.[69] In turn, that surge in refugees contributed to the political destabilization of Europe and inflamed anti-immigrant sentiment in the U.S. Similarly, in Honduras, El Salvador and Equador, climate change encouraged the spread of a fungus to coffee plants which devastated crops and the local economy and put hundreds of thousands of laborers out of work.[70] The severe conditions led to political instability and the rise of gang activity.[71] Fleeing that hardship in 2016, tens of thousands joined caravans of refugees heading to the United States, influencing U.S. politics and the 2016 midterm elections.

2. Illness, Quality of Life and Death

Modern medical science and clinical care is a miracle. Hearts, hands and faces can be transplanted. Countless diseases can be treated with sophisticated drugs. Genes can be altered inside cells. Babies can be operated on in the womb.

Yet, basic health and wellness remain a challenge. Too many people around the world lack access to affordable care. The Silver Tsunami (the wave of baby boomers turning sixty-five) will bring a massive increase in chronic disease, dementia and costs. Mental illness, drug addiction, obesity, diabetes,

69   https://www.theguardian.com/environment/climate-consensus-97-per-cent/2018/jan/15/study-finds-that-global-warming-exacerbates-refugee-crises

70   https://www.mcclatchydc.com/news/nation-world/world/article24749563.html

71   https://www.huffingtonpost.com/entry/migrant-caravan-honduras-trump_us_5ad68870e4b03c426da93a2c

heart disease and social isolation are rampant, especially in the developed world.

Communities, families and society pay an enormous price (economically and socially) when people lead lives that are less healthy, engaged and productive. Those problems show every sign of growing.

Why do people still die of malaria? Why can't we yet cure cancer or eliminate hunger? Surely, there's breakthrough growth potential for companies that help people live longer and healthier lives, and die quickly and painlessly when the end has come.

3. Lack of Economic Opportunity and Social Justice

In many ways, the world has never been more prosperous and free. Yet, barriers and threats to economic advancement and abundance are everywhere.

The wealth gap is high. Extremely wealthy neighborhoods, regions and nations can exist near very poor ones. Race and economic status can influence how much access people have to education, employment, services (like grocery stores, banks and the Internet) and even good health. Exacerbating those problems, corruption in governments and institutions remains stubbornly common today in spite of enhanced transparency and access to information.

These forces can diminish freedom, individual rights, security and prosperity. What can we do about planetary inequality, and the growing global gap between the poor and the rich? It does not seem sustainable or desirable from environmental, economic, political or ethical standpoints. With so much wealth on the planet, how can we take better care of those in need? Is a global or universal income a solid solution?

If we don't address these problems in a meaningful, market-driven way, then I fear we will pay an enormous price. Political strife, war, terrorism, refugees, disease, death … all those horrors are only likely to intensify and will undoubtedly threaten the prosperity and quality of life of the wealthy and prosperous, too.

Strategies for Addressing a Level One Problem

No company can solve a Level One problem. It is not feasible or practical for a business to end climate change or eliminate economic disparity.

A company can, however, build a practical, feasible market solution to address a sub-problem in one of the outer rings. In doing so, it can contribute to helping alleviate a Level One problem. This imbues the market solution with a very direct and real sense of higher purpose.

Tesla, as we've already discussed, did just that. Climate change is the Level One problem it has always aimed to address. Yet, climate change is too massive, global, complex and nebulous a problem to address directly. So Tesla founder Elon Musk directed innovative energy, engineering talents and business acumen to solving a secondary problem that contributes to climate change—the increase in carbon gas in the atmosphere. He then built a commercial product and a business to make that happen.

In a very similar way, Google addressed a Level One problem as its foundational purpose. Essentially, Google came into existence to make information accessible for the benefit of humankind. As CEO Sundar Puchai put it in the 2018 letter to shareholders, "Today, our mission to organize the world's information and make it universally accessible and useful is as relevant as it was in 1998."[72] Its first product was a browser. But, even as Google expands into a dizzying array of other ventures, products and services, the company continues to hew very closely to its original sense of purpose.

Scanning every book in the world. Mapping every street. Building smartphones and AI assistants. Offering video content through YouTube. Organizing emails. Leveraging healthcare data. Providing Internet access to rural communities. Google's purpose is supported by a wildly profitable business model built on advertising sales. As a result, Google has the financial fuel to do whatever it wants. It's very telling that Google stays aligned with its purpose "despite" its success.

Starting with Level One problems creates a pathway from purpose to solution via a product or service offering that can drive a business. The Level One problem creates the North Star, the greater purpose worth pursuing. It allows the company to say, "We're in business to solve X" even if it actually makes a product or service that is less grandiose. In fact, the process of breaking down Level One problems into sub-problems actually makes solutions to that problem more manageable.

The below chart illustrates how some businesses start with a Level One problem, then break that down into more practically manageable problems that they can finally address with a business solution.[73] For example, if the world's two largest bottled drink companies, Coca-Cola and Pepsi, really want to impact the Level One problem of plastic waste, that power is in their hands. I have no doubt they can build a Use-case for making that a profitable or sustainable part of business operations.

WHY → WHY → WHY →

GLOBAL PROBLEM LEVEL 1	GLOBAL PROBLEM LEVEL 2	GLOBAL PROBLEM LEVEL 3	GLOBAL PROBLEM LEVEL 4	FINAL PRODUCT OR SERVICE	BRIDGING MECHANISM (HOW) EXAMPLES	COMPANY
CLIMATE	OCEAN POLLUTION	DISPOSAL OF PLASTIC	RECYCLING	CLOTHES, APPAREL, MADE OF RECYCLED PLASTIC	RPET REPREVE FIBER (UNIFI) ECONYL (AQUAFIL) BIO-DERIVED MATERIALS	PATAGONIA H&M G-STAR RAW DGRADE HAMILTON PERKINS TIMBERLAND AND COSMOS STUDIO

73 https://www.knittingindustry.com/creative/making-textiles-and-clothing-from-recycled-plastics/

Here is an even more powerful example. Allbirds is a shoe company. They engage in a holistic view of their environmental impact and they go beyond recycling with the astonishing vision that "shoes should function like trees, [leaving] a net positive to the climate," clearly stating they are on a mission to put plastics and petroleum out of business. Sustainability, they say, is not enough anymore. It should be replaced by Accountability because "our planet deserves better".[74]

More and more companies are now following this path from Level One problem to commercial product. In the process, they are pursuing purpose in a very forceful and galvanizing way. Below are some specific ways to address the three Level One problems we've discussed.

Level One Problem: The Destruction of the Planet

Pollution is a planet killer. To alleviate it, companies can find better ways to reduce or eliminate the use of plastics. One way to do so is to turn recycled materials toward better uses. As previously mentioned, G-Star Raw uses recycled plastic in the manufacture of clothing that helps alleviate climate change with a practical solution and its own very different profitable business line.

Other companies are using recycled fabrics as raw materials to alleviate global waste. Apparently, most clothing (80 percent or so) that is donated actually ends up in landfills or incinerated. But brands like Eileen Fisher, Patagonia and Kaillo make a point of serving customers while reducing that waste, aligning purpose with a global problem.[75]

Level One Problem: Illness, Quality of Life and Death

Around the world, developed countries face a massive healthcare problem. Costs are soaring, particularly among patients with chronic illness, such as diabetes, heart disease, kidney disease, mental health problems

---

74   https://fortune.com/2019/10/07/allbirds-founders-why-we-need-to-eliminate-plastics-for-good/
       https://www.allbirds.com/

75   https://earth911.com/business-policy/clothes-recycling-4-brands/

and addiction issues. Such groups can account for 50-80 percent of total healthcare costs for a nation.

In the USA, the chronically ill and poor fall through the cracks because of the lack of universal healthcare coverage and a robust social welfare system. While Medicare and Medicaid might cover their care costs, they often lack the basics that take priority over care, such as adequate food, transportation or shelter. Without regular care or support, they may frequently seek necessary care at hospital emergency rooms, which is even more costly and fixes only immediate needs, not long-term ones.

For traditional hospitals and physician clinics, there is little incentive to care for these patients. But a new breed of for-profit healthcare company has recently emerged in the U.S. to fill this gap. Absolute Care, based in Atlanta, Georgia, actively seeks the sickest of the sick, the people that most healthcare organizations hope to avoid. They work with health insurance companies to identify those patients, then contract with the insurers to provide the patients with care for a certain cost. If they can produce quality care outcomes cheaper, Absolute Care earns the difference as profit.

Absolute provides better care by doing things differently. Most doctors see patients in 15-minute intervals with little time to understand the patient's deeper needs or issues. Absolute wants to see patients as much and as long as possible to understand them fully. They deploy care teams for each patient that include physicians, therapists, social workers, nutritionists and drivers. They transport patients who need to be brought to the clinic. They make sure people have appropriate food and housing, even supplying people with a place to live if needed.

These extensive services actually reduce overall costs by an average of 26 percent. They improve care outcomes dramatically. And they change lives, not just for the direct patients, but for their children and grandchildren, helping to revive and restore communities to health and economic productivity. In the process, Absolute Care makes a healthy profit which it uses to fund its growth and expansion to more clinics and cities in order to help solve the nation's overall chronic health crisis.

That's a perfect marriage between purpose, product and profit.

Level One Problem: Lack of Access to Economic Opportunity and Social Justice

Providing access to economic opportunity may seem like a pipe dream for a corporation. Yet, in some ways, it's as old as business itself. When Henry Ford started the mass production of automobiles in Detroit in the early 1890s, he knew his business could be an engine of transformation for America, helping bring the country out of an agrarian past and into an industrial future. He paid his workers the very high wage of $5 per day because he wanted to retain them and because he wanted them to be able to afford the cars they made. This linked Ford's success as a business with America's success as a nation, combining purpose with profit.

Today, lack of a living wage remains a huge barrier to economic opportunity for many people. Another barrier is access to banking, especially among the poor or "unbanked", as they say.

Worldwide, 39 percent of the world's population are unbanked (no access to banking) or underbanked (inadequate access to financial institutions). In the U.S., the unbanked and underbanked are 27 percent of the population.[76] This is a serious barrier to life in our modern world. It prevents people from getting paid, paying bills, establishing credit, transferring money to loved ones or getting loans.

In response to this massive global need, a variety of fintech and financial service companies have emerged. Business models vary, but many are based on Blockchain technology and access to mobile phones. Taiwan-based GMobi was founded in 2011 and currently reaches around 200 million users, predominantly in the developing world. In India, it launched Oxymoney, a mobile wallet that enables users to add to their cell phone credits and transfer money. This allows rural laborers to send money to their families. If those families lack access to computers or banks, they can pick up their money at local stores.[77]

---

76   https://hackernoon.com/how-to-overcome-poverty-by-helping-the-unbanked-723f8c915d62

77   https://techcrunch.com/2017/06/19/banking-the-unbanked-in-emerging-markets/

A Mexican fintech company called 4UNO focuses on providing needed banking services to domestic workers, as well as benefits like health insurance that employers can purchase for their employees. The insurance covers life and accident, unlimited medical phone calls, annual health checkups and four doctor visits for about fifteen cents a day.[78] Philippines-based Coins uses digital currencies to enable cross-border remittances, by which laborers working in a foreign country can send money to their families securely. Over $600 billion in remittance payments are made annually around the world, making this an enormous market with great need.[79]

Build a Better Mousetrap

The saying goes, "Build a better mousetrap and the world will beat a path to your door."

In 2019, if you link your business to purpose by focusing on a Level One problem, you can gain access to massive new markets while engaging talented employees, attracting purpose-driven investors and filling needs for committed and engaged customers. The best approach is to think big (Level One) and work backward to the product or service that can meet that need—then go build, operationalize and market it.

But this is not just a game for idealistic entrepreneurs. Increasingly, in a more purpose-focused marketplace, established companies will need to think about how their businesses impact Level One problems.

As with Patagonia, this may require performing a Level One audit on the company's business lines. Is it, through its products, processes, operations, sourcing practices, etc., acting in some way that negatively impacts a Level One problem? If so, this presents an opportunity to galvanize your workforce, investors and customer base in line with a greater purpose.

For example, to address the problem of pollution, the Danish beer company Carlsberg developed a simple solution. Rather than rely on plastic

---

78 https://medium.com/f4life/two-problems-one-solution-how-fintech-is-boosting-access-to-banking-and-insurance-for-domestic-1f728c259f60

79 https://techcrunch.com/2017/06/19/banking-the-unbanked-in-emerging-markets/

rings to secure six packs of beer together (the industry norm), the company has developed eco-friendly drops of adhesive that are strong enough to join beer cans together but weak enough so that customers can easily separate cans at home. The idea was developed by a Carlsberg designer who took it on himself to develop the adhesive at home one weekend, then videotaped the solution and emailed the CEO. The new "Snap Packs" are expected to reduce Carlsberg's plastic use by 1,200 tons a year, the equivalent of 60 million plastic bags. Carlsberg wants the approach to become the new industry norm. Now the same company goes one step ahead and presents its latest designs of Green Fibre Bottle made from sustainably sourced wood fibers, which it claims is fully bio-based and recyclable.[80]

How much this benefits Carlsberg financially remains to be seen. Indeed, its simple and cost-effective answer to a massive global problem may be so easy to emulate that Carlsberg eventually loses some of the credit in the market. But the employees of Carlsberg will always be able to look at a six-pack on the shelf or the "paper" bottle and know that they helped alleviate climate change and spread the benefits broadly. That is a powerful feeling for anyone associated with a company. It may also spur Carlsberg employees to embrace innovation in other opportunities, creating a culture of purpose-driven improvement.

In addition, by talking about its advancement publicly in the right way, Carlsberg can help "own" the issue. Carlsberg can transition from a traditional beer maker to a trendy product that is tied to efforts to save the planet. That's not a bad space to be in for a world of millennial consumers.

---

80   https://www.businessgreen.com/bg/news/3082507/paper-beer-bottles-carlsberg-toasts-world-first-sustainable-drink-packaging-designs

CHAPTER SEVEN RECAP

- Despite the explosion of science, technology and knowledge, massive problems plague the planet and jeopardize its future.

- I call these Level One problems. In my view the three biggest are:

  1. The Destruction of the Planet

  2. Illness, Quality of Life and Death

  3. Lack of Economic Opportunity and Social Justice

- Global nonprofit organizations, as we know them today, have not proved fully capable of addressing these problems.

- By focusing on these very problems in a methodical way and embedding them as variables in a company's business canvas, for-profit organizations can help. There is a methodology to do so.

- Alleviating global problems epitomizes the purpose-driven leadership model and may constitute a new path for capitalism.

Tools & Resources

Here are some indicative lists of **urgent global problems**—call them challenges or dilemmas, as identified by various groups. The detailed content of the lists and the references can be found on my site www.christostsolkas.com.

- What millennials say list:

  1. Climate change/destruction of nature (48.8%)

  2. Large scale conflict/wars (38.9%)

  3. Inequality (income, discrimination) (30.8%)

4. Poverty (29.2%)

5. Religious conflicts (23.9%)

6. Government accountability and transparency/corruption (22.7%)

7. Food and water security (18.2%)

8. Lack of education (15.9%)

9. Safety/security/wellbeing (14.1%)

10. Lack of economic opportunity and employment (12.1%)

- 80,000 Hours Club list:

  1. Risks from AI

  2. Promoting effective altruism

  3. Global priorities research

  4. Improved institutional decision-making

  5. Factory farming

  6. Biosecurity

  7. Nuclear security

  8. Developing world health

  9. Climate change

  10. Land use reform

  11. Smoking in the developing world

- World Economic Forum List of five top risks

  1. Weapons of mass destruction

  2. Extreme weather

  3. Natural disasters

  4. Climate change

  5. Water crisis

CHAPTER EIGHT

We Have the Technology

In December of 1944, a Japanese soldier named Hiro Onoda was sent to an island in the Philippines to fight the Americans. Like all Japanese soldiers, Onoda was told that surrender would be dishonorable. So he soldiered on and on and on.

I read about Onoda's remarkable story in Mark Manson's book, *The Subtle Art of Not Giving a F*ck: A Counterintuitive Approach to Living a Good Life*. Onoda had a strong personal code, a sense of purpose. He also ended up slipping between the cracks of history, and waking up on the other side. This allowed him to see the world with fresh eyes, and truly notice how much technological, cultural and political change had occurred. It also forced him to question all he believed in.

A few months after he was stationed in the Philippines, American forces took the island, capturing or killing most of Onoda's compatriots. Onoda and three others hid in the jungle and continued to harass the American war effort in any way possible. That summer, the most fearsome technological advancement in human history was unleashed on the Japanese Empire when the American forces dropped the atomic bomb on Hiroshima and later on Nagasaki. Onoda didn't know anything about that. He and his companions continued to live as primitives on their island, fighting the Americans.

Even years after the war had ended, Onoda fought on. The governments of America, the Philippines and finally Japan tried to convince Onoda and others like him that the war was over. They dropped leaflets

and messages everywhere. Onoda and others like him believed these were lies and fought on. The American forces were gone now, so Onoda fought the locals instead, burning their fields and buildings, stealing their food.

Eventually, people believed that all the lost Japanese soldiers had been found or killed. It did not seem possible, decades after the war, for anyone else to be still out there in some jungle. Then, Onoda was found in 1974 by a Japanese adventurer who had been searching for him. This man, Suzuki, finally convinced Onoda the war was over and helped him to get home. Onoda returned after spending more than half his life in the jungle fighting a war that was long over.

He didn't seem to mind that loss. He had lived and fought for a purpose—to protect his country. The country he returned to did not seem to be the one that was worth fighting for, however. Japan had changed. Indeed, it was well on its way to becoming one of the most technologically and economically advanced countries in the world. Despite the luxuries and marvels such as TV, Onoda didn't like this new Japan. The emperor was a figurehead. America, the enemy, was now an ally. People were more worried about buying cars or consumer goods than honor or pride. Onoda did not feel at home anymore. He moved to Brazil and died there a few years later.

On the other side of the conflict in World War II, a French engineer named Pierre Boulle served as a spy in Singapore, helping resistance movements across South Asia. When he was captured by the Japanese, he was sentenced to hard labor in a jungle camp. Few people survived these terrible conditions. After the war, Boulle wrote a novel about his experience as part of a prisoner of war troop forced to build a bridge. He called the book *The Bridge Over the River Kwai*, and it was made into a movie that won Academy Awards and became a classic.

Boulle wrote other novels, but the work he became best known for was a science fiction story published later in life under a false name. Boulle called the book *Monkey Planet*. Later, it was retitled *The Planet of the Apes*. In that story, astronauts leave Earth to travel to another world. One of the astronauts, played by Charlton Heston in the movie, is cynical about the planet they're leaving behind, despite its technical advances. Earth is too prone to war and conflict. When the spaceship crash-lands on a new planet, the astronaut is shocked to find it populated by intelligent apes who capture and herd human beings as if they are animals. It is a great shock, and a terrific moment, when he discovers that the planet he landed on is actually Earth. In the aftermath of a man-made catastrophe, apes rose up and took the place of humans, turning his former home into a dystopian hell.

If we were to disappear into the jungle or fly into space for twenty or fifty years, what kind of world would we return to? Surely, in that time, technology would have changed and influenced society, perhaps dramatically. In a cynical vision, like Boulle's, that technology might be a destructive or negative force, creating a culture of want and need. In a positive vision, the world might be a better, safer, more equitable and productive place. Which world is more likely? Which technologies will shape that world most profoundly?

In this chapter I want to explore nine technologies that seem potentially influential on our future. I make no claim that these nine are the most likely to affect humanity. They are only meant to spur thinking about how technology can and will shape our world. If the stories of Onoda and Boulle are to be heeded, it will be important that technology have a clear purpose if we are to create a better future.

Technology #1: Blockchain

In five or ten years, we may look back on 2009 and view it as one of the most important moments in the history of information technology, on par with the rise of the personal computer, the emergence of the Internet, the development of search engines, the evolution of smartphones and the reliance on the cloud. The advancement I'm talking about is Blockchain, something so nebulous and unusual most people don't really understand what it is or does.

Blockchain is a virtual ledger that records transactions and data. The ledger is transparent, decentralized and public, and represents a complete historical record of all transactions associated with an event, a product or service. Those records cannot be altered, destroyed or hidden; therefore, they function as a permanent "source of truth" that does not rely on being located in any place. As a result, the record is accessible anywhere, anytime. While this approach to recording information may sound simple or unnecessary, it is actually a breakthrough in cryptography. Blockchain enables transactions that are completely safe and secure. It creates "trust" in anonymous Internet transactions where no trust existed or seemed possible before. Most importantly, it decentralizes and democratizes control of an individual's information. It puts "you" in charge of your own data, eliminates the need for middlemen (like banks), and creates the kind of transparency that will shine a bright light on the world's darkest corners.

Today, Blockchain has many practical uses.[81] For example, it can help health plans or drug manufacturers trace a drug from production through distribution and sale to the end-user, allowing the companies involved to determine whether that person actually takes the drug or how they are affected by it, positively or negatively. Similarly, Blockchain is used in many other supply chain situations. For example, the world has a huge problem with food fraudulence—the expensive fish or extra virgin olive oil you enjoy in an upscale restaurant may actually be substitute products—and food wastage. Blockchain can help securely verify the provenance of an item, so you know where it came from and where it's been along the way. Likewise, Blockchain can help us understand how or where food is going uneaten, opening the way to transforming waste on a global scale.

For those who have heard of Blockchain, chances are that happened because of Bitcoin. In fact, Bitcoin is only possible because of Blockchain, its underlying technology. Bitcoin is a truly virtual currency, stored only in

---

81   https://www.telegraph.co.uk/connect/better-business/business-solutions/blockchain-applications/

the cloud. At first, Bitcoin was largely attached to dark web activities, such as occur on Silk Road, an online service for selling drugs. Later, as early adopters proliferated, digital transactions normalized and the currency became more mainstream. The value of a Bitcoin rose and fell (sometimes sharply) like the value of any traded commodity. This alarmed observers and reassured them that Bitcoin followed some conventional rules after all. Yet, there was also something enticing about its magical power to exist outside financial institutions. The mainstream is beginning to catch on, and sophisticated economies like Singapore, Dubai and Iran are experimenting with cryptocurrency while Canada, the UK and Israel are researching the possibility. On the other hand, Germany, Switzerland and Japan are among the countries that have experimented with and rejected cryptocurrencies.[82]

Bitcoin and Blockchain represent a potentially seismic shift in the control of economic resources and information. They eliminate the need for intermediaries. Since the 1500s, financial transactions have been largely channeled through financial institutions like banks. This makes these institutions centers of power. The powerful control them. The powerful access them. And they exert great power over national economies and the state. For the first time in history, Bitcoin and all other cryptocurrencies shift some of that power away from centralized banks or governments and into the hands of individuals.

One of the biggest problems in today's world is the mobility of money. Worldwide, over 2 billion people do not have adequate access to financial institutions.[83] Banking is also costly. Transaction fees, late fees, handling fees, etc., may be small but they add up, and banks seek to manipulate processes to maximize those fees and extract billions from customers. Crypto transactions have no fees or miniscule fees. They free users from paying to spend and deploy their own money.

The impact on access to economic opportunity is profound. Mobile money has been around for some time, and in many ways has revolutionized the

---

82   https://cointelegraph.com/news/state-issued-digital-currencies-the-countries-which-adopted-rejected-or-researched-the-concept

83   https://medium.com/@connectjob_/fintech-vs-blockchain-be8acfedcc5c

economies of developing nations and communities. But even mobile money is based on established financial institutions that control those transactions and charge fees. Crypto allows anyone to transact with anyone else, safely and virtually for free. This can enable people to pay their bills, save money, lend money, start businesses, buy goods and services without fear or cost.

As I mentioned, Blockchain goes well beyond cryptocurrencies in that it revolutionizes the way information is stored and exchanged. Think of how this might help us overcome some of the data challenges of today. For example, one of the biggest problems in healthcare is the power to control and access patient health records. Billions of dollars have been spent in the United States alone building record and transaction systems that can allow access, coordination and flow of data. They are costly, insecure, vulnerable and do not function well. Most do not communicate well with one another. This is an enormous problem that makes healthcare more expensive and less safe.

Blockchain decentralizes those records and enables easy communication across different digital platforms. It is also more secure and less vulnerable to hacking. And since Blockchain is a transparent historical record of all transactions associated with that data or that person, it lends itself to creating a lifetime health record for an individual, one that is not trapped in a single institution but follows the patient wherever he goes. This is the long-imagined dream of health information. And it puts the power of that data in the hands of the patient, not the institution.

What other applications can you imagine for Blockchain? What societal problems will it solve? What business models can emerge? Can you imagine a world without banks and health plans? What organizations or services would emerge into that vacuum that people would gain more value from?

Technology #2: CRISPR/Cas9

On July 25, 1978, a baby girl was born in England. Although approximately 335,996 other children were born that day, Louise Brown was special. Her cells were cultivated in a petri dish in a process that became known as in vitro fertilization. Once the cells had grown, they were implanted in her mother's womb, and Louise was born nine months later—the world's first test-tube baby.

The media went crazy over the sensational story of an "invented" baby. Police security was needed at the hospital and at Louise's home. Even the pope criticized the decision of the parents to tamper with nature. Although Louise was a normal baby and child in every other sense, her fame followed her everywhere. In 2018, Louise turned forty. She still receives hate mail occasionally.[84] In the meantime, over 8 million babies have been born using the same technology.

In November 2018, a Chinese scientist named He Jiankui used in vitro fertilization technology to conduct another scientific experiment. He applied CRISPR, a tool for "editing" genes in cells, to change the genetic code of two babies. Specifically, he manually disabled a gene associated with AIDS/HIV to make the girls resistant to the disease. The scientific community was outraged by this manipulation of human DNA and the creation of "designer" babies.

CRISPR stands for "clustered regularly interspaced short palindromic repeats." These genetic sequences are found in bacteria. Cas9 is an enzyme that uses these sequences to cut specific strands of DNA from genes in other organisms. Scientists can apply Cas9 very deliberately and directly to edit genes as they wish.

The uses of CRISPR seem limitless. CRISPR potentially could:

- Rid malaria from the mosquitos that transmit the disease to humans

- Repair the deterioration of muscular dystrophy

- Eliminate a patient's cancer genetically, without applying toxic chemo-therapy or drugs

- Create organs in pigs that can be transplanted to humans

- Develop new designer pharmaceuticals

---

84 https://www.independent.co.uk/news/health/test-tube-baby-40th-anniversary-world-first-reaction-ivf-louise-brown-a8454021.html

- Treat blindness

- Edit humans[85]

Bluntly stated, humans have never had more power to change life. Does this represent the ultimate threat to humanity, or the biggest gift or both? Will the ethical considerations override the scientific possibilities? Imagine a company finding a way to leverage CRISPR to improve human health. Perhaps a disease-free, super-healthy, super-intelligent being will be born in the next few years. Perhaps people, with a ready supply of genetically modified organs, tissues and body parts available, can essentially become immortal. What other previously insurmountable problems can CRISPR finally solve? What businesses will make those solutions commercially available?[86]

Technology #3: The Internet of Things/Internet of Bodies

In 1964, an obscure Canadian philosopher named Marshall McLuhan wrote a book called *Understanding Media: The Extensions of Man.* McLuhan believed that all tools are extensions of the human body. The hammer is an extension of the hand. The flashlight or telescope is an extension of the eyes. The car is an extension of the legs. The computer is an extension of the brain.

Writing about McLuhan's theories, the American academic John Culkin observed, "We shape our tools and thereafter our tools shape us." Human beings, in other words, quickly develop a reliance on their tools that makes those tools indispensable. Who, these days, can imagine being without their smartphone for even a few hours? A tool that we didn't even have twenty years ago is now an essential part of our lives, shaping our habits, brains and even our personalities.

---

85   https://www.popularmechanics.com/science/a19067/11-crazy-things-we-can-do-with-crispr-cas9/

86   https://singularityhub.com/2019/05/02/crispr-used-in-human-trials-for-the-first-time-in-the-us/

Prepare for tools to become extensions of the body in an entirely new way. Thanks to the Internet of Things, billions of devices are now connected to the Internet. This means that almost anything can be turned into an intelligent digital device. A refrigerator, a pen, a car, a plant vase … all can become nodes of data, monitors and robots doing what we ask them to do. A smarter, more efficient, more interactive world awaits.

The Internet of Bodies is around the corner. People can swallow pills, equipped with sensors and processors, that will monitor their health internally. They can put on smart contact lenses that monitor glucose levels and help diabetics manage their conditions with a new level of precision and ease. Devices inserted into the ear or the heart or the spine can help a deaf person to hear, monitor their heart condition or walk again despite paralyzed limbs. Of course, with data breaches a daily occurrence now, concerns about personal data privacy are understandable. Perhaps new implanted IoB devices will be vulnerable to hacking and even control by outsiders. Yet, the power of technology to improve, enhance or heal the human body is incredibly tantalizing.

Imagine a microscopic device that can exist inside your body, constantly monitoring you for disease or adverse health conditions.[87] Imagine your car driving you to work and picking up your groceries and children while you're at the office. Imagine your smartphone, taking time away from you when you're not using it, to apply its computational power to solve massively complicated problems that improve life on the planet.

What approaches to this technology will solve the biggest problems and have a powerful impact on the market? What businesses will be able to take advantage of these opportunities?

---

87 https://singularityhub.com/2019/07/10/cancer-killing-living-drug-is-made-safer-with-a-simple-off-switch/

Technology #4: Artificial Intelligence and Robotics

In 1770, a Hungarian author and inventor named Wolfgang von Kempelen built a chess-playing machine called the Mechanical Turk. Sitting across a chessboard, the turbaned mannequin battled human opponents by moving its own pieces. The level of play was quite strong, and the Turk won more than it lost. A spectacle of amazement, the Mechanical Turk toured much of Europe and America over the next seventy-five years playing chess champions and such notable figures as Napoleon and Benjamin Franklin. Although many suspected there was some trick or hoax involved, the mechanics of the machine were extremely convincing. It was only much later that researchers figured out that a chess-playing human sat inside the Mechanical Turk and used the levers to create the illusion of artificial intelligence.

Two centuries later, IBM built a computer actually capable of beating the world's greatest chess player. When Big Blue defeated Gary Kasparov 3½ games to 2½ in a 6-game competition, it signaled to the world that artificial intelligence had finally arrived. Kasparov, who detected real intelligence and creativity in some of Deep Blue's moves, suspected IBM cheated by inserting human decisions and interpretations into the play. He demanded a rematch, but IBM retired Deep Blue and moved on to developing other applications of AI. Kasparov might have had a point. Twenty years later, Big Blue, IBM's AI cancer-diagnosis computer was accused of very poor results in diagnosis and treatment suggestions, which were corrected by further input from its human handlers.

When I was an engineering student thirty years ago, AI was considered a very promising technology. Back then, we wrote algorithms that attempted to imitate how the human brain works. Trying to code that way proved to be impossible, and AI didn't progress much. In the last ten years, that approach has changed. Now, instead of replicating human thinking, we've realized that the best way for AI to learn is to let it observe. So we've combined computer processing with sensors, monitors and other mechanisms for data input. We don't try to define the difference between a cat and a dog, for example; we feed the computer lots of images of cats and let it write its own rules. This kind of self-learning capability is at the heart of the AI explosion; and when it is combined with enormous quantities of data and tremendous computational power, we create the possibility of a machine that can make predictions about the future far more quickly, cheaply and accurately than humans.

After all, human beings can't process, remember, interpret or draw patterns from such large and fast-moving streams of data. We need algorithms to do the work for us. An algorithm is a step-by-step process that produces insight or can even make judgments or decisions. Computers rely on the complex interplay of many algorithms to do the work we want them to do. From the beginning of the computer, we've wondered whether that network of algorithms could become so intelligent that it would seem human. Alan Turing said, "Suppose non-conscious algorithms could eventually outperform conscious intelligence in all known data-processing tasks—what, if anything, would be lost by replacing conscious intelligence with superior non-conscious algorithms?" His Turing test posited that we could assess whether machines can actually think by engaging them in conversation. If they're indistinguishable from a human conversation partner, then real thinking is taking place.

Today, machines may not be able to "think" like a human, but thanks to AI, they can certainly learn. That's the promise and threat of the rise of AI. Yuval Noah Harari, the author of *Homo Sapiens* and *Homo Deus*, says that all living organisms are already made up of algorithms, from humans to dogs to viruses. The only difference with machines is that living organisms rely on biochemical algorithms which have "learned" through evolution over millions of years. Questions about the difference between AI machines and humans, Harari says, come down to confusion between the nature of intelligence and the nature of consciousness. Intelligence gives us the ability to solve problems. AI is exceptionally good at that, and becoming better than humans. Consciousness is the ability to feel things in an intelligent way. Humans are still distinct from AI in that sense. Superintelligence without consciousness is the likely future of AI.

According to HackerEarth, AI is currently being applied in five different areas.[88] These are:

- Reasoning—solving problems through logic

- Knowledge—forming conclusions based on data

- Planning—setting and achieving goals

- Communication—interacting with humans through language

- Perception—taking in information through sounds, visuals and other sensory inputs to draw observations and present insights

In essence, then, AI helps make predictions and suggest actions. The applications of these capabilities are limitless and pervade our world. AI is integrated today into almost all areas of human endeavor and business. It's part of finance, healthcare, distribution, supply chains, transportation, manufacturing and entertainment. AI is responsible for making stock trades, diagnosing illnesses, moving goods more efficiently, driving cars automatically, making complex machines, and even choosing the movies, music or food we should buy or select.

If AI might replace or augment human thinking, robots leverage that intelligence to potentially replace or augment what humans do or would like to do. Kate Darling of the MIT Media Lab defines a robot as "a physical machine that's usually programmable by a computer that can execute tasks autonomously or automatically by itself."[89]

Why are robots so exciting? Because robots can move about and perform tasks like humans, it must feel like we are creating a type of life. Certainly, robots are valuable to humans because they can free us from mundane, dangerous or precision-driven tasks, and do them much better.

Robots are working in factories, warehouses, farms and mines. They're operating as retail service workers, soldiers, pharmacists and brain surgeons.

88   https://www.hackerearth.com/blog/innovation-management/applications-of-artificial-intelligence/

89   https://www.wired.com/story/what-is-a-robot/

They're cleaning houses, defusing bombs, operating drones and caring for the elderly and physically disabled.

The ability of robots to do tasks better than humans is tantalizing. The potential of robots to replace humans in all manner of work, even work that seems to require uniquely human capabilities, from pharmacy to journalism, worries many of us. If robots can be put to work to solve our biggest problems, what would those problems be? In the environment, robots could potentially help us clean up pollution that humans can't or don't want to go near. In terms of access to economic opportunity, perhaps robots can help the disabled function physically so they can participate in the workforce, or help an otherwise struggling farmer or a business owner be more productive at lower costs.

In 2016, a robot named Sophia was activated by a Hong Kong-based company. She can manage fifty different facial expressions and engage in conversation. That ability to connect through language and reflect or project emotion makes a major difference in the sense of humanity in the robot. In 2017, Sophia became the first robot to become a citizen of a country. She now has seven siblings.

Plenty of storytellers have looked at robotics and imagined a dark future for humanity. Just think about the *Terminator* movies. AI may be an even scarier prospect. Before he died, Stephen Hawking warned that humanity's biggest threat was AI. "Whereas the short-term impact of AI depends on who controls it, the long-term impact depends on whether it can be controlled at all." Hawking didn't think the real risk was in AI becoming malevolent toward humans, but that it would be so competent humans wouldn't be necessary anymore.[90]

Imagine a different future in which AI and robotics help foster a better world rather than limit our potential.

90 https://www.vox.com/future-perfect/2018/10/16/17978596/stephen-hawking-ai-climate-change-robots-future-universe-earth

What can we do to turn AI and robotics towards solving humanity's biggest challenges and problems?

Technology #5: 3D Printing

3D printing has been around in some form since the early 1980s. The basic technology that is used today, called fused deposition modeling, was invented in 1988. In the thirty years since, 3D printing has been impeded by technological challenges and high operating costs. In the past few years, the technology has improved even as the cost has dropped dramatically.

The excitement of 3D printing is that it eliminates the need to manufacture at scale, and enables the economic production of a single product when and where it is needed. Theoretically, a farmer in need of a tool, a doctor in need of a prosthetic, or an entrepreneur in need of a prototype could design and manufacture that item with absolute precision. This gives any individual with access to a 3D printer the power of a factory and the resources of a manufacturing company. 3D printers can also solve the problem of distance. Remote communities and developing countries seem poised to benefit the most.

The applications of 3D printing are probably limitless. Manufacturers use 3D printing to develop prototypes and parts or even produce and sell products while customers wait. 3D printing has powerful educational possibilities, allowing students to learn how to design and build objects on their own. The technology could even find its way to space, allowing a space station or planetary colony to build what it needs, despite the lack of raw materials.

On a social level, 3D printing democratizes manufacturing, making it more possible for more people and communities to produce what they want, cheaply. No doubt, this distributed technology platform will empower people to get what they need to do their work or live their lives while also unleashing great entrepreneurial potential. A 3D printer could print a house, for example, in twenty-four hours. Another potential impact will be the rise of creativity and do-it-yourself design and invention. Once, only highly trained architects, engineers, industrial designers and craftsmen could design and create buildings, machines, elegant devices, and so on. Now, any individual of any age or experience can become his or her own designer with the ease with which children can manipulate photos today.

The downside of 3D printing may, like robotics, lie with the people who no longer are needed to work in factories or in stores. To counter the global problems with inequality that will likely result, do we need to implement a minimum universal income? The ideal purpose of technology is to help solve problems, not create new ones; yet, "creative destruction" has always gone hand-in-hand with innovation. Where there is change, there is the need to adapt.

Technology #6: Virtual/Augmented Reality

In the popular TV show, *Star Trek: The Next Generation*, one of the great sources of escape and play on the spaceship was the Holodeck. In this virtual reality room, the ship's crew could do or experience almost anything. They could go back in time to visit an ancient ruin while it was functioning. They could participate in a famous story like Sherlock Holmes as though they were living the drama. They could generate a world or an environment or an adventure that was unplanned, and let that experience unspool naturally.

Historically, radio, film, TV and computer games have introduced us to the experience of artificial environments that felt increasingly "real" to the beholder. Virtual and augmented reality seem likely to be the next stages in that evolution. The giant tech companies sure think so: They're making enormous bets through their investments.

VR has powerful possibilities to offer. As a tool for gamers, it can create an immersive game-world that will "place" players into the game worlds they long to inhabit. As an educational tool, VR can help students experience life in another point in history or explore a great museum on the other side of the world or interact with a program of a great philosopher like Aristotle as if he is the guest lecturer. As a training tool, VR can let surgeons practice on virtual patients or explore complicated procedures or even the body itself, while also enabling pilots and soldiers to train for realistic and dangerous scenarios. As a communications tool, VR can enable people to interact with each other "in person," despite great distances, while saving time, resources and reducing energy use and pollution.[91]

Imagine the changes that can come in many different industries—travel, movie watching, wilderness trips, sports, education. Suddenly, you wouldn't need to experience something directly; you could do it virtually. The way we work together might change, too, as physical offices become irrelevant. People might visit hospitals virtually first to be diagnosed, preventing exposure to germs and disease or greatly alleviating the stress on emergency departments.

On the downside, virtual reality is a potentially highly addictive technology that might suck users in while making the "real world" seem a humdrum and unfulfilling place. We've already seen the impact of social media and smartphones on people's attentions.

Technology #7: Social Media and Global Connectivity

Even before the World Wide Web, since the early use of the personal computer, people have congregated in virtual communities. The first such communities were known as bulletin board services (BBS). They allowed people from around the world to "dial in" to a particular server, and participate in a text-based chat discussion on any number of subjects or themes. They became very popular as ways to access information and engage with people interested in similar topics. More than anything, they created a sense of community among the members and participants. Some of those early communities like the WELL were passionate places for debate, sharing, information exchange and activism.

The early Internet browsers made this experience even more vivid and easy, while moving communities away from single servers into the broader network. Businesses like Friendster, Myspace and, eventually, Facebook became the new iteration of online communities. Facebook

---

91   https://www.nytimes.com/2017/07/27/climate/airplane-pollution-global-warming.html

emerged as the behemoth, linking friends, acquaintances and interested strangers across a web of connections while also serving as a platform for countless communities focused on specific issues or shared interests. Other services like LinkedIn, Twitter, Reddit, Second Life and Instagram offered specialized experiences or forums for different purposes or types of people. For example, LinkedIn focuses on the professional aspects of our lives, while Second Life allows people to escape their lives by presenting themselves in avatar form. Reddit is largely text-based, while Instagram is almost completely visual.

In their early days, modern social media platforms were considered a frivolous but surprisingly intimate way to connect with other people. Old friends from high school. Colleagues around the world. Fellow researchers, artists, and so on. Starting with the Arab Spring uprisings in Egypt and Tunisia and later in the uprising in Ukraine, social media became viewed as a great enabler of grassroots democracy. Resisters of authoritarian regimes could communicate through unofficial channels, share information, learn news and make plans. During the 2016 U.S. presidential election it became apparent how vulnerable social media networks were to manipulation, hate, extremism and fake news.

Are social media platforms good or bad? Do they facilitate communities or undermine society? Can they be productive not only in a social sense but in solving humanity's problems or enabling economic and political solutions?

Whichever way social media goes, there will be much room for growth of services, uses and numbers. How can global connectivity facilitate serious crises handling? How can purpose-driven businesses leverage such platforms to solve big problems? Students of subjects can gather to improve their knowledge and understanding of a subject. Professionals can advance their insights into less-explored areas of their field.

The potential and the pitfalls of social media and global connectivity remain very real.

Technology #8: Growing Food

Food production, distribution and waste are immense problems today, putting pressure on society, the economy and the environment. Technologies that alleviate some of this pressure are now increasingly available.

Today, half the world's population lives in cities. By 2050, that will rise to 70 percent.[92] How will we feed 2 billion more people than now, most of whom will live in urban centers, far from food production?

Today, large-scale agricultural production on farms is very hard on the environment, especially in the developing world where most population growth is occurring. Agriculture often starts with clearing land for crops or livestock, which contributes to climate change because of deforestation. Agriculture is also hard on soil nutrients and composition and requires enormous quantities of water, which may not be readily available and may become even more scarce soon. To supplement soil and grow healthy produce, farmers use highly toxic (often petroleum-based) fertilizer as well as pesticides. This increases pollution and inefficiency. Some of the most environmentally intense produce, like cows for dairy and beef, and corn for corn syrup and oil, are the very things we consume the most. An argument can be made that cow flatulence, for example, is more harmful to the environment than vehicle exhaust.[93] Agricultural animals consume almost as much produce as people.

That's only the first stage. Once produce is ready for market, it must be transported. This means moving refrigerated and highly packaged goods long distances to sell in urban centers. More fuel is wasted with the transportation and refrigeration. More pollution results from all of the plastic packaging. The quality and taste of food also degrades when it is stored, distributed, repackaged, shelved in stores, brought home and refrigerated.

92 https://www.un.org/development/desa/en/news/population/2018-revision-of-world-urbanization-prospects.html

93 https://animals.howstuffworks.com/mammals/methane-cow.htm

Then there is food waste during and after delivery. One third of the food that is produced is wasted every year, enough to feed 2 billion people. In the wealthiest countries, consumers throw out 40 percent of all food that is wasted.[94] Some countries are trying to regulate food waste. Diverting food would have as big an impact as changing diet. Overeating is also a major source of food waste.[95]

Technology is helping and will have an increasing impact going forward. GPS technology, for example, can make farming much more productive and efficient. Lab-grown meat holds the promise of an alternative that is far less burdensome on the environment, ethically sounder and perhaps able to give more people needed protein one day.[96]

Another approach to growing food might be even more sustainable and scalable. A number of new investor-backed startups are experimenting with hydroponic technology that allows people to grow produce very quickly and efficiently in cubes in their own kitchen. With four or five cubes, a family could grow enough vegetables to consume a salad every day of the week. The vegetables would replenish rapidly, providing a constant supply of food.[97] IKEA is currently marketing these vegetable production tools for home kitchens.[98]

This system would help reduce reliance on large farms and inefficient distribution and retail channels. It could also reduce overall waste. The system is potentially intelligent as well. One intelligent hydroponic cube can "learn a lot" as it adjusts light, nutrient and soil conditions for optimal growth. Hundreds of thousands or millions of cubes, connected together through the cloud, can learn very quickly and potentially make substantial leaps in productivity and efficiency. Grocery stores are also getting in on

94   https://www.nytimes.com/2017/12/12/climate/food-waste-emissions.html

95   https://www.sciencedirect.com/science/article/pii/S0308521X16302384

96   https://www.washingtonpost.com/national/health-science/burgers-grown-in-a-lab-are-heading-to-your-plate-will-you-bite/2018/09/07/1d048720-b060-11e8-a20b-5f4f84429666_story.html

97   https://www.voanews.com/a/smartphone-grow-vegetables-indoor-cube/3185347.html

98   https://www.independent.co.uk/extras/indybest/house-garden/gardening/best-home-hydroponics-kits-gardening-indoor-herb-garden-a8461671.html

the act, growing produce in stores or on top of buildings, to reduce waste, inefficiency, pesticides, water use, etc.[99]

Technology #9: Solar Power

Since the conversion of coal-fired ships and the arrival of the automobile, the world has been addicted to fossil fuels. In the century since, oil has driven our economy. It has made great fortunes, caused economic booms and busts, catalyzed regional conflicts, inspired unlikely alliances, changed society and polluted the atmosphere to such an extent that extreme global climate change is likely irreversible. Our addiction to oil has been so over-powering that rather than save the planet by turning our attention urgently toward alternatives, we continue to seek new ways to extract and use fossil fuels as though nothing was wrong.

For centuries humans have pondered how to tap the sun's energy as a source of fuel. An efficient, cost-effective conversion mechanism has been lacking until recently. Solar power has been around since the late 1800s, but it only began to take hold as a potential alternative in the 1990s. Worried about peak oil, the environment and lingering fears of the next oil shock, solar panels were adopted by many large office and industrial buildings. They were expensive, bulky and difficult to take advantage of, however.

In the past decade, despite cynicism of those who thought it would never be cost-effective, solar power has begun to take off. The industry is high-growth. The number of people employed by the solar industry has doubled since 2010, while prices for solar panels have dropped by around 60 percent.[100]

As solar cells become cheaper and more efficient, their use will continue to spread. Perovskite solar cells, an alternative to silicon, promise to be cheaper still, once they become available for commercial production. As technology improves, solar panels may become ubiquitous. Conversion

---

99   https://www.businessinsider.com/infarm-creates-a-mini-lettuce-farm-for-grocery-stores-2016-4

100   https://www.cleanenergyauthority.com/blog/the-future-of-solar-energy-01232017

cells could be "painted" onto the surfaces of walls or cars. They could power smartphones, computers and every vehicle or tool we use. It's conceivable that oil will be made anachronistic very rapidly as the solar economy takes over.

Imagine what business opportunities could result. As humans become more reliant on solar power and less addicted to oil, they will need a new infrastructure of energy filling stations, batteries, and power sources. Perhaps roads could be equipped with electricity recharging pads. Maybe a few entrepreneurial types in a community will find ways to service the electricity needs of their neighbors, supplanting the local power utility.

"The Cause of and Solution to All Our Problems"

Human beings have always used technology to solve urgent problems and achieve critical goals. The hunter-gatherers developed weapons and tools which helped them kill larger, faster animals and forage for food more effectively. The first agrarian civilizations harnessed cows and developed hoes and irrigation systems to grow crops more productively. The Romans built a network of roads and aqueducts to serve the needs of their empire. Those constructions still influence the locations of cities, the prosperity of regions and the flow of trade two thousand years later.[101]

Until today, however, nothing in human history compared to the Industrial Revolution in terms of the explosion of technology, innovation and change. Over the course of several centuries, the world became replete with new devices, technologies and systems. Steam engines. Factories. Giant trade ships. Extensive railroads. Communication systems like the telegraph and telephone. Financial systems like banking, currency and stocks. The electric power grid and countless electric devices. All of these technologies burst into prominence because they served important needs. All of them got exploited and accelerated by new businesses that grew fast and large, almost overnight, many of which still exist today. Societies

---

101   https://www.dailymail.co.uk/sciencetech/article-5673247/Roman-roads-contributing-spread-prosperity-scientists-claim.html

transformed under the pressure these new technologies exerted. Lives changed, families changed, communities changed. The impacts were never always or completely positive. Sometimes different solutions, technologies and rules were necessary to correct problems that resulted. Sometimes those new solutions and technologies led to still more problems.

Consider the need for light. As the Industrial Era took hold, work changed. People who once relied on daylight spent more time inside or in the dark. Candles and oil lamps were the primary source of illumination. The cheapest candle wax and oil was rendered from animal fat. But animal fat exuded unpleasant odors, spewed thick smoke and spattered grease. The quality of the light was also poor, and sometimes house fires resulted. The best available alternative, we soon discovered, was whale oil.

Almost overnight, the traditional whale hunt became an industry. In America, long-standing whaling communities in Massachusetts and Cape Cod suddenly emerged as global centers for thousands of fishermen and many prosperous merchants and financial collectives. The well-stocked ships they funded set out on voyages that could last two to five years while the fishermen on board chased giant sperm whales around the world. When those fisherman finally encountered a whale and the hunt began, the garrison of fishermen turned into soldiers and launched attacks on one of the largest creatures ever to roam the Earth. After the fight was over and the dead sperm whale was tied to the side of the hull, the whaling ship turned into a floating factory, and the fishermen carved out the blubber and rendered it into oil in a giant furnace on the deck. The flames of that furnace burned brightly for many nights. Then the whaling ship would move on, and the whale's carcass would be left behind to float away.

The world's first oil crisis developed because sperm whales became scarce. The majestic beasts became harder to find, even as the number of whaling ships increased. No doubt, extinction loomed. Then, in 1854, at the height of the whale hunt, a chemist in Canada named Abraham Gesner invented a new type of fuel called kerosene. Gesner's process distilled kerosene from coal and later from petroleum. The American oil industry started because of the industrial world's insatiable demand for light.

Kerosene's reign as an illuminant was short-lived. Edison's light bulb and the electricity grid took over the market because it was easier and safer to turn on a switch than light a lamp. We quickly found other uses for kerosene, however, in a new industry.

Henry Ford was credited with "inventing" the automobile. But he was one of many thousands of inventors striving to produce a "horseless" carriage in the late 1800s. Some versions used steam power, others electricity. The diesel- and gasoline-powered engines were late to the game. But finding a solution was becoming a necessity. In part, this was because horses were an environmental disaster. The horse crisis.

The world's major cities were clogged with the horses that transported people in carriages and trollies. Horses created traffic jams, but unlike cars, they also produced waste and disease. In 1900, New York City streets were polluted every day with 40 dead horses, 2.5 million pounds of manure and 60,000 gallons of urine. When the automobile came along, it was seen as a environmental savior.

In other words, just as the invention of kerosene helped save the majestic sperm whale from extinction, so the invention of the automobile made living in major cities, at least for a time, healthier and cleaner.

This is the story of technology. Crisis leads to solution. Solution leads to business model. Successful business model grows in scale as a brand-new market opens up. Modern global giants like Standard Oil (Exxon) and Shell emerged to meet the global need for kerosene and later for petroleum, just as the great car manufacturing companies rose out of Ford's innovation. Yesterday's savior, however, can become tomorrow's threat. Today, millions upon millions of gas- and diesel-fueled cars and trucks are responsible for a significant percentage of the pollution and greenhouse gases that threaten to cause devastating global climate change. Temperatures are rising. Wild fires are burning. Drought, flooding and disease are forcing millions of people around the world to become refugees. It will only get worse unless something changes.

What will we do to save the day now? Maybe the electric car will prove to be the answer, or perhaps some other technology will offer a very different kind of solution, capturing carbon from the atmosphere or giving us the ability to turn environmental pollution toward some productive use.

The point is that technology takes off when crisis is at hand. The biggest opportunities arise because of the greatest need. Right now, I believe our biggest problems, as I discussed in the previous chapter, concern environmental challenges, health challenges and access to economic opportunity. Are there technologies in existence right now—like kerosene or the automobile—that can alleviate those needs?

The impact of technology is notoriously difficult to predict. Assessing a particularly new and exciting technology, it can be easy to overestimate its potential for changing the world, just as it can be easy to miss how that technology might "turn against us." Given the global scale of the problems we face and the urgency of our need for solutions, the technologies described in this chapter may present significant opportunities for new high-growth businesses—the Standard Oils, General Electrics and Fords of the future. Hopefully, they will also save us from ourselves.

CHAPTER EIGHT RECAP

■ ■ ■ ■ ■ ■ ■ ■ ■ ■

- Technology can help address Level One problems in a multitude of ways.

- There are nine technological streams with transformational potential:

  1. Blockchain

  2. CRISPR/Cas9

  3. The Internet of Things/Internet of Bodies

  4. Artificial Intelligence and Robotics

  5. 3D Printing

  6. Virtual/Augmented Reality

  7. Social Media and Global Connectivity

  8. Growing Food

  9. Solar Power

- Today, the potential of technological enablement is so profound we can best capture it in a simple phrase: "Whatever you can imagine, you can do."

Tools & Resources

To better understand the role technology can play in seeking solutions for our Level One problems, below are some good places to go (for all links visit my site www.christostsolkas.com).

- Read *Fast Company*'s article "5 Ways Artificial Intelligence Can Help Save The Planet". It talks about

  - Autonomous energy and water networks

  - Climate modeling

  - Real-time data dashboards

  - Disaster resiliency and response

  - Earth bank of codes

- Read a very interesting paper from WWF Australia published in 2017 that talks about smart cities, the IoT, VR and AR, Blockchain, Electricity Generation and Storage, AI, Autonomous Vehicles, Agri Tech, Food Tech, Ocean Tech and the Sharing Economy.

- Read a ZDNet article by Greg Nichols tackling the top 10 technologies which can help the planet.

- Get the e-book from Singularity University titled *Feed the World: How Exponential Tech Can Create an Abundant Future.*

- On the preventative side, Machine Learning and AI can help us to anticipate and better manage future disasters, according to an article of Seth Guikema in *Scientific American*, you have to read.

CHAPTER NINE

Putting It All Together

A few years ago, I spoke about purpose, crisis and innovation at a conference in Europe. It was a big event with some world-famous people as keynoters. I was humbled but excited to be sharing the stage on one of the days. The talk went well. I could see people nodding, smiling, taking notes. They asked questions. They got it. Here are the titles of the PowerPoint slides I used:

1. **Crisis**

   Where purpose is born

2. **Innovation**

   = Purpose x Crisis

3. **Growth**

   = Purpose and innovation at scale

4. **Business Model**

   Purpose ⇔ Global Problems ⇔ Customers ⇔ Innovation

5. **Technology**

   Helps you get there/Operationalizes innovation

6. **Leadership**

   Purpose is the new leadership

7. **Impact**

   How success is measured

8. **Performance**

   It pays your bills

In my talk, I gave examples of different companies that are following this approach, many of which I have discussed already in this book. I spent much of my time talking about leadership, particularly the challenges leaders face today in motivating employees and winning in the market, and the way purpose is the foundation of lasting impact and real significance.

In the reception afterwards, two people approached me with questions. The first was a young woman from Sweden who'd trained in agriculture and food science. I'll call her Ilsa. She'd always been idealistic about food and sustainability, but her education had really focused on making the old system function more efficiently. That didn't seem like a big enough goal for her, given the world's global problems. A year ago, however, she'd met some people online who were developing an artificial meat process and wanted to form a new company together. They'd asked her to come on board. She'd hesitated before, but now she wondered if she should give up her old job and join them. She was clearly excited about this idea, and I could understand why. You don't have to be a vegan to recognize that the production of meat, particularly beef, is brutal on the environment. By many estimates, cows are one of the main global contributors of CO_2 to the atmosphere because of their flatulence. And creating pasture land for cows by clear-cutting forests and jungle in developing countries continues to devastate the environment. An innovative business selling artificial meat that tastes great and is affordable could save the planet while helping to solve the problem of hunger, too.

Ilsa was fired up by my talk but still overwhelmed by the practical business side of that challenge. How do you change the world when you're just three people with big dreams, a very alternative idea and no clear path to market?

I asked her where she fit on my quadrants.

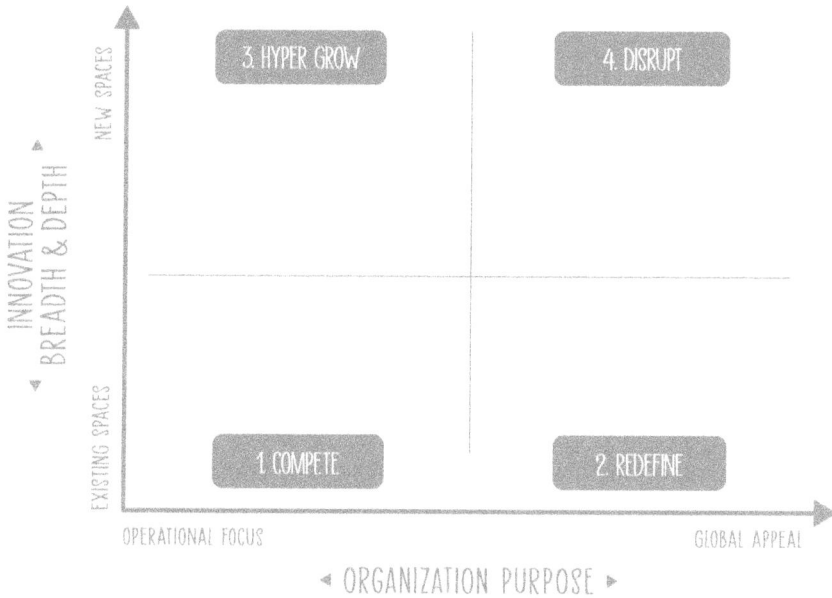

She said that she initially thought the company was very much in the quadrant that focuses on global need in a white space area (Quadrant 4). However, when she really thought about the market she realized she was still competing against more traditional organic and specialty food suppliers. If she couldn't play their game well, her company wouldn't make it. In a few minutes, I helped her come up with some focused questions about what her customers want, how big the market might be, and how the product could reach them. Very quickly, she felt as though she was armed with a way to develop a business model that could support their purpose and compete with a commercial product in the real world. This put her business closer to the quadrant of global appeal in an existing space, but still "high" up in the quadrant in terms of white space and innovation.

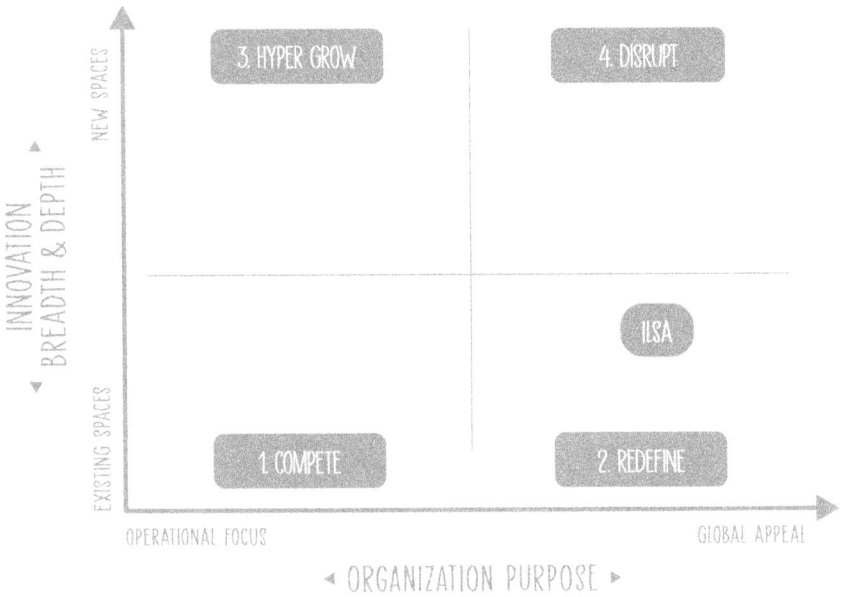

Seeing this on the chart calmed her fears quite a bit. She and her partners could still change the world, but their idea wouldn't seem as "out there" or "radical" to investors who wanted to support something that could make them a return. In fact, she was beginning to think bigger than ever in terms of the company's potential valuation and how much funding they should seek. I wished her luck and told her I looked forward to seeing news of her company in the years to come.

The second person who approached was not a millennial in hip clothes. He was a tall man in his mid-forties from Germany, wearing a poorly fitting suit. He introduced himself as Max, the CEO of an engineering company with around eight hundred employees. As a very left-brain thinker and practical manager, Max wanted to know how he could bring to life a sense of purpose for his company. Business was good. You could say it was booming. But like many good CEOs, he also worried about what he couldn't see coming, and he had a sense that what I was saying about purpose was a blind spot for him. His company wasn't facing any particular crisis, at least not a direct one. He was somewhat worried about political issues, including Brexit, a new administration in Germany, and the possibility of global trade wars.

But he didn't see how his company could shape, change or even prepare for those possibilities. He was more curious about purpose. Could he bring purpose into his company and make a big difference on growth, market share and impact?

I asked him what the purpose of his company would be. He thought about it for a second and said, "Maybe our purpose is to have happy employees." In Germany, this made sense. German companies are a lot more employee-centric and -empowered than in the U.S. and Britain. Happy employees could lead to even better results. As former Southwest Airlines CEO Herb Kelleher often advocated, if you hire good people, make sure they care about the same things you care about (safety, service, doing the job right) and let them have fun, your business will be okay. Your employees' engagement and willingness to solve customers' problems will lead to substantial competitive differentiation and long-term success. This didn't feel right to me, though, so I said to Max, "Is that why you lead this company—to make your employees happy?" As he considered my question, I pressed him again. "Do your highly talented engineers come to work for your company to be happy?" No. He agreed that this wasn't the case.

He tried another tact: "Maybe our purpose is to develop the best engineers in the world." I understand why he went there. Talent is hard to come by. Driven people with technical expertise (whether salespeople, marketers, physicians, engineers, etc.) have a tendency to seek organizations that continue to develop and build their skills. They are hardwired to learn and grow through on-the-job problem solving and professional development. Yet, that didn't feel right to me either. "Is the purpose of your organization to be a school?" I asked. He agreed that it was not. And insisted that he would keep thinking, and let me know if he came up with anything.

A few weeks later I got a message. He wrote that after much soul-searching and discussions with his executive team and key employees he realized something. As a contractor, the company doesn't really have a product or a direct impact on the world. But the company's clients actually do. Reviewing clients, it was easy to see which ones operated in areas that made his people feel good and which didn't. A car parts manufacturer client, for example, was an industry leader in environmental sustainability. Helping that company meet its goals made the people in his organization feel great. Another client made military hardware which it sold mostly to the Middle East. Despite the revenue, no one in the organization felt good about that relationship, especially given the extent of recent military conflict.

"We decided we're in business to help **our clients** make the world a better place," he wrote me. "So, we're going to be a lot more choosy in the future about the clients we work with and the projects we apply our talents to. We've started to develop a list of industries we work in and how our clients can have an even bigger impact on the world. We also developed a list of companies we might prefer to drop because they are not focused on global problems. When I socialized this with our teams, I got some pushback about lost revenue, but most people were extremely enthusiastic. I'd say it energized us a great deal. Now we have to figure out the details. But we've already come up with some interesting ideas and approaches that we've never tried before. I'm excited about that, and even the holdouts seem willing to try."

I felt good about this development and the previous conversation with Ilsa. Very quickly, two organizations were now thinking differently about their work. They were energized by that change. It was creating new pathways and possibilities. By drawing a line between business and global impact, they were also strengthening connections with their people, customers/ clients and investors.

Personally, I believe both those companies will be more successful financially and socially as a result. Now, let's dig into the path your company can consider following.

1. Crisis

Crisis is where purpose is most often born.

It was through crisis that I learned about purpose. But in thinking about this book and, in particular, this final chapter, I debated whether purpose should be first or whether crisis should be first. While it's obvious a company should have a clear sense of purpose before any crisis, in practical reality, it often doesn't. Crisis can focus a company on what really matters.

John Kotter, the incredibly influential business thinker, laid out this formula thirty years ago. In his 8-Step Change Model, Kotter declared that change only really takes effect when some underlying crisis forces people, companies and customers to adapt. In my business career, I've seen the truth of this from many different levels and perspectives. Try motivating anyone, even yourself, to change without some cause or need to do so. Chances are, whatever your best intentions, you just won't follow through or feel the motivation to stick with it. Think about motivating and shifting an entire organization to a new software system or a new accounting system or a revamped product design or better manufacturing processes without some fear or urgent opportunity driving the change. You might as well practice herding cats first.

Crisis can spur change. But it's also a powerful motivator to seek out a meaningful purpose. If a crisis is big enough, you might need a clearer sense of purpose just to survive. As I described at the beginning of this book, I was "lucky" twice in my career to confront a crisis as the leader of an organization. First in Greece and then in Ukraine. In both cases, economic and political forces well beyond our control completely overturned our normal business plans.

In the case of Greece, I discovered the power of purpose as I lived through the crisis. I was in despair before then, and my people felt lost as our business profitability evaporated overnight. To manage that confusion and lack of direction, I turned to purpose and brought in some ideas and approaches that helped us focus on a meaningful path, develop courage and resiliency, and formulate a plan to take steps to save our company and our jobs.

In the case of Ukraine, I brought that understanding of purpose into my new role as head of that territory. We got to work right away on developing our purpose. The crisis at that time was sort of an ordinary business crisis. We weren't reaching our business goals. I recognized that many of my leaders did not have a lot of motivation. And we didn't feel united or aligned. Developing a clear purpose for the group helped us come together and begin to speak a common language and feel closer as a team. It also helped me identify and position key people in leadership roles that stretched and developed their skills. These people became my most valued lieutenants later on.

Then the BIG CRISIS hit in the middle of that work when the protests became violent and the Little Green Men invaded. This threw Ukrainian society and our company into turmoil. Suddenly, the purpose that we'd come up with around business goals and team alignment didn't serve our more urgent needs. We needed to develop a new, more relevant purpose around keeping everyone safe and attempting to sustain normal business operations. I believe that the second purpose was built on the first. If we hadn't done the work of introducing the power of purpose earlier, it would have been harder to do it later. So I'm grateful for the lessons I learned in Greece that I brought to Ukraine.

Crisis helps. It's really difficult for human beings (as individuals and in organizations) to truly and deeply understand the need for purpose until they confront a crisis. Until the crisis comes, the need for purpose is more academic than urgent. We may believe or think that purpose is morally or ethically a good idea, but we don't necessarily see it as a lifesaving need or a desperate solution.

There are a few simple reasons why:

- We tend to coast when the going is good. We get very busy managing the day-to-day and can't always see the forest (purpose) for the trees (business objectives, daily challenges). When the crisis hits, we are suddenly confronted with very big questions like,

  "What really matters?"

  "What (resources, people, plans) do I need to save and what do I need to let go?"

  "Why is it important for me, my team or the organization to keep working so damn hard during this very difficult time?"

  The answers point to purpose.

- Sometimes we believe we are working or living with purpose but we are really not. This is not our fault. It is, again, human nature. It takes real discipline, daily practice, and lots and lots of awareness to live, work or operate according to a greater purpose without losing track of that purpose, forgetting about it or falling away from it. When the crisis hits we get reminded in a hurry. We either realize that purpose has been missing or we discover that we've wavered. The crisis serves as a reminder. All the difficulties are conspiring to help us figure out what's really important.

- The purpose we're living or working by is not actually your real purpose, or maybe it's no longer valid. This happens all the time. Companies get very lofty ideas when they determine their purpose, but when they operate and make decisions in the real world, they often do so in ways that have little relevance to that purpose. When the sh*t hits the fan, they don't turn to their purpose because it's not actually real, or they realize that their purpose no longer feels relevant. What's a company to do? Well, if purpose really does help a company navigate uncertainty, change and threats, then it's time to figure out what that purpose should be. Once again, crisis can be a gift.

A sense of purpose is not intellectual or ethereal. You feel it in your guts. You rely on it frequently, like a touchstone, to make good decisions. You use it to gain clarity when there is confusion all around.

The good thing about a crisis is that it interrupts old patterns of thought or ways of living and doing business. A crisis makes it necessary to question everything that used to work and figure out new solutions and new ways forward. When the old ways suddenly don't work anymore or don't mean as much given new realities, we need to get real (authentic, genuine, clear-hearted) about what actually does matter. Alcoholics Anonymous talks about hitting bottom. Seth Godin says entrepreneurs reach the dip. That's the point where you look up (often in despair) and say "What *does* matter?" Organizations, communities, leaders and people need the same moment of truth. Some, of course, would argue "Why wait for a crisis? Just do it now."

2. Innovation = Purpose x Crisis

Crisis can help define the problem you need to solve. For me and my team in Ukraine, the crisis made it very easy to decide that survival and business-as-usual should be our purpose. For a financial firm during an economic crisis, a new sense of purpose might mean evaluating and changing current business practices. For a mature-beverage manufacturer, the crisis might be that the processes of manufacturing and distribution the company has relied upon for many decades threatens the environment. As we discussed earlier, this could be related to excess water use or the problem of obesity because of sugar or the devastation of pollution generated by so much plastic. Adding to that hypothetical crisis, maybe the government starts taxing sugar, eroding the company's profits.

Facing a crisis, even if it doesn't directly and immediately threaten the organization, inspires a response. If the crisis is serious enough, however, that response is likely to change current business practices. When crisis meets purpose, innovation is almost always the result.

When my team and I looked at purpose-driven startups, we stumbled across the link between purpose, crisis and innovation. Studying larger companies next, we quickly determined that the same formula applied. I think it's an intuitive concept to understand. As we discussed above, people find it hard to change and grow without a crisis and a renewed or new sense of purpose. In the same way, a person might struggle to lose weight until they face a severe health crisis. Recognizing that they really want to stay living for years to come, that purpose becomes a powerful force for changing an old path. For an organization, that's the definition of innovation.

The classic startup motto is: "Give me a problem and I will find a solution."

The world certainly has plenty of problems today. In 2015, the United Nations came up with its list of Sustainable Development Goals. In 2018, a

Danish company called Sustainia turned those goals into a list of business problems. They included reducing global inequality, reducing consumption and production, preserving the oceans and slowing down climate change.

What can businesses do to address such global challenges? As *Fast Company* noted, companies "can actually create solutions that improve lives and develop new markets. In other words, being responsible isn't some moral choice, but rather it's smart strategic planning."[102] Solutions to global problems can be drivers of innovation and growth.

A report by CB Insights, "2019 Game Changers", focuses on startups that are making a mark by tackling global problems.[103] The startups chosen are "high-momentum companies pioneering technology with the potential to transform society and economies for the better." Categories included AI, superbug killers, ecosystem engineering, autonomous vehicles, net-zero buildings and defense against disinformation. CB Insights identified three startups in each of those twelve categories that it saw as having the potential to be game changers.

Massive global problems represent massive market opportunities. Think about the problem of plastics. Much of the effort put into recycling plastics is useless, researchers now believe. Two-thirds cannot be recycled at all. Seventy percent ends up in landfills.[104] Growth in plastic waste will be overwhelming in the next thirty years if we don't do something about this problem now. Will regulations, policy and public education be enough? It hasn't been so far. Instead, we need the innovation and ingenuity of thousands of companies that can profitably convert or divert our need for plastics toward better, more environmentally sustainable ends. Likewise, companies like Adidas that pledge to use only recycled plastic can have a huge impact on the environment, improve the bottom line and connect better with customers.[105]

---

102 https://www.fastcompany.com/40526823/4-of-our-biggest-global-problems-are-big-business-opportunities

103 https://www.cbinsights.com/research/briefing/2019-game-changing-startups/

104 https://www.independent.co.uk/voices/plastic-waste-wish-recycling-bins-black-environment-green-shopping-a8548736.html

105 https://money.cnn.com/2018/07/16/news/adidas-using-recycled-plastic-only/index.html

FORECAST OF PLASTICS VOLUME GROWTH, 2014-2050

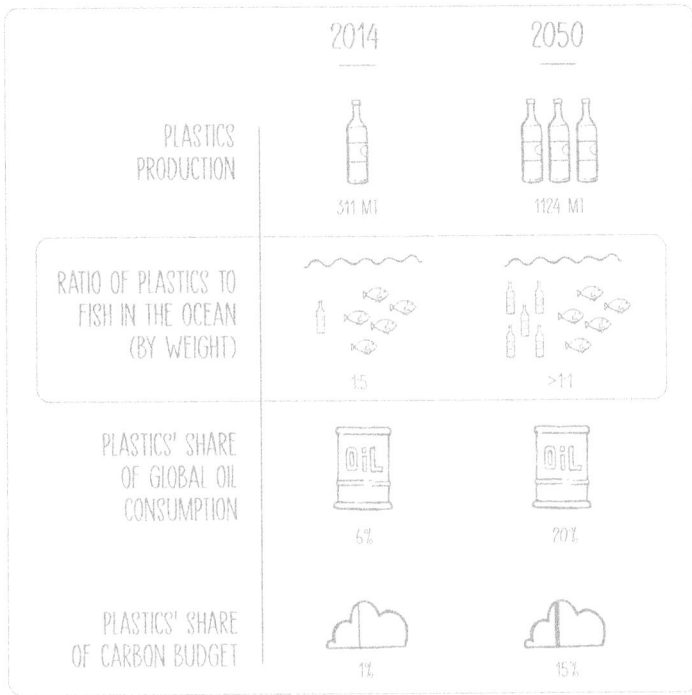

SOURCE: WORLD ECONOMIC FORUM, 'THE NEW PLASTICS ECONOMY', 2016

3. Growth = Purpose and Innovation at Scale

Innovation is about where you are going, but exponential growth comes from bringing purpose and innovation to scale. Take another look at the quadrant to see how using purpose to move up the Y axis can lead to significant market expansion or the establishment of entirely new markets.

The vast majority of established organizations find themselves by default in the lower left quadrant. They are competing in existing spaces by attempting to raise their game operationally. So, MacDonald's is trying to sell more burgers than Wendy's. Or Ford is trying to earn higher margins than Toyota. Even Apple, it seems, despite its renown for innovation, is just trying to make more money by selling slightly better smartphones than competitors. Frankly, when it comes to the handset, Apple has stalled out. Markets get crowded. Customers lose excitement. The money can still be great, but it's unlikely that the connection between people, product and customer will stir the passions in quite the same way. An explosive surge in growth is unlikely. There's no reason for it to happen.

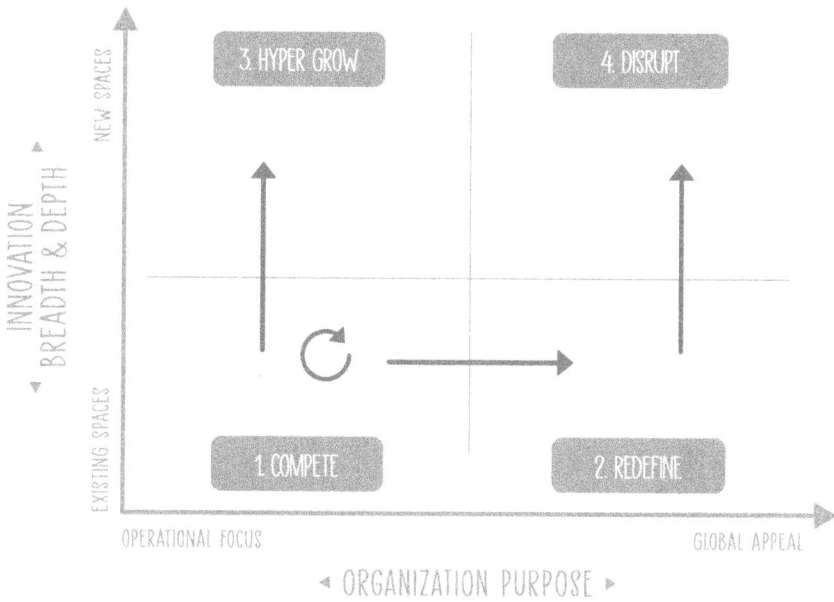

So, what's a company in a mature market to do? For years Apple has been rumored to be coming out with a new kind of TV or an Apple car. Would these products fire customers up? Maybe they'd help Apple surround the customer more than ever, but I doubt they would charge the company with the kind of energy that shot its valuation and brand prestige into the stratosphere starting with the iPod and continuing with the iPhone. No doubt, Apple CEO Tim Cook knows this, too, and he's under tremendous pressure to continue Steve Jobs' legacy of exciting innovation.

Cook is a bit inscrutable in this regard. Though an incredibly competent CEO, he cannot possibly replicate Jobs' personality and passion. However, if there is anything Cook has spoken passionately about, to my knowledge, it has been health. Steve Jobs' death from pancreatic cancer seems to still move him deeply, and certainly Apple was shaped by Jobs' life and death.

I find it fascinating, as a result, that Apple's boldest move in recent years has been its entry into healthcare. That move started slowly and relatively quietly (for Apple) with the introduction of the Apple Watch which had some health monitoring features. Behind the scenes, Apple kept making low-key moves in the healthcare space, developing new technologies, bringing in influential talent, acquiring some related companies. Recently, however, Cook spoke boldly of Apple's bigger plans in a statement that was genuinely Jobs-like in its radical quality. "If you zoom out into the future," Cook said, "and you look back, and you ask the question, 'What was Apple's greatest contribution to mankind?' It will be about health."

Now, that is a bold pronouncement for a giant company known for IT, entertainment and creativity. But if you take Cook at his word and think about what that means for Apple, you can recognize that he's talking about shifting out of Quadrant 1 (where the market for handsets is now) and into a new area. How far will Apple go? Does its move into healthcare represent a shift into Quadrant 2 with a redefinition of existing product lines for more global appeal? I would argue No. If Apple stopped at the Apple Watch and promoted a health and wellness campaign for employees and customers or somehow attached Apple's products to healthy lifestyles or more efficient hospitals, that might be the case, but it doesn't appear so. Likewise, Apple is not inventing an entirely new product category suitable for Quadrant 4. Instead, Apple seems to see tremendous growth potential in bringing its data and interface technology to the healthcare industry as it already exists. In this way, just as Amazon disrupted distribution companies or Airbnb threw the hotel accommodation industry into turmoil, Apple seems bent on bringing tremendous efficiencies and customer focus to healthcare customers. As a result, I would put Apple's new healthcare business line squarely in Quadrant 3.

How big should your innovation be? It depends on what quadrant it falls into. If it's a new twist on an existing product line, that's Quadrant 2. If it's a total new way of doing the work, that's Quadrant 3. And if it's a whole new offering that few have introduced or considered before, then you're getting very close to Quadrant 4.

Where do the biggest opportunities for you lie? I've argued that shifting upwards in the quadrant is essential for exponential growth. As I also already suggested, positioning your company in Quadrant 4 is a tough game. It may be where the world's biggest problems or needs can be found, but that doesn't mean it's where you'll find the biggest business opportunity in the short-term. Even Apple's most prominent innovations were variations on existing products. It's always played well in Quadrant 3. Apple's move into healthcare seems consistent with Apple's long-standing tradition. Such an approach, if successful, would no doubt satisfy investors, disrupt the healthcare industry, and delight patients.

4. Business Model is Purpose ⬄ Global Problems ⬄ Customers ⬄ Innovation

A successful purpose-era business model brings your purpose, global problems, innovations and customers together. Here's a simple story about a very small problem that had the potential to become a practical idea with the right business model.

An experienced executive I'll call Monica returned to her company's headquarters in Rome after a long assignment in the U.S. At the office, she discovered that parking in the center of the city is a daily stress. Everyone wants a company parking spot but there are only so many to go around, and those spots go to the top executives first. All the rest of the employees need to find spaces on the street nearby or deal with public transportation.

One day she had an idea. Even though all of the company's parking spaces were assigned, she noticed that many spaces were often open because executives travel a lot. It seemed silly to let those spaces go to waste when others need them, she thought. In her own small team, for example, there were four assigned parking spots, but fifteen additional people had nowhere to park. Why not develop a small project to monitor when assigned spaces will not be used and let people who need a spot know? She asked a couple people on her team to come up with a simple system and test it with the group.

She figured they would jump on her suggestion, but the people she had asked to work on the problem didn't do anything. When she checked back a few months later, they agreed to get right on it, but nothing happened. About a year after that, she learned that a rival company in the same city had come up with a similar idea and acted on it. Now, businesses in the downtown area were regularly using a parking share app that was attracting customers and capital.

This really frustrated her! Her people had an opportunity to do something innovative but procrastinated and blew it. Why? Because an idea that potentially met a need lacked a business model.

Services like Airbnb and Uber create value by using resources more efficiently. But this concept is not just for second homes and family cars, it applies everywhere. Parking spaces are a good example. Wherever there are "givers" and "receivers" or "owners" and "renters", there is an opportunity to create a two-sided market where both benefit.

I read an article recently on "Platformization" which recommended turning existing products, processes or services into revenue-generating platforms. The authors talked about reimagining a global fulfillment process to look more like Amazon and less like SAP. Pretty much any sharing economy business model could become a platform.

Automakers are transitioning from being primarily manufacturers to becoming mobility solutions companies, focused on car sharing, bike sharing, and public transport to help them grow deeper connections with customers in the future, while transforming vehicles into smartphones on wheels. Amazon Web Services has been a huge growth engine for the company functioning as a platform service for supplying data storage in the cloud for customers and competitors alike.

I understood Monica's frustration at seeing "her" idea get executed by another group. I've often felt the same way. Today, business innovation doesn't always follow traditional rules. Good ideas can show up unexpectedly. If you don't follow up on those ideas, somebody else with more time, initiative or motivation will beat you to it. Execution is the difference between great ideas over coffee or beer and the next big business concept or growth sector.

To move her idea for an app prototype toward a platform, Monica would have required more knowledge, expertise, budget and pairs of hands. For every Facebook or Dropbox, there are dozens or hundreds of companies that simply didn't scale fast enough to turn their good idea into an awesome product.

Here's the really funny thing. Why did Monica's group fail to execute on her suggestion? It turned out, the people she asked were already monitoring spaces and using them occasionally for themselves! As a result, they were reluctant to develop a more public, open system and lose their informal benefits. People are not always resistant to change merely because ideas are new. To understand how to motivate them, you need to determine what they actually value and what matters to them.

How do you get them to think even bigger and go far beyond the problem-at-hand to solve related problems? The team that developed the parking space app at the rival company didn't stop innovating. They built their app to help convert drivers to greener commutes by increasing carpooling and public transportation. Making a positive impact on the company and even the community got them excited because it gave them a sense of purpose.

Why stop there? A parking app promoting green living could easily promote healthy living and wellness. It could encourage biking, tie into wearables like Fitbit, and create an online marketplace for healthy businesses or services to market to employees.

Money, aligned interests and incentives help, but the kind of extra effort, brain power and entrepreneurial zeal needed to build a brand-new business is catalyzed by a sense of greater purpose. Purpose-driven innovation can help people connect the problem they're trying to solve to much bigger community, societal or global problems. As the scale of focus grows, so grows the scale of opportunity. By tying a parking app to a real purpose, you can eventually create a dynamic platform that makes the world a better place.

Here's how I would advise someone like Monica to come up with a business plan in the future:

- Identify a two-sided need that many people share.

- Figure out the real market drivers for the "buyers" and "sellers".

- Scheme out a platform that will help bring buyers and sellers together.

- Identify what other related needs those buyers and sellers might also have ... build the ecosystem.

- Develop a scaling model.

- Tap into something bigger—a sense of purpose shared by your buyers and sellers—that your idea can fulfill to motivate you into action.

With those questions answered, you may have enough ammunition to convince others—partners, employees, investors—that this is an idea worth pursuing.

The big shift for established corporations is to stop thinking about purpose as a philanthropic or social responsibility campaign—and start thinking about purpose as the key to critical innovations and massive potential growth. Purpose can be woven into your business model in a variety of different ways. Here are some suggestions:

- **Buy One Give One**

   Companies like TOMS Shoes pioneered this approach. Customers buy a product knowing they are also buying something for a person in need.

- **Replace Purposeless Assets**

   A company begins to transition from a harmful product to a product in line with purpose. For example, car manufacturers can shift from gasoline combustion engines to diesel or electric vehicles.

- **Employ Those in Need**

   Some companies focus on giving jobs or education to people in need. Intel, for example, trains refugees to be coders.[106]

---

106 https://www.fastcompany.com/40529447/the-intel-foundation-is-betting-it-can-transform-refugees-into-tech-workers

- **Lead a Trend**

  Purpose can be tied to business model by taking a stand and setting a positive trend: a tech or garment manufacturing company that won't employ labor in unfair conditions, for example, or an influential clothing designer like Stella McCartney who won't use leather.[107]

- **Impact Investing**

  Capital was once viewed as neutral, its only duty to seek positive returns. No more. Impact investors leverage capital to achieve purpose-driven change in the world. For example, SolarHome was founded to supply cheap, renewable electricity to people in developing countries who lack access.[108]

- **Partner with Charities**

  A company can leverage its core competencies to focus on social sector issues. For example, Salesforce employs a 1-1-1 philanthropic model that leverages technology, people and resources to improve communities.[109] They view this work as a growth market, and measure progress like they would any business line. They also actively support other businesses, including startups, in pledging 1 percent of their people, technology and resources in similar ways, enhancing their impact and reputation.

- **Offer Free or Inexpensive Versions for the Needy**

  Some companies offer extremely expensive products and services at reduced costs to needy consumers. For example, Ivy League colleges that charge up to $100,000 per year for tuition often offer free education and certification to students around the world via MOOC courses.

---

107 https://www.peta.org/videos/stella-mccartney-takes-on-the-leather-trade/

108 https://kr-asia.com/greg-krasnov-of-solarhome-on-southeast-asias-solar-energy-opportunity-startup-stories

109 https://www.salesforce.org/pledge-1/

Likewise, pharmaceutical companies that charge high prices for drugs in the U.S. may offer free or price-reduced versions of those medicines in the developing world.[110]

5. Technology Helps You Get There

Today, technology is no longer a barrier to making an idea happen. If you can think it or dream it, you can probably find a technology to do it.

In Pittsburgh, for example, cameras and proximity sensors monitor traffic flows to adjust traffic lights and thereby reduce traffic jams which waste fuel and harm the environment.[111] In healthcare, a startup called Cota Healthcare crunches immense quantities of data to develop better treatment paths for patients with cancer.[112] The energy industry uses drones to inspect pipelines and wind turbines, report on emergencies and even deliver supplies to hard-to-reach areas.[113]

What can a food company do to combat obesity, diabetes and other related chronic illnesses? Nestle decided to bring the power of personalized medicine to bear on its customers' nutrition. The Nestle Wellness Ambassador platform allows customers to send pictures of the food they eat to Nestle, along with DNA and blood tests to assess susceptibility to chronic illnesses. With that information, Nestle provides personalized nutrition advice and supplements. When such services are conducted across millions of customers, the data promises to provide deep insights into the connections between nutrition, lifestyle and genetic code.

Some years back, a food technology company called Linfa developed because of the marriage of three technologies. The original idea was to grow vegetables in the home using elegantly designed hydroponic chambers. These could be stacked in a kitchen, allowing the person at home to grow a substantial amount of produce year-round. The purpose of the company

110   https://www.ncbi.nlm.nih.gov/pmc/articles/PMC5725781/
111   https://sustainablebrands.com/read/product-service-design-innovation/how-ai-machine-learning-are-solving-global-problems
112   https://www.cotahealthcare.com
113   http://info.industrialskyworks.com/blog/how-to-solve-the-biggest-problems-with-oil-and-gas-projects-using-drones

was to enable fresh vegetables to be grown anywhere with minimal environmental impact from fertilizer, soil erosion and transportation. The problem was that the hydroponic chambers depended a lot on the quality of the light and the skill of the grower.

So, the team wedded their hydroponic idea to a second technology for data-generating light. With this sophisticated LED system, the quality of the light in the chamber could be monitored exactly and altered to improve growing results. Suddenly, Linfa turned a device for dedicated hobbyists into something with more mass-market appeal.

Then, it took it a step further and developed a way to share data among all customers. In this way, the hydroponic system could become smarter, figuring out from thousands of sources what approaches to growing vegetables (light, soil, nutrients) worked best.

Most companies spend some time worrying about which technologies will disrupt their industries. Technology has advanced so quickly that the question is almost meaningless. The real question should be, what urgent global problems do your customers want you to solve? Once you have clarity around purpose, the technology will likely be easy to find.

6. Purpose is the New Leadership

Today, trust in traditional leadership is at an all-time low. People view CEOs and politicians with suspicion—not in spite of their professional experience and competence, but because of it. Maybe this is because they associate traditional leaders with the devastating financial collapse of 2008 and all the job losses, corruption and tough times that went with it.

In contrast, people are more enthusiastic about leaders who are clear about their purpose. Such leaders stand for something meaningful, and they are able to create a deeper connection between their own aims and their followers/employees and customers. On top of that, they are often keen to disrupt business-as-usual and fuel growth. This feels exciting and significant to be around.

Although I am not a supporter of President Donald Trump and his populist agenda, I recognize the power of his very simple, purpose-driven message: Make America Great Again. It's hard to tell how real it is for Trump, a master brander, but he delivered that message repeatedly to his core supporters and electrified them. In contrast, Hilary Clinton could not really move her supporters with any specific emotionally charged agenda outside of her own historic attempt to become America's first female president.

Trump also connected better with his supporters because he knew emotions are always more energizing than facts. Steve Martin, the author of *The Science of Persuasion*, says that although we all think we are influenced by facts and coherent arguments, we are actually far more influenced by what we believe others around us are doing. For example, the way hotels use arguments about environmentalism to try to convince guests to reuse their towels is less effective than telling guests that most customers in this specific hotel, or even room, reuse their own towels.

In a similar way, Trump appealed to voters by pressing emotional triggers. Corporate CEOs who rely on traditional speeches, marketing ads and memos that pass through legal are unlikely to connect with employees, customers and even shareholders going forward. No one is interested in the same old narrative. They want a human touch with next-door-neighbor kind of messages.

Ricardo Semler became CEO of his father's Brazilian company, Semco, when he was only twenty-one. Semler tried to reinvent his family-owned business by doing lots of management consulting-type things. He broadened the portfolio by acquiring new businesses, and he fired all the old managers and brought in new ones who had very tough performance standards. It worked—for a while. But Semler didn't think it was sustainable. Nobody liked working for the company, even him. It was too stressful.

So Semler did something really different—even crazy for the corporate status quo. He turned the company into a purpose enterprise that put people first. To show he was serious, he got rid of all the rules and let the people take over. No set working hours. No project plans. Total transparency. People could decide what to do, how to do it, when to get it done by, and how much they should be paid. They even gave their managers performance reviews, not the other way around.

Amazingly, Semco became successful. It grew every year for twenty years, became a more profitable business, and the people were happy.

In its own way, a company like Google has done the same thing. Give people purpose and let them be free. This takes a special type of leadership. All the old attributes of leadership—expertise, experience, practical know-how and position—seem less credible and meaningful today. As people have lost faith in leaders and leadership, they've begun to look for something different. They seek values and principles they can believe in, embodied in leaders who seem to live those values authentically. Customers want the same from the companies whose products they buy.

The desire for meaning can be dangerous. Followers can be attracted to powerful ideologies—such as Nazism and ISIS. Yet, followers are also attracted to ideas and people that drive positive change. Purpose-driven leaders are not satisfied with small goals; they want to make moon shots happen. If they don't have the expertise, resources, or talent to do it, they go find it.

As more employees, customers, investors, and influencers are drawn to this type of leadership, it will be important for all leaders and decision makers to understand and compete in the marketplace for purpose.

Companies and leadership programs are already starting to get organized around this theme.[114] The movement has begun. The world is ready. Leadership is dead. Purpose is the new leadership.

7. Impact is the New Measure of Success

In an economy that increasingly elevates and rewards purpose-driven companies, how can you target objectives and measure success? There is clearly one key metric that stands before all others: Impact. How much impact is your company having on alleviating the urgent need it has set out to resolve?

This starts, first, by identifying that urgent need. Then you must assess how far you go toward meeting that need. To think in this way, I like to flatten out my four quadrants by focusing on customer-focused needs versus

---

114 https://teams.movingworlds.org

global or human-focused needs. Placing those on an X-Y axis, it becomes easier to identify where purpose-driven companies cluster.

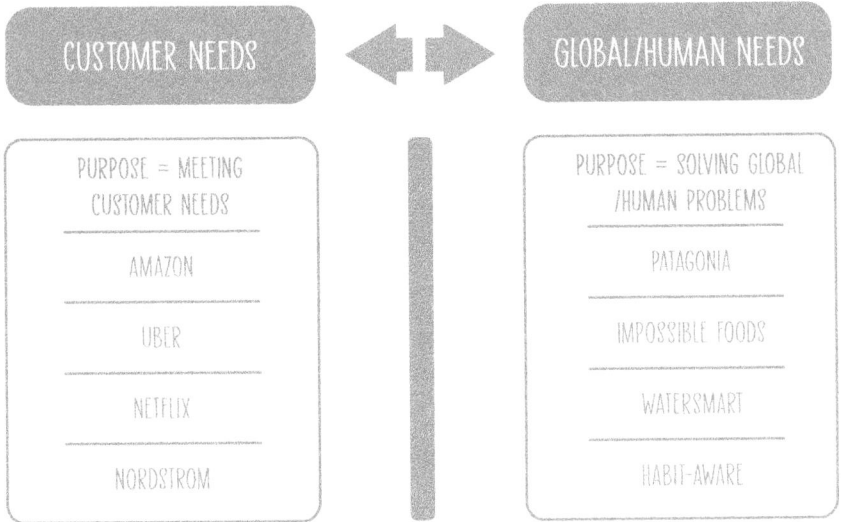

CUSTOMER NEEDS	GLOBAL/HUMAN NEEDS
PURPOSE = MEETING CUSTOMER NEEDS	PURPOSE = SOLVING GLOBAL /HUMAN PROBLEMS
AMAZON	PATAGONIA
UBER	IMPOSSIBLE FOODS
NETFLIX	WATERSMART
NORDSTROM	HABIT-AWARE

Let's look first at companies meeting customer needs. Almost every competitive company claims they are in business to serve their customers. Their notion of the customer can be defined broadly, to range from B2B to B2C. Few companies truly move the needle for customers in a transformative way. Most rely on a conventional mix of providing some service or product in an existing market while using branding, marketing, sales and attentive service to push that product or service to customers. Even though customers might feel strong brand loyalty or preference for one product/service over the other, the offerings and the companies are relatively interchangeable.

This is old-school capitalism. In this new purpose era, companies meet customer needs at a whole new level. Amazon is the face of this movement. According to Amazon's own purpose statement: "Our vision is to be earth's most customer-centric company; to build a place where people can come to find and discover anything they might want to buy online." It's easy to prove that Amazon has succeeded marvelously in that regard. The self-described world's most customer-focused company stops at nothing (including profitability) to deliver new services that delight customers.

Uber transformed customer expectations for transportation convenience and ease, gaining huge market share in the process. Netflix did the same for TV entertainment. Nordstrom has transformed the customer experience of retail by combining customer data, digital technology, creative local stores and personalized services.[115]

On the other end of the spectrum, there are purpose-driven companies that are worried less about the customer's market demands and desires, and far more about their human needs or the needs of the planet as a whole. For example, Patagonia, the clothing and outdoor equipment manufacturer and retailer, has always been at the vanguard of environmental activism. More recently, it has put "saving our home planet" front and center as its corporate mission. Patagonia's HR is empowered to hire people who are committed to that mission. Sourcing strategies have been revamped to serve rather than impede planetary needs. Politically, the company is backing candidates with committed environmental strategies. And the company continues to vigorously support grassroots activists and public land-conservation efforts.[116]

It's not easy for a legacy manufacturer and retailer to have a transformational impact on a global or human need because such companies still must compete in the old world. The closer your business model aligns with the need you seek to alleviate, the more likely you will be at achieving impact. This is why it's easier for new companies to find the technology, market, funding and business model that helps it target those purpose-oriented needs directly.

Impossible Foods, mentioned in Chapter Six, is a company that has developed plant-based meat substitutes that taste so much like real meat customers find it easier to switch over. By satisfying customers' taste for meat with a meat substitute, Impossible believes that it can drastically reduce environmentally inefficient use of land and water and the production of environmentally harmful emissions. Recently, Impossible Foods launched

115 https://www.forbes.com/sites/blakemorgan/2019/03/26/the-10-keys-to-nordstroms-digital-transformation/#1476fd564aa0

116 https://www.fastcompany.com/90280950/exclusive-patagonia-is-in-business-to-save-our-home-planet

a new burger, the "Impossible Whopper", through fast-food giant Burger King. Not only does this give Impossible a giant new customer with lots of new revenue, but it significantly advances the goal of broadening the consumption of meatless burgers—helping to save the environment and improve human health.[117]

WaterSmart is a software service that assesses water use, predicts demand and helps identify and track waste. The company uses sophisticated analytics and AI to analyze the consumption patterns of millions of users. This could well turn out to be invaluable information in reducing waste. Investors have backed the idea with a recent $7 million raise. Whether WaterSmart can achieve its purpose remains to be seen. However, it's powerful to see a purpose-oriented company identify a significant global need, address it with sophisticated technology and satisfy a base of customers (in this case utilities) willing to pay for that service. This is business model meeting purpose in action.[118] As TechCrunch notes, "The good news is that the commercial market for water solutions is bigger than you might think, and that venture-stage companies in water perform better than many investors and entrepreneurs realize."[119]

HabitAware tackles a problem on a more human level. Millions of people have self-harmful body-focused repetitive behaviors like hair pulling or skin picking. Traditional medicine and therapy does a poor job helping the sufferers alleviate their problem. A husband and wife couple with direct experience developed a simple bracelet and software solution that enables its customers to track their behavior, interrupt those patterns and rewire their brain. Filling an important need, the company has been remarkably successful raising money, gaining public attention and support, developing an intuitive and powerful product, and marketing and selling it directly to consumers. Another example of purpose-driven business plan in action.[120]

---

117   https://www.nytimes.com/2019/04/01/technology/burger-king-impossible-whopper.html

118   https://www.watersmart.com/about-watersmart/

119   https://techcrunch.com/2015/06/22/turning-water-problems-into-business-opportunities/

120   https://habitaware.com/pages/about-habitaware

Over the past five hundred years, the world has changed dramatically. It has probably changed just as much in the past twenty years. All of that change has accelerated because of technological advancements. Though many worry about change, the problems of the globe have never been more solvable. What are the "impactful" challenges that remain to be solved? War, disease, violence, hunger, thirst? If you can dream a solution today, you can find a business model and a technology to fix it.

The great thing about this approach to business is how much enthusiasm it engenders among shareholders, customers, employees, stakeholders and observers. Think of the "goodwill" and share premium that Elon Musk, Tom Mycoskie, Steve Jobs or other visionary purpose leaders have generated for their businesses. Stakeholders want to create new legal frameworks for you. Regulators want to help you. Banks want to finance you. Consumers and customers seek out your products or services. Talent seeks out your organization for employment. You are in the news more often.

Marketers understand this link well. (Perhaps this is why genius promoters like Musk and Jobs have been so far ahead of the curve.) They see and leverage the connection between purpose, customer need, brand and business model—to a T.

8. Performance Pays Your Bills

A close friend of mine taught me a lesson many years ago. He had just graduated with a degree in pharmacy and was expected to begin work at the family drugstore business. Success meant making dad's small enterprise grow faster, maybe by opening up a couple of new stores ... That's it. My friend George, however, had noticed the growing market for homeopathetic medicines. In his view, people were looking for milder treatments with less toxic effect on the body. This became his new passion.

George developed therapeutic and beauty solutions that didn't include any chemicals except for botanics. He leveraged the beauty and bounteous nature of Greece and its ancient history of medicine in his marketing. Because of his deep knowledge of drug commercialization, he decided to avoid grocery stores or supermarkets. Instead, he started small, just selling his new products to independent pharmacies. His friends from university and his personal network of pharmacists became his biggest allies.

Consumer response was fantastic. Within a couple of years, he proudly showed me his revenue graph and how he'd manage to double his sales year over year. I was amazed. Enthusiastically, he told me that this had been his plan from the beginning: every year to double sales.

Ten years later, he developed his brands so nicely, both in the domestic but also in the export markets, including the U.S., that he was able to sell a majority stake of his business to a Chinese fund, and he is now one of the most successful and well-recognized entrepreneurs in Greece. In addition to his natural talent to build brands, I think his "never give up" mentality proved to be one of his biggest assets.

Today, some of the highest-profile leaders and CEOs engage in social and political causes, following a "purpose-driven" strategy over bottom-line results. Many of those leaders have stepped down from their roles because of poor company performance. While they were successful in creating a purposeful brand and vibe around a special cause, they failed to meet bottom-line promises and forecasts. WeWork, eBay, Uber are among the latest examples.[121] Other companies with grandiose claims that they are helping the world include Lyft, Snapchat, Etsy and others. Salesforce, on the other hand, offers a contrary example. Marc Bennioff's company has enjoyed stellar growth both organically and through acquisitions, while also contributing meaningfully to its social agenda.

Clearly, putting purpose uniquely above and separate from other concerns is a recipe for failure. But some people insist that business performance must come first, and social impact and sense of purpose is a luxury that can be indulged in accordingly. In my view, performance and purpose must be balanced and integrated. Performance pays the bills. Purpose feeds the commitment and energy. Delivering on both can be measured by revenue and social impact. If they both get achieved, then purpose has been effectively integrated into the business model, into the DNA of the whole organization. Such businesses, I believe, are the ones built really to last and thrive.

---

121   Source: https://www.nytimes.com/2019/09/28/business/wework-juul-ebay-ceo.html

Putting It All Together

It's one thing to believe in purpose, define it, and dream about it. It is another thing to put purpose into action. How do you bring it all together and get started?

INNOVATION AND PURPOSE - HOW TO REINVENT YOUR COMPANY

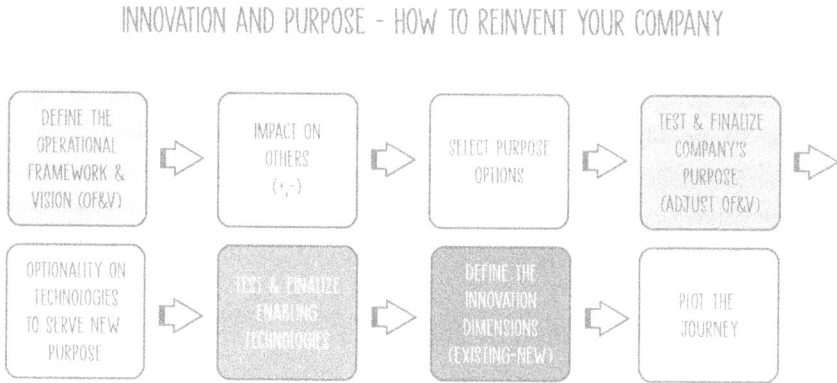

When I work with founders and top executives, I bring them through the following eight practical steps:

Step 1. Determine Location

Decide where you currently operate in the quadrants. Is that where you want to be? This is the start of the larger journey, and it helps to tie purpose to business model to market together from the beginning.

Step 2. Admit Current Impact

If you're in an "old-school" business this isn't going to be pretty. What is the current impact of your product or service? Honest answers only. My soft drink, for example, doesn't deliver happiness; it contributes to obesity. My plastic cases don't just help customers get their products in top condition; they help pollute the world. In all seriousness, you may have good impacts and bad impacts. Start with the truth and you can find your truth.

Step 3. Develop Purpose Options

If your business or company is going to do something very different to maximize positive impact, what would that be? Can your automobile reduce CO2 emissions? Can your plastic company change the way plastic is used or recycled?

Step 4. Road Test Your New Purpose

If your new purpose is to reduce harm, for example, do you have the technological and business means to do that now? If not, what will you need to do differently? Perhaps you will need to hire new scientists or reengineer your manufacturing processes or work closely with customers to meet their critical needs.

Step 5. Adopt Technology Enablers

Often, transformational purpose requires technology. What will you need to help you get where you want to go? The Internet, AI, robotics, Blockchain, solar power … you name it. Come up with a list of gaps that only technology can solve, then go out and find the technology. It's waiting for you.

Step 6. Test Again

Does your new formula work? Does your business plan fit your purpose? Have you identified the right customers and markets? Are you meeting those needs with impact? Do you have the technology in place to make it happen?

Step 7. Set Destination

Now that you know where you are and the impact you want to have, where do you want to go on the growth quadrant? Does it make the most sense to play in existing spaces, or should you venture forth into new spaces?

Step 8. Plot the Journey

You're ready to get started. You know where you want to go and you know why. So what do you need to get there? The most important thing is to find and attract the right people. As leader, you will need to communicate your message of purpose and impact over and over. You will also need to continue to assess and adjust your action plan. Often, this involves small tweaks every day. But you also can't be afraid of major pivots. Startups understand this better than established corporations, but it's hard no matter what. It takes a great deal of vision, conviction and persuasion to enable an organization to change its business model or approach to the market, even for the right reasons.

The most important piece of the puzzle, however, is you. Do you want to lead with purpose? Once you answer that question, you can find your answers for all the other questions.

More CEOs and leaders are taking social matters seriously.[122] There's no question that the times have changed. Have you changed, too? You can gauge this by assessing what really matters to you.

Maybe what matters is your family or your health or your passionate hobbies. In such cases, you might choose to step out of the business arena and devote yourself to a personal pursuit. Perhaps you're burned out, or just not feeling it anymore or there's something else that you really want to do to feel right. There is nothing wrong with that. Everyone deserves to be happy, engaged, fulfilled and to feel a sense of significance and compassion in their lives.

On the other hand, maybe what matters to you is something external and bigger than you. If that purpose is a problem or a quest that only a business or organization can solve or a need or a potential that only a business or organization can meet, then you have a different kind of answer. You might need to become what I call a purposeful leader. This is someone, at any level of the organization, who inspires, motivates, organizes, strategizes, coaches and directs the people around him or her to accomplish a larger, purposeful vision.

This is not an easy road. Companies that are striving to embrace purpose must undergo significant change to get there. It also creates a tangible dilemma. Being purpose-driven sets a company apart from competitors in a broad sense and helps them be more dynamic and innovative. I believe it is a source of real competitive advantage. However, companies that are purpose-driven are viewed differently by customers, employees and the stock market. Because they are purpose-driven, people assume they should always act with values and ethics in mind. It almost doesn't matter whether their purpose is aligned with a particular issue or not. Perception and expectations count more.

Purpose, in other words, can make you a target. If your purpose-driven company fails to take a position on controversial issues, customers can get very emotional and criticize you. If you take a public stand, you can get attacked by other customers. In particular, navigating areas where societal, political and business priorities clash is incredibly difficult. As the world becomes more chaotic, uncertain and polarized, this need for meaning and purpose will only grow. Accordingly, societal, political and business clashes are likely to increase.

As the great Peter Drucker said, "Free enterprise cannot be justified as being good for business. It can be justified only as being good for Society."

Purpose is a very serious business.

In fact, I believe it will be the most serious challenge you have ever taken on.

It will also be the most fulfilling, supported and connected journey of your life.

CHAPTER NINE RECAP

- Hey, did you like what have read so far? Do you want to move forward?

- If you have not bumped onto a serious crisis yet, why wait? Discuss about the issues you face (i.e. enemies and supporters exercise in Chapter Four) with your people and brainstorm on possible purpose directions.

- Assess where your company stands today and how it impacts the world. Reverse the negatives. Can you become good by attacking one of the Level One problems that looks relevant to you? Integrate it with your business model.

- Where do you want to be in the future? Do you want to go for moon shots or short jumps? Brainstorm to identify relevant technological enablers. Check your assumptions with employees and customers. Refine. Craft your plan with phases and a few metrics.

- Join the team of believers, changers and likely disruptors.

Tools & Resources

Purpose and Business Model Matrix

As discussed in this chapter, there are various ways to attack Level One problems or subcategories of them. After selecting a problem and integrating it with your business model, you will encounter the critical question "HOW?" For example, I am the founder of a software company, and I would like to help communities in need to prosper through job opportunities. In the below 2X2 matrix I have plotted four different ways to do that.

PURPOSE & BUSINESS MODEL MATRIX

LEVEL ONE PROBLEM:
ACCESS TO ECONOMIC OPPORTUNITY

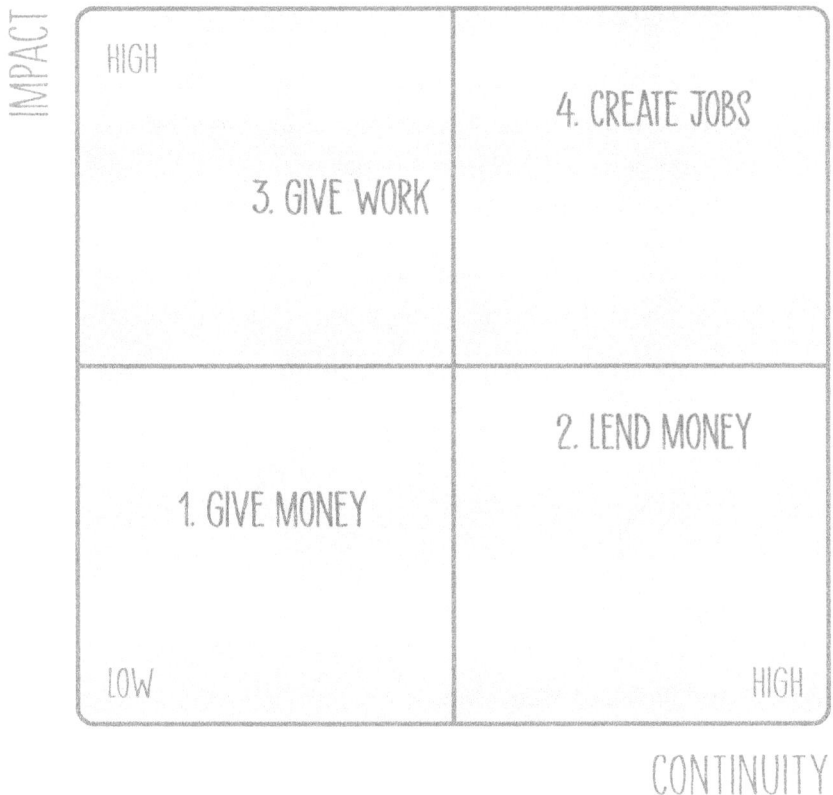

1. **Give money.** In any form, from charity to a 1 percent pledge. While a traditional approach, impact is minimized in my view, making sustainable success less likely.

2. **Lend money.** Lending to local software entrepreneurs in very affordable terms can operate like the famous microloans pioneered

by Muhamad Yunus and described in Chapter Six.[123] This creates more sustainable development, but impact is still light because some loans will fail and contribute to a cycle of poverty. Funds might also be misused.

3. **Give jobs**. This is in line with what Leila Janah has done with her company Samasource https://www.samasource.org/ which is nicely described in her book *Give Work*. She offered classroom training of people in Africa and India on coding with the aim to create out-sourced jobs. Another good example is the Intel Foundation, which just gave the International Rescue Committee $1 million to retrain one thousand German-based refugees for technology-related jobs.[124]

   It is a very impressive idea and hard work. It can certainly have impact and some sustainability. The weak spot is that the work that needs to be done by intermediaries or NGOs to organize, funnel and maintain the flow of training and outsourcing.

4. **Create jobs**. In my view, this is the most powerful way to deal with inequality and unleash opportunities for people to access growth and prosperity. It is based on the assumption that this very objective is part of a company's business model and operations. As a result, it can be potentially highly impactful and sustainable. The greater the success of the company, the more jobs this can create.

Think about these two dimensions and design or repurpose your organization accordingly.

---

123 https://godmoneyme.com/2013/04/16/five-problems-with-microlending/

124 https://www.fastcompany.com/40529447/the-intel-foundation-is-betting-it-can-transform-refugees-into-tech-workers

EPILOGUE

For the last five years or so—coincidentally, the same period that I have been working on this book—I have been trying to go deeper into my life, examining, among other things, the trail that we each leave behind. Is it important to leave something behind or not? What is the role of luck in the way our life unfolds? Can we help our trajectory in a positive way by being prepared and ready to grab opportunity when it appears?

I've also reflected on how our experiences shape us, and what bad luck actually means and whether that's something to be avoided or embraced. For example, I have had a lot of "bad luck" in my career, so much so that one of my colleagues used to call me a "black swan", because wherever I went, a crisis soon followed.

Through my experiences, reflections and the writing of this book, I've concluded that crisis is not bad luck, but good luck. It's a gift, and your best trainer. Whatever doesn't kill you makes you far better than before. It makes you think. It forces you to turn off the autopilot we can all tend to rely on and hold the steering wheel yourself. Sometimes it pushes you to rediscover qualities from your youth that were sleeping while you pursued a professional career. It reacquaints you with the importance of risk taking, companionship, experimentation, play, positivity and the sense that "anything and everything is possible."

Ultimately, crisis may be the biggest gift any of us ever get because it helps us discover our inner self.

For a team, crisis helps teach that each member has special qualities beyond their résumés and assigned roles that might go unused, untapped or unrecognized otherwise. In overcoming emergencies, you get pushed to use everything and everybody in the best possible way. Hierarchies and organizational structures just don't matter suddenly. You put together new, simple systems that actually work. You need to be fast and effective. And beyond everything else, you develop a sharp and vital sense of purpose. It doesn't need to be there forever. A team's purpose can alter. But for a time, it matters very much.

For an organization, crisis teaches that the collective group can have an important role to play in a broader context, maybe even globally. Together, you can have an impact on the world. The bigger the crisis, the bigger the gain. The more people you positively affect, the larger the opportunity to grow and flourish. There is a kind of magical reciprocity in that formula: The world pays you back for the purposeful efforts you make. And we have more than enough problems in the world these days to tackle. Just pick one.

Next comes the how: the operationalization piece. What approaches can you use to fulfill the needs of your current customers, understand their wants that are not yet expressed, and serve them in ways that will benefit the general public and even the planet? It is not always obvious. It takes courage, "tent time", imagination, and science to come up with quality answers. Being innovative for the sake of innovation is a short and unfulfilling trip. It won't take you far.

For sales, entering new markets or white spaces might feel scary at first. But there are ways to start small, prototype and test prior to selecting the final shots. There's no need to be afraid.

Chances are technology will also be necessary. We are lucky to live during the heart of the Fourth Industrial Revolution. I am a firm believer that today "whatever we can imagine, we can do."

Technology decentralizes and democratizes decisions, relations and transactions. It creates personalized products, goods, services, even medicines without human hands. It connects people, brains and bodies in unthinkable ways. It uses the gifts of the sun. It enables you to use your senses remotely and to live experiences without being there. It facilitates the production of food and other essentials of life without burdening the planet. It corrects nature and helps us to realize the eternal dream for a longer life. What a world has become possible! Just need to grab hold and make it happen.

Am I being too visionary? Maybe. But I see such things happening around us all the time. We just need to move out of our self-limiting beliefs and write new stories with new rules. If we use some of these ideas, we can build the world anew. In the process, we'll live happier lives and leave a better planet to our children.

If not us, then who else? If not now, then when?

That's a question I hope you answer, starting now.

■ ■ ■ ■ ■ ■ ■ ■ ■ ■ ■

Oh, before I forget. I want to give you an update on my colleagues from Ukraine …

Tatiana got promoted as a managing director in a large territory in Latin America. After significant achievements, she left the company to create her her own future back in Ukraine.

Artem, promoted twice, now serves as an area vice president in Saint Petersburg, Russia, managing huge resources and challenges.

Roman advanced in two consecutive jobs, attaining number one status in territories of greatest importance and responsibility and then left the company to pursue his own dream.

And me, though I still live in Lausanne, Switzerland, I've left the company, too, in order to forge my own path in business and, hopefully, the world.

ACKNOWLEDGMENTS

In the beginning it was a speech and an article in HBR, then a blogpost, and another one, and so on. I was encouraged by some people I respect very much to continue writing even though the corporate environment I worked in at the time was not accustomed to one of their executives engaging in such a public and honest dialogue. I put all of my writings together on a website, without any agenda or objective, just hoping that like-minded people would read my thoughts and engage with me in return.

Eventually, the volume of material grew and took on a sense of direction. I began to feel I had something larger to contribute. Should I write a book? Could I? I asked my friend and collaborator, Keith Hollihan, for his opinion. He was positive. Keith is an amazing person with whom I share similar life stories and he was at least as crazy as me. Thank you, Keith, for this amazing journey.

The next problem was the storyline. I soon realized that putting together a variety of thoughts, ideas and stories does not make it a book. My friend, coach, and mentor, Phil Harkins, sat next to me to help, offering not only his sharp, experienced eye but also his natural empathy and his willingness to be there for me unconditionally. Thank you, Phil, for your support, friendship and insights over the years.

My teams in Athens, Lausanne and Kiev helped me to become a better professional and person. Their help and support are reflected in each and every line in this book. I am listing their names below in no particular order, though I fear I might forget somebody. Thank you ALL. *Chapeau!*

- Athens: Vasilis Nomikos, Christos Harpantidis, Costas Salvaras, Jackie Taylor, Leonidas Tolis, Vassilis Nomikos, Nikitas Theofilopoulos, George Partsakoulakis, Romina Siaterli, Walter Veen

- Kiev: Tatiana Karpova, Artem Krivtsov, Andreas Mosel, Roman Khrushch, Natalya Trifonova, Nataliya Davydova, Piotr Cerek, Malcolm Healey, Victor Borovkov, Denys Strobykin, Liviu Vornicu, Nadezhda Redkina, Emil Krustev, Iryna Zhukova and Iaroslava Tereshkova

- Lausanne: Hugo Vilchez, Klavs Berzins, Christos Kiritsis, Tyrone Kearvell, Darek Kiersztan, Magda Drag, Anil Turan, Joao Costa, Aldo Podesta, Christian Rivette, Mike Halparin, Philip Goldhammer, Alexandra Gorra

I want to express my heartfelt appreciation for all the friends who gave me precious feedback on ideas, concepts and even full chapters. Margarita Albanezou, Romina (again), Anil (again), Andrii Kladchenko, Sushim Gupta and Bohdan Nahaylo. I cannot forget you.

Also, huge appreciation for all my followers in social media and from the website.

Ellie Bakopoulou from MILK Athens, and Alina Bonn from Agency 94 took excellent care of logos and looks. Alina was the cornerstone of all marketing and PR activities related to the book.

Without B.G. Dilworth for coordination and advice, Ronda Rawlins and Michele DeFilippo from 1106 Design for the whole publishing process, Sheri Gilbert for all approvals required, and Andreas Aggelopoulos my favorite cartoonist illustrator from Patras who designed all sketches and charts, publishing wouldn't have been possible.

Finally, I would like to express my love and gratitude to my family, Stanka, Dimitris, Elena, my little Sebastian, Yannis, George and Eleni, with whom I not only share a name but a life, too.

ABOUT THE AUTHOR

Christos Tsolkas is an Independent Business Advisor and Entrepreneur.

He has spent more than 25 years in positions of significant responsibility (General Management, Sales & Marketing) with multinationals in the Fast-Moving Consumer Goods sector, leading senior teams to achieve high performance and change. His educational background is Chemical Engineering & Business and he is dedicated to continuous learning.

Christos has had the unique opportunity to lead organizations in the midst of extreme crisis, not once but twice, including when the Greek Economic Crisis of 2010 unfolded rapidly and when the Ukrainian Crisis of 2013/14 devolved into violent geopolitical conflict. In both cases, Christos stabilized business operations and maintained the morale and security of personnel while positioning brand portfolios for strong growth. Most importantly, he leveraged each crisis to catalyze the development of his management teams, enabling the organization to not only weather those storms but thrive.

Christos is a turnaround specialist and a creative thinker, keen on internal startups and digital platforms. He is driven by the potential of new ideas to transform businesses, grow markets and inspire people. An author, blogger and passionate speaker, Christos was born in Athens, Greece and has lived, and worked across Europe. He currently resides in Lausanne, Switzerland.

Visit his personal blog www.christostsolkas.com
✉ contact@christostsolkas.com
in https://ch.linkedin.com/in/christostsolkas
🐦 @ChTsolkas

www.ingramcontent.com/pod-product-compliance
Lightning Source LLC
Chambersburg PA
CBHW050528190326
41458CB00045B/6747/J